Future Proof Leadership

Transform Your Behavior, Thoughts and Communication with NLP, Rational Thinking Models, and Emotional Intelligence for Recession-Proof Productivity and Relationship Management

By

Jonatan Slane

© Copyright 2019 - All rights reserved.

The content contained within this book may not be reproduced, duplicated or transmitted without direct written permission from the author or the publisher.

Under no circumstances will any blame or legal responsibility be held against the publisher, or author, for any damages, reparation, or monetary loss due to the information contained within this book. Either directly or indirectly.

Legal Notice:

This book is copyright protected. This book is only for personal use. You cannot amend, distribute, sell, use, quote or paraphrase any part, or the content within this book, without the consent of the author or publisher.

Disclaimer Notice:

Please note the information contained within this document is for educational and entertainment purposes only. All effort has been executed to present accurate, up to date, and reliable, complete information. No warranties of any kind are declared or implied. Readers acknowledge that the author is not engaging in the rendering of legal, financial, medical or professional advice. The content within this book has been derived from various sources. Please consult a licensed professional before attempting any techniques outlined in this book.

By reading this document, the reader agrees that under no circumstances is the author responsible for any losses, direct or indirect, which are incurred as a result of the use of the information contained within this document, including, but not limited to, — errors, omissions, or inaccuracies.

Hello,

As a successful leader you´re no stranger to long workdays. But you also want and need to level up a lot of your leadership skills, without adding a lot of extra hours

Skills you need to use on a weekly basis:

- Self-awareness, having a clear vision and goal so you don´t get distracted
- ***Decision making based on sound logic*** instead of on your emotions
- Smoother communication, both 1-to-1 as in groups
- Negotiation skills, to get better and more profitable deals

This all will lead to better personal results and **higher profits in your business.**

So, if you want to improve your leadership skills in a efficient and effective way:

- Go to:

http://futureproofleadership.businessleadershipplatform.com/

OR Scan the QR Code below

- Download the 3 PDF´s

- Print the one you want to start with
- Put on a visible place like your monitor at work, or the bathroom mirror at home
- start reading it daily, add it to you routine and experience the improvements

To your success!

Enjoy the book.

Jonatan Slane

Business Leadership Platform

www.businessleadershipplatform.com

Table of Contents

Part 1: Emotional Intelligence for Leadership — 9

Introduction — 11

Chapter 1: Understanding the Foundation: Human Emotions — 17

Chapter 2: The EQ Models — 27

Chapter 3: Introspection — 33

Chapter 4: Extrospection — 43

Chapter 5: Week 1: Intro- Basics- Self-Awareness — 59

Chapter 6: Week 2: Basics of Self-Control — 73

Chapter 7: Week 3: Intro: Basics to Recognizing Emotions in Others — 93

Chapter 8: Week 4: Intro: Basics: Social Skill — 105

Conclusion — 133

Part 2: NLP for Leadership — 137

Introduction — 139

Chapter 1: NLP Explained — 149

Chapter 2: Vision — 171

Chapter 3: Thinking, problem-solving and decision making — 185

Chapter 4: Productivity and time management — 215

Chapter 5: Communication, negotiation, and presentation — 235

Chapter 6: Anxiety and stress management — 259

Chapter 7: Motivation — 273

Conclusion — 289

Part 3: Thought Models for Leadership — **295**

Introduction — 297

Chapter 1: Why We Use Models? — 303

Chapter 2: You Want to be Right — 321

Chapter 3: Answering All These Questions — 343

Chapter 4: Optimizing and Systemizing Productivity — 373

Chapter 5: Negotiation and How to Make it a Win-Win — 407

Conclusion — 425

Bibliography — **429**

References — **431**

Part 1: Emotional Intelligence for Leadership

4 Week Booster Plan to Increase Your Self-Awareness, Assertiveness and Your Ability to Manage People at Work

Introduction

Everyone wants to improve their job, to get better at what they do. It's a part of what makes us human. We desire innovation and the ability to overcome unique challenges. And that involves investing our entire selves into what we do. Perhaps, you are looking for ways to improve and develop further at work. There are many ways that we can improve our various situations by having the right attitude and work habits to promote productivity.

One of the ways of developing productivity is by becoming emotionally mature in handling different situations. We have to develop emotional intelligence, to know how people are feeling at work, and think of different ways that we can improve the workspace at the office and promote worker happiness and satisfaction. That is one of our responsibilities as managers. It is to find ways that we can engage our employees and bring them to higher productivity and achievement so that we can promote our products and services and allow our customers to be happy. Therefore, it is crucial that we find ways to connect with our workers' emotional needs and it is helpful to have emotional intelligence.

There are different benefits to developing one's emotional intelligence. For one, managers can learn to handle their teams better. Managers can learn what motivates their team and how they become emotionally sensitive to different issues. They can also learn how to handle demanding colleagues, who can be hard to deal with their emotional reactions and constant negativity at work. Additionally, emotional intelligence allows managers to create a working environment, where employees are developing positive and meaningful relationships with their peers. For employees, the benefits of gauging emotional intelligence can be helpful, because they can use social skills, the right emotions at the right time. They can then get things like pay raise or promotion so that they can live happier lives. Finding the right motivations is a critical factor in increasing satisfaction in different people. Therefore, it is one of the best ways of getting people to perform well at work.

The history of emotional intelligence research began with Peter Salovey and John D. Mayer. These two researchers created the term emotional intelligence. They started a research program to highlight different measures of emotional intelligence in people. In one study, they discovered that when a group of people saw an emotionally-stirring film, those that had higher emotional sensitivity were able to recover much more quickly than the ones that didn't. Within another study, people who were able to assess emotions accurately were able to adjust to changes within their social life and build positive social networks.

In the 1990s, Daniel Goleman wrote a book, Emotional Intelligence (1995), which argued that emotional intelligence is more important than IQ in determining the success of an individual. He regularly coaches others about the different competencies involved in relationship management. And he says that when someone focuses on improving their awareness of emotions, they will be able to see better health benefits and improvement in their relationships. The research of Daniel Coleman has helped people as they have discovered the importance of emotional intelligence and how it can help develop a sense of community within different social circles.

This book is called Emotional Intelligence for Leadership, and it is going to show you all the different ways of developing emotional intelligence that will help your team to thrive with happy employees who will produce excellent work in your company. We will talk about various aspects of emotional intelligence, including self-awareness, self-regulation, social awareness, social skills, and assertiveness to become more productive. Having all of this knowledge will help you to become a better manager and to get more done with less time and energy. Within this book, we will give examples of the work environment with different stories to illustrate our points and provide a real-life scenario that you can understand completely. We want to allow this material to come alive as you are reading it, so you will have fun and learn a lot in the process.

In our opinion, success is less determined by IQ (intelligence quotient) than it is by EQ (emotional quotient). You can have a high IQ and have a low EQ. The thing is, emotionally sensitive people can make a big difference in the workplace. They can foster a sense of community in others and witness the success of different colleagues in a company. A survey by Career Builder in 2011 found that 71% of hiring managers said that they thought an employee's EQ was more important than their IQ. Also, 75% said that they would promote a person with a high EQ.

Moreover, more than half (59%) reported that they would not hire a person who had a high IQ and a low EQ. Employers use EQ as a way of assessing if an individual has leadership potential and can make an impact in the workplace. It is something that employers want in their candidates, to meet the needs of the other workers. It is also something that employers can use to build effective relationships with their employees. This aspect also helps them to develop their mindset in how they can be active managers and have a good relationship with their employees.

There are two parts to this book. In the first part, we'll talk about emotions and self-awareness. We will discuss the basic human feelings, as well as the more advanced ones. We will also go into depth about EQ and what it means. We will even talk about the implications of EQ for your private life and social life. In the second part of the book, we will give you a four-week emotional intelligence booster plan, which will provide you with a project to work on. We will provide you with different strategies to work on for different emotions so that you can train yourself in emotional intelligence. We will advise you to work on it one emotion at a time so that you can hone the craft of emotional regulation and awareness of others, which will make you more productive at work and also help you in your relationships with others in your company.

We believe that this book will give you all the tools you need to succeed in emotional intelligence and provide productivity and joy in your company while satisfying you, your colleagues, employees, and clients.

Chapter 1: Understanding the Foundation: Human Emotions

Emotions are an essential part of who we are as humans. They are a fundamental part of our framework and make-up and demonstrate the depths of our feelings and thoughts. They influence how we live our lives and have meaningful interactions with others. Our emotions powerfully impact how we act in our lives, and they can quickly overtake us and push us to do actions that are entirely off the edge. The people who surround us can influence our emotions. When a person has pain or anxiety within a problematic relationship, a friend can help encourage them in their lives to go forward. Another example of emotional responses to situations includes gossip. Whenever people gossip about another, other people may have a negative attitude or feeling toward that person. Also, a person who is always negative and exhibits feelings of anger or frustration can affect others around him or her.

Throughout history, psychologists have tried to classify the emotions that people experience. One psychologist, Paul Eckman, named six basic emotions that are experienced by people in all cultures. Let's look at these emotions here in more detail.

1. **Happiness**

Happiness is the experience of feelings of joy, gratification, satisfaction, and contentment. There has been extensive research carried out about happiness with the advent of positive psychology. Most people want to live happy lives. Happiness is characterized by different expressions such as smiling, body language in a relaxed way, or a positive and pleasant tone in speaking (Cherry, 2018). Happiness is one of the basic human emotions, but people in this world tend to make it a lot more complicated than it should be. They think that gaining material possessions, acquiring wealth, or having a beautiful home or car, or having a high-paying job will bring happiness to people.

Research has demonstrated that the experience of happiness influences your physical and mental health. Happiness has been linked with longer life expectancy and increased overall satisfaction with life. On the other hand, unhappiness has led people to experience more loneliness, anxiety, and depression.

2. Sadness

Sadness is an emotion that involves a person feeling in a low mood state with feelings of grief, disappointment, and other feelings. It is something that a person experiences from time to time. However, during periods where it's at its worst, it becomes a depressive episode. Sadness is an emotion that can be either a passing emotion that includes crying or getting upset, but it can become more serious whenever people experience intense sadness due to a variety of factors. That said, sadness can lead people to avoid people, self-medicate with alcohol or illegal drugs, or dwell on negative thoughts. These types of compulsive behaviors can easily become addictions that will make a person stay in a low or depressive state.

3. Disgust

Disgust is another one of the six basic emotions. It involves turning away from something that a person finds revolting or unbearable. Disgust usually includes a physical component, including vomiting, wrinkling your nose, or moving your upper lip. Feelings of disgust arise from different things, including an unbearable smell, taste, or sight. Some people believe that this emotion originated from the reactions to foods that have gone bad which might harm a person. When a person eats a food that has gone bad, he usually responds with disgust.

4. Surprise

Surprise is often a fleeting sensation that a person feels whenever he is startled by something surprising. It can be a surprise birthday party or someone that scares you unexpectedly. You may feel positive or negative feelings about surprise. Surprised expressions include widened eyes, opening one's mouth, raising the eyebrows, jumping back from a situation, gasping, or screaming. Furthermore, a surprise is an emotion, which can trigger a fight-or-flight response (Cherry, 2018). In this case, the person either wants to stay and fight the emotional response or leave the situation. Surprise can have a powerful effect on how a person reacts to different situations and lives his life.

5. Fear

Fear is an emotion that a person experiences when faced with some danger or experience of a fight or flight response. In this type of emotion, the person becomes tense, his heart rate increases and a person has a primal instinct response to a situation of either staying and fighting within the situation or leaving the scene. The fight or flight response is useful in helping protect people from danger or threats to a person's safety and physical wellbeing.

6. Anger

Anger is an emotion that involves feelings of frustration, hostility, and aggression toward another person. It can also be part of a person's fight and flight response to a situation. When a person is moved by anger, he will have expressions of frowning or glaring at a person. He will want to move away from another person. Also, he may yell at another person. A physical response includes turning red in the face or sweating. Anger can lead a person to act out in violent ways, such as striking another, kicking, or throwing and destroying things.

Many people think of anger as a negative emotion; however, it can have some benefits, because it can make people seek justice in situations where there is the unjust treatment of others. People who are motivated by a cause can take action united in their anger at a given situation. On the other hand, anger can be harmful and cause significant damage to a person's health. It has been linked to different diseases, including heart disease and diabetes. Finally, some angry people engage in risky and harmful activities such as aggressive driving, alcohol, or smoking cigarettes.

Advanced Combination Emotions

In addition to the underlying emotions, there are other advanced emotions, which are combinations of a few feelings. For example, emotion optimism is a combination of anticipation and joy. Its advanced opposite is a disappointment. Optimism is a positive emotion that involves happiness, but it also consists of anticipating the future and looking to the possibilities. It is much more than mere happiness; it has a forward component that involves the future. Another emotion that is a combination of different emotions is awe, which is a combo of fear and surprise. When you are in awe of the situation, you stand both amazed and in fear of something. Perhaps, this is a natural wonder outside, or it is a fear of God that a person may have. To be in awe is a complex emotion. Another combination of emotion is contempt, which is a combination of disgust and anger. It involves a certain level of anger against something but also a disgusting reaction to a person for doing something wrong or upsetting. Another combination of emotion is remorse, which involves a mixture of sadness and disgust. When a person is remorseful, he is regretful of his actions and feels both sad and disgusted at the same time. So, it also has a layer of complexity to it. Finally, love is a complex emotion involving both happiness and trust. A person feels happy with another person, but also trusting and accepting of another, so it is something that has a combination of feelings.

As you can see, the advanced combination emotions have a lot more to them than what meets the eye. They combine the effects of at least two emotions. For example, a high school student may feel disappointed when he gets a bad grade on a chemistry test after having had studied for 10 hours for it. He feels both sad from it but also a bit surprised at the score from it.

Why Do We Experience Emotions?

We experience emotional changes based on our environment, a change inside of us, or both. Emotions change rather quickly and can last from a few minutes to a few hours to a few days. They depend on the situation a person is in. The function of an emotion is to bring something to our attention and get us to produce a response (Josh Clark). Psychologists don't agree as to whether it is an involuntary response or if it is based on a judgment that a person makes based on evaluating their situation.

Emotions motivate us in our lives. They incite us to change and action. For example, when we feel disgusted over what our government is doing about immigration regulation, we feel incited to petition for change. Another example is with anger. When we are angry, we feel compelled to fight and stand up for what is right. Alternatively, when we're fearful, we want to run away from a dangerous situation. Emotions motivate us to stay right where we are and enjoy our lives, in particular, if we are enjoying our lives. However, they can also produce in us a response that can be either positive or negative to a given situation.

Additionally, emotions enable us to empathize with others. When we see someone grieving, we feel for them and want to comfort them with our presence and safety. Thus, emotions enable us to form strong connections with others within a social context. All the basic emotions can be worn on a person's face. As a result, they are overtly present to others when we are talking to them. Emotions then become social cues that we use to get our points across and communicate about different matters.

Emotional Response vs. Logic and Decision-Making

You may not realize it but many of our decisions are motivated by emotional responses, rather than by logic, and this can lead to different kinds of situations. A person may have just received his paycheck and get excited by the money in his bank account and then go on a spending spree and use up a lot of his money and then get into trouble with his finances toward the end of the month. Because he was motivated to spend his hard-earned money on frivolous things. It was driven from an emotion of excitement of receiving the money in his bank account. Consequently, he loses his money and may become sad or disheartened.

Another example of an emotional reaction is that a government elects a strong right-winged politician at the time when there is intense terrorism, and people want to elect someone who can crackdown on immigration and protect the citizens. People are motivated by fear to elect the politician, who will protect them from terrorism by trying to enact laws that will protect border control. People are fearful and thus want to choose a politician, who would have a strong stance on immigration. In the 2016 election, there was a lot of emotional motivation to the decisions made by people, based on their fears and anxieties. This incited them to elect people such as Donald Trump. Not to get political. However, it is true that people become very emotional when they talk about political things.

On the other hand, a person may be motivated by a rational decision to save money when receiving a bonus. Instead of responding with an emotional reaction of going out and spending all the money on things, the person may put the money into a savings account, knowing he will use it to spend on a vacation or a new car. That would be the logical and rational decision to make in that situation. For the second situation with the election, the people would make their decision to vote, not based on fear, but instead, they would decide by looking at the platforms of the candidates, analyzing the perspectives and policies, and in other ways. Consequently, they would make their decisions based on the empirical evidence available and not based on their emotions.

It is easy to make decisions based on our emotions because they can be strong and powerful and influence our behaviors. However, it is crucial that we pay attention to how we can respond to situations less emotionally and more with logic and rational thinking, because if we are not careful, we may do things that we regret and get ourselves into trouble. Therefore, it is vital that we have both emotional sensitivity and rational thinking to make the best decisions in our lives. It is also true that emotions can lead us to make the right decisions, if we are in a distressful situation, for example with a fight or flight response.

To conclude, emotions are an essential part of what makes us human. They drive us to action and response. Although they are powerful and influential, they can lead to adverse reactions and consequences. It is vital that we find ways of dealing with our emotions that are constructive and useful to our wellbeing and that of others.

Chapter 2: The EQ Models

Emotional intelligence is the ability to "perceive, control, and evaluate emotions." The term was made famous by a man named Daniel Goleman, but Michael Beldoch coined it in 1964. Emotional intelligence is a person's ability to monitor one's own and other people's emotions, to distinguish between different emotions, and to use information about the emotions to guide a person's thinking and behavior. To make the concept of emotional intelligence clearer and more logical, three models were developed, the ability model, mixed model, and the trait model.

1. The Ability Model

Salovey and Mayer developed this model. They said that emotional intelligence enables a person to think about emotions to enhance their reasoning skills. It discusses a person's abilities to gauge and understand people's emotions and to regulate them. This model says that there are several different abilities.

   a. Perceiving emotions. With this ability, the person can read another's emotions throughout both verbal and nonverbal communication.
   b. Reasoning with emotions. With this skill, a person can reason through different situations and figure out how

to solve a problem using the emotions. It enables a person to be attentive to what is going on around them and react appropriately based on their surroundings.

c. Understanding emotions. Emotions are complex and they have many different meanings that help us to understand how a person is going and how they are reacting to a given situation. Emotions themselves have different colors, and they have interactions with each other frequently. Because each emotion is connected to a specific behavior or response, you can deduce why a person acts the way they do in a given situation. For example, if a person's angry, their reasoning might be that they were not treated fairly. The possible action associated with this emotion would be to get revenge, withdraw, or attack another in this situation. As you can see, emotions are linked together.

d. Managing emotions. In the ability model, the person must learn how to control his or her responses to the various emotions that he or she perceives or experiences in his or her life.

2. Mixed Model

Daniel Goleman created 25 emotional characteristics, which include many different aspects of the emotions, including teamwork and collaboration, service orientation, and motivation for success (Slaazar, 2017). It's called a mixed model because it includes not only information about emotional intelligence but also aspects related to personality traits. Here are some examples of how this is used.

1. **Self-awareness**: This is the ability to recognize that you are experiencing emotion at the time of speaking. We have to acknowledge how we are feeling at a given time and know-how to manage our complex emotional patterns. Self-awareness involves two key aspects:
    a. Self-confidence in a person's unique abilities
    b. Emotional awareness in understanding a person's emotions and their effects
2. **Self-regulation:** To deal with our issues of regulation, we have to self-regulate through doing activities that will help us to face stress and conflicting emotions. Examples include walking, prayer, and meditation. Self-regulation involves a certain level of personal integrity, creativity, adaptability, and conscientiousness.
3. **Motivation**: To do something well, you have to have a goal in mind. Motivation enables a person to pursue his or her dream. Positive thinking is an integral part of this kind of ability. Within this ability, a person can be optimistic and confident, ready to tackle any challenges, in pursuit of his or her goal.
4. **Empathy**: This is a person's ability to relate to the emotions of others and understanding how they feel. When a person feels compassion for another, they can

understand and help others who are in need. They can also fulfill their requirements by helping to encourage them in whatever they are dealing with.
5. **Social skills**: For this skill, you need to be able to work and collaborate with others and communicate effectively. In addition, you will need to know how to resolve conflict and build relationships and rapport with others around you.

3. Trait Model

Petrides and his colleagues developed the trait model in 2009. It differs from the previous two models in that it shows that people have emotional traits or self-perceptions that are part of a person's unique personality (Salazar 2017). Emotional intelligence is an individual's ability to examine himself or herself in light of his or her emotional skills, as mentioned in the ability model. The traits that a person has are based on a person's self-perception but are not measured in any scientific way. This model has to explore all the facets of a person's personality before it can be useful in evaluating a person's emotional intelligence.

Conclusion

To sum up, each of these models is important to getting a person to realize the ability to monitor and recognize the emotions that they are experiencing. It also helps the person to have a higher degree of self-acceptance and self-awareness of factors, such as personality and ability to understand the experience of emotions. The models help a person to deal with the complex feelings that they have from day-to-day and understand how their personality affects their emotional responses to the given stimuli.

Chapter 3: Introspection

In this chapter, we are going to look at introspection as we look at ourselves and how we experience various emotions in our lives.

Within our emotion cycles, we have to look deep within ourselves to see how our personality affects our emotions. According to the preceding models we have looked at, personality shapes a big way that we can deal with our emotions. Moreover, one way our personality manifests itself is through our self-confidence and self-esteem.

When we have negative self-esteem, this impacts how we experience our emotions. Also, when a person is negative all the time, his or her emotions will manifest themselves in negative ways. Therefore, it is crucial to recognize that a person with higher emotional intelligence will recognize that their self-esteem impacts the way they view themselves and how they experience emotional cycles from day to day.

When a person has positive self-esteem, he or she will experience emotional cycles more positively, because they will be comfortable with themselves and not feel the need to worry about aspects that they have not accepted about their personality and attributes, and such. People with positive self-esteem have a higher degree of self-acceptance and will be more apt to forgive themselves for mistakes they have made or offenses that they have made against others. This also impacts how a person will experience their emotions throughout the day.

As we go through introspection of ourselves, we have to ask ourselves, how do we know that we are experiencing emotions. It takes a degree of self-awareness that is important to figure out what kind of emotions we are having at a given time. To access this self-awareness, we need to think about how we respond to a given situation and assess whether or not that was motivated by some emotional reaction or if it was based on logic. For that, you have to examine the facts of a given situation and assess what they are. One way to track how you are doing with your emotional awareness is by keeping an emotions journal. Every day, you can write in it how you are feeling at different moments in the day and highlight what happened. Think about what events happened that day, which may have triggered your emotions and provided you with some powerful response to the given stimuli.

Emotional Self-Regulation and Self-Control

Children must learn how to manage their emotions and usually do this in a safe and supportive environment. However, adults must control their emotions alone and have to have a high degree of self-control to function as productive individuals in society. In particular, an adult must deal with the negative emotions that can easily overwhelm and discourage, including anger, anxiety, and frustration, to prevent any negative responses that can result in regrettable behavior. Self-regulation enables a person to recognize the stimuli that are causing a person to act out on their emotions and helps them to keep them in check and respond in appropriate ways that will help them in a given situation. There are different techniques that a person can practice, to improve in this area of emotional wellness. That includes meditation, mindfulness, and other ways of managing stress. With emotional regulation, a person learns how to reduce the intensity of the experience of emotions. For example, a person who is mourning the loss of a loved one might recall a happy memory that helps them cope with the sadness that they are experiencing. Alternatively, an angry person can think of happy thoughts or amusing things that will help them to laugh off the situation. Emotional regulation involves an element of distracting the person from the situation to cope and to aid in response to a given situation. It is also known as "down-regulation," which is useful for playing down the emotions to calm and soothe a person into responding in appropriate and constructive ways.

Additionally, emotional regulation is used to control impulsive behaviors, such as spending too much money. We all know people who buy impulsively on the Internet and then lose money because they have spent too much. Everyone has the same emotional experience of receiving a paycheck and then wanting to buy merchandise afterward. Emotional regulation helps a person to recognize the excitement and respond to it in an appropriate way that does not result in a harmful overspending habit that can lead from the given situation. If a person recognizes that they need to pay bills and cannot resort to overspending, they will stop and not spend on that next handbag or pair of shoes, but rather keep the money safely.

On the other side is the up-regulation of emotions, which plays up the emotions, based on a given situation, including times of distress, for example, when there is a fire or a danger that surrounds a person. This type of regulation is essential whenever there is a presence of danger and initiates a "fight or flight" response. It is used to give a person a degree of anxiety or excitement that is appropriate in responding to a situation and helps a person to escape or help others get out of a situation.

A Real-Life Example of Self-Regulation

Emily was a high-strung individual. She was a hardworking administrative assistant. She always did her job and to a high standard and yet she always felt inadequate and that she could do better. Emily had become quite the workaholic type, who would constantly work on projects and never stop in the evening. Every day she would think about work, and she had no work-life balance in her life. Therefore, she was tired every day and then the one thing that was getting her through the day was caffeine, and that was causing her to lose sleep because she was taking too much of it in her system.

Although she was quite organized, Emily tended to procrastinate on one or two items on her agenda, especially the things that she didn't want to do. One day, it was the management of her task app on the computer and things piled up on the task app. Then, it was her desk, which also started to accumulate things on it. After having procrastinated on these little items, Emily had a panic attack when she realized that she had forgotten a few of the tasks from her task app that should have been done yesterday. When she realized it, she was shocked and went into panic mode. It was so difficult for her at the time, she screamed and went crying to the ladies' room; it was a case of a nervous breakdown that she was having.

The thing is, however, Emily would have these cases of nervous breakdowns once every few months and they would become pretty ugly. Emily realized that she was having a hard time, so she talked with one of her colleagues about what to do, and she learned some coping strategies for knowing how to handle her emotions and also how to avoid going into full-on panic mode.

Emily's colleague advised her to write down what it was that was making her stressed and feel that she was going over the edge. She needed to make notes about how she was feeling at the time so that she could refer back to them later. Then, she told her how to stop herself from going off into panic mode by diverting to something different and distracting from the situation. She also advised her to do meditation and practice mindfulness afterward. Emily later became more acutely aware of how she could handle her emotions and control herself before going off the edge with panic attacks.

After four months of therapy, Emily was able to come up with ways that she could manage her emotions better and then she was able to handle the various stressors that she had by writing things down, prioritizing what absolutely needed to be done on a given day, and doing things in an organized way.

How to Manage Negative Behaviors and Exert Positive Responses

The way to respond to negative emotions is simple; it's learning how to exercise a degree of self-control and try to ramp up the positive responses to the emotions. Rather than reacting to a situation, the person learns how to externalize their frustration or anxieties by focusing on what is positive in a given situation. For example, rather than getting into a shouting match with coworkers or swearing profusely, a person can use positive words to encourage someone else or externalize through writing their frustrations. Finding ways to be creative in getting out your emotional energy is essential because if you don't get it out some way, it is going to blow up and it won't be pretty. Therefore, it is vital that you find some good ways to do this and to be innovative in how you respond to different situations. Whenever you experience a negative emotion, you should recognize it as being the emotion you are having at a time, analyze it and see if it reflects the reality that you're in, and then choose an appropriate action that will be constructive and helpful. This won't always happen in a few minutes. It might happen instantaneously. The important thing is to train yourself how you are going to react rather than finding yourself still blowing up in a given situation and causing both strains to you and your relationships with others.

Positive responses are the best way to deal with the negative emotions we experience. You may have heard that you can cancel a negative with a positive. One positive word can infuse your life with a lot of positive energy and response to a given situation, while a negative word can give you a lot of stress and anxiety. Therefore, it is vital that you keep everything positive and uplifting for your health and wellbeing. One way to be more positive is to use motivation. This aspect allows you to focus on motivating yourself to be a better person by setting goals and by seeing the bright side of things. When you set a goal or target for yourself, you will always be looking to achieve something and will go after it with your energy. This will infuse your mind with positive energy that will make you feel good and will counter any of the negative thoughts that may enter your mind.

Practical Example

Let's give an example of how a person uses creativity to manage negative emotions and integrate positivity. Henry is a lazy worker, who always gets by with doing nothing. On most days, he arrives late to work, a bit hungover, tired, and smelling as if he had not taken a shower the night before. When he's working at the cafe, he always finds ways of sneaking out back to have a cigarette, because he's bored out of his mind. One day, he was out having a cigarette with a few colleagues, and he started out of the blue cursing his luck and saying "I suck. I can't believe that I live here in this place. I will never amount to anything. My life has no meaning! Sometimes, I don't give a _____ but today I really don't." Then, a coworker named Isaac from the cafe told him something very important.

Isaac told Henry, "Look, Henry, you've got to pull yourself together. You need to get a goal or vision for your life. I know you feel hopeless right now. However, I believe there is something that you can go for in your life, some kind of goal or dream that I want you to pursue. Do you think you can?" Henry said, "Nope. I have no dream or vision." Isaac replied:

"How about you do this? Write down things that you want in your life and think about how you can get those things and write down a goal that you want to achieve." Henry then wrote down some things that he wanted to do to get better in his life. That included stopping smoking and drinking and having a girlfriend. Isaac said: "see there, you do have something you want in your life. I know that you can accomplish these things if you really set out to do them." After this talk, Henry felt very happy, and he thought that he could take the necessary steps to stop smoking, take up a sport, and do some positive things.

So, what happened in this situation? Isaac, who is the inspirational motivator in this scenario, believed he could do something for Henry. He could instill in him an inspiration to have a dream. Henry was feeling hopeless, sad, and angry, all at the same time and then he felt happy after he had a dream and goal for the future, so it was a successful time.

Conclusion

To sum up, it is vital that you find creative ways of responding to negativity in your life, which includes positive emotional responses to the negative thoughts that may come across your mind. Looking further at yourself and having a high degree of self-awareness and acceptance will help you realize your natural tendencies, evaluate whether or not your emotional responses to situations are helpful or healthy, and come up with action plans or goals that will enable you to be more positive in responding to given situations that involve your emotions.

Chapter 4: Extrospection

Getting to know yourself and how you emotionally react to situations is an integral part of the process of self-awareness and knowledge. Equally important equally essential and valuable is getting to know about the emotions of other people and how they are feeling and reacting to different kinds of stimuli and situations. The opposite of introspection is extrospection, and within this type of awareness, a person can understand how people around them behave and interact with one another. There are different aspects of extrospection.

Recognizing Emotions on Others

The most basic fundamental way to understand people is by reading their emotions, which includes body language and facial expressions. People communicate a lot more than just with the words that they say, but also with how they speak, how they behave and demonstrate interest or disinterest in conversations. People will make eye contact, nod their heads, give verbal cues and grunt and other signs of understanding, agreeing, and disagreeing. Within conversations, many different signs communicate the level of energy and interest. Learning to read how people accept or reject your words is an essential sign of emotional maturity. It is crucial to understand how a person is feeling when talking to them.

The Difference Between Empathy and Sympathy

Empathy is a way of feeling the different emotions of the people around you. It is a way in which a person can fully understand, accept, and identify with the person who is experiencing an emotion. Think about the person who is grieving the loss of their grandmother. You are in the position of having lost your grandmother or grandfather, and you know exactly how it feels to lose someone special to you. Therefore, it puts you in the position to counsel, listen to, and comfort the person who is going through this challenging stage of mourning the loss of a loved one. Empathy involves shared experiences that a person must feel the pain of another person, to completely identify with the other person. When a person says, "I feel you" or "I feel your pain," it is a sign of empathy and identification with another person, who is hurting somehow.

Another example is if a friend loses a job and has no money and is unable to pay his bills. You, who have already lost a job once and had no money at the time, can immediately identify with this person and offer to help him out. You feel empathy for your friend because you have been through the same or similar situation. Consequently, you can identify with the feelings and emotional responses of your friend. This puts you in the best position to comfort and restore your friend. Thus, you help him out by buying him a meal the day he lost his job, and you also might lend him some money, as well.

On the other hand, sympathy is when a person identifies a person's feelings of distress or suffering but is unable to know what a person is going through. It is somewhat like compassionate pity for someone in which a person may feel sorry for another but also comforts them. At the same time, they don't have the actual life experience that enables them to understand fully what another person is going through emotionally. An example is a doctor who is giving care to a patient who is suffering from cancer. Doctors have to be emotionally sensitive and aware to be competent and supportive caregivers.

Example of Empathy

Vicky always knew what it was like to be a proofreader and that it always involved looking at extensive data collections for long periods every day and staring in front of a computer. She was the supervisor of all the proofreaders within the editing company. There were several interns in that group, and she remembered what it was like to be on the job for the first time. She had squinted at the screen for long periods and sometimes had eye strain that she had to deal with, which was painful. Vicki also remembered the time when she completely misread a whole text and missed a lot of the errors in grammar on one page. This happened once when she was a young proofreader and had no experience in the job. She was mortified at the time and felt complete shame and remorse as a result of the experience. She feared for her career. She thought she might be fired over it. However, her supervisor told her it would be all right and that they could correct the mistake.

When Jason was first hired as a proofreader, he had no experience in the field and was feeling woefully inadequate and thought he would not be able to complete the assignments that he had. He had to proofread thousands of words per day, and it was so mentally and physically exhausting to look at two screens every day. He knew that it was a challenge to do that. And one day, it happened. He skipped a whole section of proofreading that had important data that had been either omitted or erroneous. The client who was in charge spotted the error and returned the document to the editing company, livid as a result of the problem. Jason's supervisor recognized it and played the middle man between the two, but she also came to Jason and said, you know Jason you made these mistakes and I need to follow-up with you about it. When Jason heard that he had made so many mistakes, he was also mortified and felt so bad. A lump descended into his throat, and he could hardly breathe. When he talked to Vicky, he was losing his energy and felt so bad about it. He was feeling shame and remorse, as a result of what he had done. However, then Vicky gave him the negative feedback that he had been waiting for her to unleash at him. As Vicky was giving the input, there was gentleness and tenderness in her voice that made it possible for her to share with him in a way that would be positive and uplifting. She made him feel a lot better because she had empathy for him. Vicki knew precisely how it was to be new to proofreading and to make mistakes in the work. Therefore, she was able to side with Jason and realized that he could do better next time. Vicki was an advocate for Jason and told the client that the proofreader was new and that it was his first time doing this type of assignment.

After that communication, the client came back with a note of understanding that showed empathy also with Jason and his first experience. It was a positive resolution to a difficult situation. This type of scenario is an example of emotional empathy. Vicky had compassion for Jason because she knew exactly how he felt and how he had a bad day. She also had compassion for Jason and knew that he could improve in the future if he applied himself. Jason also felt sorry for what he had done but was able to get better after that episode. All ended well.

Having Social Skills

A key aspect of developing sympathy or empathy with others is by improving your social skills. This means being in tune with how others are in your life. You're able to have better relationships with people through developing your interpersonal skills. If you want to make other people like you, you're going to have to know how people think, act, and behave. That also means understanding others' sense of humor and style of communication. Not everyone communicates the same way, so it is best to learn how to communicate effectively across different lines. When you have the social skills to help with communication, then you will be able to seamlessly do many things with others, which will strengthen relational ties and enable you to have fun in the process.

Social skills include the ability to relate to others and their interests. It means taking a vested interest in what others think and feel in their lives. Social people are always interested in what others have to say and have higher self-esteem. Because they exude self-confidence and are seeking to meet others with similar and unique interests, they know how to communicate their thoughts and feelings to others. Whereas, people without good social skills will struggle to find ways to relate to others and quickly get offended or hurt by others, especially when it comes to jokes and humorous things that they may not readily get.

A crucial part of interpersonal communication is knowing how to relate to others' feelings and how they think and behave. The way to do this involves getting to know others and their tastes. That said, it also takes some creative thinking. It is important to note how well you respond to people's emotions in times of conflict or other things.

Reading Others' Emotions

Reacting to others' emotions is a vital part of how you can make meaningful relationships. However, it is not always helpful. A lot of times, it is quite harmful. For example, a group of men arguing in a bar after having drunk a lot can result in some severe communication that may result in injury on both parties. One man might call another a dirty name, and the other man would get very angry and react in anger to the name-calling and make a violent turn to the evening. It could result in destructive behavior and physical injury. Emotional reactions in their worst form can occur in acts that are shameful and harmful. That was an example of the worst kind of emotional response.

However, what about reacting to other's sense of humor or jokes? Sometimes, people will make jokes or inter-racial slurs or different offensive remarks that can invoke anger in a person and cause a great deal of discord among people. Laughing has a way of bringing people together to enjoy an amusing joke; however, it can also be very offensive to some people and cause them to react in anger or frustration at the laughing person. This is where learning others' communication styles is very important. It is crucial that you find ways of relating to other people's emotions and sense of humor because that will be the way that you can make friends with others.

Also, you have to understand whenever others are feeling sad and how you can react to their sadness and provide comfort and support to them. In particular, when someone else is having a tough time at work or school and needs someone to comfort them, you can provide the necessary support that your friend needs because you are there for him or her and can do all things for them. Being a good friend involves sharing in the joys with your loved ones, as well as the challenging times. It requires a person to have maximum emotional sensitivity.

How to Leverage Positive Emotions in People

When you observe how people behave, you will notice how they act when they are experiencing positive or negative emotions. Usually, when a person is displaying a positive feeling, their faces will light up, they will smile or laugh, and there will generally be a positive, exuberant, and upbeat tone in their voice. Usually, positive people are entertaining to be around and can make you feel their positivity everywhere you go. They tend to give people lots of energy.

Moreover, when you're around a positive person, you will feel how they give their energy and help you experience warmth and joy in your life. The way to leverage positive emotion is how it has an impact on you personally. Does it give you energy and move you forward? Does it bring you excitement, anticipation, or joy? Then, it would be a more positive emotion that you would be experiencing from that person. Often, with positive people, you will want to get closer to them and spend more time with them. Positive people are great to be around, and they can help you improve your self-esteem and confidence.

How to Deal with Negative Emotions in People

On the other side of things are negative people. They bring us down. They always suck our energy and time and tear down all the positive energy that we may exude. Negative people radiate negative energy and emotions. Most of the time their energy is negative. Think of the Negative Nancy at the office who curses as soon as she arrives and complains about every little thing. She then causes other people to complain and gripe. Moreover, pretty soon, the whole office is filled with Negative Nancies and Neds. It is evident that negative emotions tend to zap people of energy. They also demoralize situations where people are perfectly content and happy because they cause people to doubt their ability to have a good time and enjoy their lives because they emphasize the negative. Emotional reactions such as anger also cause the person to become stressed and anxious, which ups the blood sugar and other things. It creates a great deal of stress for everyone around you.

So, what should you do when you're within these situations? Well, if you have someone who is angry and is not in a good mood, it's best to let that person get some fresh air by himself or herself. It's a good idea to run away from a situation that may cause friction or even an outright explosion. Therefore, avoidance and running away can be a good solution. Distancing yourself from people who exude negativity is also a good policy. The truth is, negative people, get their energy from sucking out the positive energy out of people. They love to tear others down only to feel better about themselves. They are insecure in themselves and don't have any self-esteem, so the way they get theirs is by ratting away at someone, complaining, gossiping, and other ways. Negative people will almost always have something to complain about, so perhaps a good idea to get them going on something that is not their hobby high-horse of negative talk is by changing the subject. If a person is getting emotional or angry or depressed about something, you should offer to change the subject within a conversation to something a bit more light-hearted, fun, or enjoyable. That way, you and your interlocutor can have a more fun time and benefit from having happy times together. Instead of walking away, you can stay and get your interlocutor to feel positive about something that he or she loves. Find something that is passionate or exciting to talk about, and you will see how enthusiastic the situation will become.

Negative people are tough to deal with. They are not always easy to be around and cause you a lot of stress and strain. It is best to find ways of changing the subject, avoiding, or even running away from them because they will suck the energy and life out of you. Think about whenever you have a great project that you want to do, and you're really excited about it, and you tell your friend, who tells you not to try it because it's not worth it. Then, the wind in your sails is taken out, and you feel depressed and discouraged. Don't let negative people bring you down. They want to do it, and they will do anything to get after your positive and upbeat emotions. Also, they want to turn it around and make you feel bad about yourself. It can be a good idea to avoid that person if you can.

Let's look at an example of how to handle a negative person.

Joe is a person who continually complains at the office, and he invites people into his gossip about coworkers and his boss. He goes out drinking every night until 5 am and loves to talk about how much of a good time he has had the night before. He tends to yell at you whenever he finds something, he disagrees with you about and gets fired up. One day, he had a conversation with a coworker named Daniel. They talked and talked, and Joe was getting riled up about something, and

Daniel said, "let's talk about something else." So, they continued to another topic. But then Joe started yelling at Daniel for another topic. Daniel said, "I should be going actually. Sorry, I have an appointment." Daniel then left the conversation. Eventually, Joe's negative energy was sucking the life out of the office, and he was fired after a long haul.

How was this dealt with?

Daniel realized he wanted to be a good friend and listen to Joe and talk but also knew how negative and emotional Joe could be. He tried to change the subject of the conversation to something that was not so sensitive and then it backfired. Joe then got emotional, and Daniel left. Later, Joe was fired, and his negativity must have had something to do with the situation.

Conclusion

What can we take away from this discussion on extrospection? The way to truly relate to others is to understand how they think and feel. That involves analyzing how they think, feel, and react to different situations. This is the way to understand best where a person is coming from because the way to truly be relational is to understand the feelings and emotions of different people. Emotional sensitivity is very powerful these days with the extensive play of Facebook and how people interact with people on the web. It can get gruesome at times online because people find ways to tear each other down and say truly awful things about others online, even though many times, they would not behave that way in real life. However, the thing is, with communication on the Internet, it has made it easier than ever to make emotional responses. In addition, it exacerbates the situation, because often, people are made stressed or angry from what they read online.

Reading other people's emotions is an essential skill to have when you are focused on others. You learn what makes people sad, angry, or happy, and it can be great in bringing people together. But it can also make people go in opposite directions. It is vital that you find ways to relate to others through the emotions, because it enables you to have a spiritual connection with another person, almost like kinship in which you talk about something together, and it stirs in you an emotional bond that can lead to close friendship. This is not to say that all close friendships operate from this perspective, but it means that emotions are essential to bringing people from different backgrounds together to share in experiences with one another. When you can connect with another person's emotions, then you can bring out the best in the other person and find ways of interacting that are meaningful and productive.

Finally, it is essential that we move to be others-centered in our extrospection. Being aware of our own emotions is important, but it is vital that we move to how we relate to others and form relationships so that we can have a good time with our friends, coworkers, family members, or anyone else who is in our circle.

Part II: Introduction: Four Week Emotion Intelligence Booster Program

In this section of the book, we are going to go into how you can enhance your emotional sensitivity to help you hack your way to getting that promotion and success in your workplace. We know that you want to get ahead where you work, and we want to give you the tools to do that. So, we are going to provide you with a step-by-step guide to raise your emotional intelligence (EQ) and give you the right tools to enable you to be successful in your goals and aspirations for your life.

Let's begin with the emotions themselves. Choose one emotion for every four weeks that you want to work on. Begin with the basic emotions, and then you can move on to the more subtle and advanced emotions as you go along. We want you to go through each emotion one at a time. Moreover, for every emotion, you will take four weeks. If your intended goal is not reached for each emotion, you should repeat multiple times the exercise. Throughout your journey, we advise you to keep a journal of your thoughts to record how you're doing with it.

In the next chapter, we will highlight each step of this journey that you can take to get on your way to better emotional intelligence. We will show you how you can use this knowledge to your advantage, as you seek to be a better employee or manager within a company. We hope that this information will be helpful to you, as you try to understand the emotions better. In each part of this journey, we will guide you through the ups and downs through different anecdotes that will illustrate our points. So, let's go on this journey together.

Chapter 5: Week 1: Intro- Basics- Self-Awareness

At the beginning of this journey to emotional understanding, we should begin with how you experience emotions and your way of recognizing them. You have to become self-aware and examine how you are experiencing emotions from day to day. It all begins with self-regulation of the emotions.

How Do You Recognize the Emotions and Feelings Within Yourself?

One way to be self-aware is to write down your thoughts that you experience from day to day. Get a journal and start writing down all your passing thoughts, especially the ones that are causing you stress or anxiety. You should learn how to recognize when you are feeling angry or sad and take note of what you think triggered or caused this negative emotion to come about.

You should think about how you are reacting to each situation. For example, if you were angry, perhaps you became enraged and started shouting or throwing something. Alternatively, if you were sad or depressed, you went to your room and cried it out. Another example is that when you got the news that your friend was getting married, you immediately jumped up and down and started shouting. Once you have gauged how you responded to each situation, then you can evaluate how you responded to the scenario. Think to yourself: "was this an appropriate response?" "Did I act out in the right way, or could I have responded differently and more positively?" Or, perhaps, you experienced a positive emotion that helped to solve a situation. For example, maybe you were able to solve a problem yourself that you thought was really difficult, then you discovered there was a simple solution and could laugh it off and think that it was no big deal. Often, we can learn to laugh at ourselves; it can help us to have more joy and peace in our lives. It is also a part of self-acceptance that enables you to reach your goals and accomplish the purposes of your life.

To fully understand, how emotional regulation works, we have to look at some concrete examples of self-awareness.

Negative Emotional Reaction Example 1:

Immanuel was often a perfectionistic worker. He tended to be hard on himself and at times would self-flagellate as a result of the mistakes that he made. He had very high standards for his life because he had attended a renowned university with an honors degree and knew that he could accomplish all the purposes for his life. Like many people who were high achievers, his perfectionism made it hard for him to deal with the negativity that inevitably would enter into his mind at times. Immanuel constantly dealt with the fear of failure and "imposter syndrome." This would infiltrate into his work at the office as a paralegal at one of the leading law firms of Boston. Immanuel was a big picture INFJ man, who often liked to look at big ideas rather than details. Although he had a good deal of detail-orientation, he tended to make small mistakes that he would internalize and self-implode after recognizing them. He would get stressed and worried about it. One day, he was doing his daily data entry tasks, and he was swamped doing it when he realized that he had cut off a whole field of data and that it got lost. He was mortified at his mistake and was fearful, anxious, and deeply sad at what had happened. Immediately when he made a mistake, he became depressed and was very upset at what had happened. He didn't eat for a few days afterward and cried at home because of his mistake. He also became worried and experienced a flood of intrusive negative thoughts that caused him great stress. Eventually, he was able to correct his error, which was a slip of his attention, but he was greatly worried about his job and whether or not he would get punished for his action. His boss told him it was no big deal and that this was just one mistake that he had made and that it would be okay.

Was This Response Appropriate?

It was ok for Immanuel to feel sorry about making a mistake. However, the extent to which he responded to the situation went overboard and caused him stress and anxiety. He entertained the negative thoughts that flooded into his mind after the incident. In addition, he internalized the negative emotion, which was not properly dealt with and so he was suffering quietly. He was not able to externalize his negative emotions properly, so he became depressed.

How Could He Have Responded Differently?

Immanuel could have responded differently by countering his negative thoughts through some emotional regulation. Instead of responding with anxiety and stress and bottling up his feelings, he could have countered negative thoughts by telling himself: "it's okay, you made a mistake. It happens to everyone. You're still a great worker and talented. You've had a lot of great experiences, and you are well-qualified for this job, but you just made a mistake." He should have tried to spot these intrusive thoughts and responded with some positive thinking. Immanuel could have also gone to a trusted friend and talked to him about what had happened. The talk therapy could help him to cope with his feelings of disappointment and discouragement.

The takeaway from this story is that to manage emotions properly; it is essential to get them out in the open, to share them with others. It is important also to note the self-coping strategy of handling negative emotions, including positive self-talk that can help a person to avoid going off into unhealthy expressions of emotions.

Positive Emotional Response: Example #1:

It is common knowledge that the best workers are those that are happiest and are the most satisfied with their work. When a person is satisfied with their work, they feel good and want to do their job. They are absent less to work due to sickness, and they are much more productive than their less happy counterparts. When a person is doing well and enjoying his or her work, then they will produce the best work possible, and it is a win-win for the employer and the employee. When the workplace treats the employees fairly, and with decent compensation, then all workers are happy. So, whenever a person is happy at work, he will do a good job. Let's give an example of a person who is happy at work and is doing a good job.

James truly enjoyed his work as a project manager at an editing company. He was passionate about writing and found it profoundly satisfying work. He wanted to produce the best results for his clients. Because James enjoyed his job, he wanted his employees to feel the same burst of excitement when it came to working on a project. So, he treated his employees fairly. He never contacted them during their off-hours. He respected others greatly and didn't want to demand too much of his employees. James wanted his employees to enjoy a work-life balance and not make their lives simply work-work-work and no play.

Why Was James So happy?

Well, for one thing, he enjoyed his work. He was paid well, which makes a difference, but it is not the only factor in making work satisfying. James liked what he did and enjoyed project management, and he was good at delegating tasks to his employees. However, at the same time, he used his happiness to make others happy. James wanted his employees to enjoy their work just as much as he did, so he did his best to ensure that they were doing well by encouraging them and offering them quality feedback on their work.

What Does Happiness do for Work?

When a worker is happy, he will do a much better job in producing results. The example of James shows the productivity of an individual who finds satisfaction in his work. This is not the case for the majority of workers. Most people working are not happy with their work. They only go to work for a steady paycheck and nothing else. One article finds that ¾ (75%) of all American workers are unhappy at their jobs. That is a saddening statistic to have. And the thing is, the majority of work that people do is mundane, boring, and uninteresting. This causes many workers to become disengaged and not productive at work. But when you have one person who is deeply satisfied in his work, you see that this can affect how others also experience this enthusiasm and passion. James was aware of his own happiness as a worker. And then, he chose to give out his positive energy to others. It began with a positive experience of emotion and then led to his outward expression, which impacted his workplace and community. Positivity: it's infectious and exciting.

Negative Emotional Response Example #2:

The next example is one in communication, which is one that is very important to consider in workplace situations. Wilson is the head manager of his translation company and is in charge of communication for the different project managers. He had one issue of communication in which he did not communicate with everyone in his office and instead did a lot of one-to-one contact with different individuals. As deadlines started to pile up on people, some of the project managers were missing their deadlines, because Wilson did not effectively send out the deadlines to all the project managers. This led different project managers to get very angry at Wilson for not adequately communicating the deadlines and for only doing it one-on-one. One project manager, Amy, was visibly upset and she yelled across the room to Wilson: "You idiot! Why did you not send out the notices to the project managers?! You're so inconsiderate! I can't believe you!"

Looking at Amy's example, she got agitated and became angry with Wilson for his poor communication style, but instead of approaching Wilson directly, she vehemently screamed at him from across the room to get his attention. Moreover, then, everyone in the room was shocked to see this display of emotion.

What Could Amy Have Done?

Poor communication is a crucial factor in workplace conflict and hostility. It causes friction within the most productive of workplaces. However, it can be a factor in getting people riled up with their emotions. Amy could have recognized her negative emotion and contained herself and simply gone up to Wilson and confronted him directly, but she was so upset that she screamed at him from across the room. In addition, Amy could have gone with one of her colleagues to him and talked to him about this problem and perhaps the issue could be resolved then. However, it is up to Wilson to resolve his problem of poor communication with his colleagues. He needs to get his act together. That said, Amy needs to come up with a way to healthily confront her colleague rather than exploding in emotion. Perhaps, she could have written an email to him and then arrange to have a meeting with Wilson privately. This would have resolved the issue.

A crucial part of recognizing negative and hostile emotion is realizing when you're starting to get riled up. With Amy, she needed to control herself and regulate the emotional response which was beginning to escalate over time. If she had known how to deal with her negative emotions, she would have responded more positively and dealt with the issue by talking to another coworker, confronting her manager, or writing an email. This would have aided her in coming up with ways to do this.

Positive Emotional Response #2:

In another example of an emotional response, we can see how positive emotions can influence others and lead to success in conflict resolution. Jill made a mistake in communication with her colleague. She told one of her other colleagues about a project but misstated the facts about it. Jill then communicated a different story to another colleague, and they got confused about the matter. She was very frazzled with herself over the miscommunication and felt sorry for what she had done. Instead of getting upset about the matter, however, she told herself: "everyone makes mistakes. This is the first time this has happened. I will apologize to colleague #2 and tell them the fact of the story." Jill then apologized to the second colleague and explained the real facts about the project. There was conflict resolution, and the situation was much better. Jill was able to forgive herself, and then her colleague also overlooked the situation and thought it was no big deal.

What Did Jill Do in This Situation That Helped?

Jill was a bit frazzled with herself. That is understandable, as everyone makes mistakes. However, she did not beat herself up about it, nor did she blame someone else about it. Instead, she owned up to her mistake, apologized, and then forgave herself for what she had done. In the end, she was able to move on, and her customer was too. Often, we can be our harshest critic and can be hard on ourselves. However, in this case, Jill was comfortable with herself, and she did not have a problem with apologizing over the issue and resolving the conflict of communication. It was a good result and a positive response to the emotion that she was experiencing.

Conclusion

We hope you've been able to see the importance of self-awareness and understanding when you are experiencing emotions, particularly negative ones. In the workplace conflict resolution is so essential to creating a harmonious atmosphere for all workers. There is nothing worse than when you have a workplace with hostility and alienation among the workers. When you create a positive working environment for your colleagues and subordinates, it can make the difference between a toxic workplace and a positive and upbeat company. We now want to provide you with some daily note-taking sections to guide you through the process of recognizing emotions. There will be one section for each day of your week.

Notes:

Day 1: How are you feeling today?

_____

What happened today at work? Did anything upset you?

_____

Were there any triumphs or success stories this week that you can write about?

_____

How did it make you feel?

_____

Day 2: How are you feeling today?

_____

What happened today at work? Did anything upset you?

_____

Were there any triumphs or success stories this week that you can write about?

How did it make you feel?

_____

Day 3: How are you feeling today?

_____

What happened today at work? Did anything upset you?

_____

Were there any triumphs or success stories this week that you can write about?

_____

How did it make you feel?

_____

Day 4: How are you feeling today?

_____

What happened today at work? Did anything upset you?

_____

Were there any triumphs or success stories this week that you can write about?

_____

How did it make you feel?

_____

Day 5: How are you feeling today?

_____

What happened today at work? Did anything upset you?

_____

Were there any triumphs or success stories this week that you can write about?

_____

How did it make you feel?

_____

Chapter 6: Week 2: Basics of Self-Control

In this chapter, we are going to talk about how you can use your emotional responses to maintain self-control in your interactions with others. This is especially important when you are talking to different colleagues, subordinates, and clients.

Every emotion we have is a response to a situation that we come across in our lives. It is always purposeful and meaningful. There is a reason that you are experiencing a particular emotion and it is valid. All feelings are valid. At the same time, our emotional responses are what either become a positive or negative reaction to the different stimuli that we may experience in our lives. You should listen to your emotions, but you also need to learn how to regulate how you respond to them because it is vital that you have a plan in place to deal with complex and negative emotions that can be overwhelming and difficult.

One way that we deal with negative emotions is through the "fight or flight" response in which a person reacts to a situation based on their emotional reaction. They do not have time to reflect; they respond. For example, when a person is in a dangerous situation and sees a bear in the woods, his initial instinct is to run from the danger in fear. That is a natural response to the emotion of fear. Every time a feeling occurs, it is vital that you observe how you are feeling at a given time and observe how it is. A crucial step in dealing with emotions is to identify what it is that you are feeling and see if what you think reflects the reality of a situation. You must validate the accuracy of your feeling with empirical evidence.

As humans, it is challenging to regulate our feelings and emotions. However, we have the power to influence our feelings in positive ways. When we develop our emotional intelligence skills, we can regulate how we will respond to overwhelming emotions, such as anger or anxiety.

About Emotional Regulation

One of the most crucial parts of emotional regulation is recognizing the negative emotions that we have objectively. We must see that it is normal to feel one way and we shouldn't make a moral judgment against the negative emotions as if it is terrible to experience such things. Sometimes, our emotions are triggered by a sense of justice, and when we see unjust actions and behaviors, we want justice to be served. For example, if you get angry at how a person is being treated at the workplace, you have the right to get mad about it. A sense of justice can produce a kind of "righteous" anger in that you may realize that something is wrong, and you want to correct it. However, what you do with this emotion matters.

Emotional regulation at work is going to help you to put all your emotions in check. You'll have to go through the process of getting your feelings in check. Furthermore, there is a step-by-step process to get there. Let's look at how you can achieve emotional regulation at work.

Label Your Emotion

One of the first ways you can deal with your emotion is by labeling the emotion and understanding what it is that you are feeling. This is a technique that is used in talk therapy such as cognitive-behavioral therapy or dialectical behavioral therapy for people dealing with various mental health challenges. Primary emotions are the body's way of reacting to triggers that might cause a person stress. For example, if you see someone being mistreated at work and they are getting maligned or criticized by the management, you have the right to feel angry about it. You can identify what it is that is triggering the negative emotion in you: injustice and think about ways you can deal with that emotion.

Example of Labeling the Emotion

How do you label an emotion? Immediately when you start feeling an emotion, you talk about what it is that you are feeling. When you begin to feel depressed or down in the dumps, you can tell yourself, "I think I'm starting to feel down today. Maybe I should go for a walk or run and get those endorphins flowing again." Alternatively, when you're starting to feel stressed about an upcoming deadline, you could tell yourself, "I'm feeling nervous about this upcoming deadline. I think I need to get to work now."

Identifying the emotion is an essential step in the process of self-regulation because once you know exactly what it is that you are feeling and why you can come up with ways to manage the symptoms of what you're feeling. You can formulate the most positive response to the situation.

Letting Go

The next step in emotional regulation is letting go. As humans, we often become entangled in our emotional cycles and can't manage to pull ourselves out of it. Rather than letting go when we hold a grudge against someone, we hold onto it and clutch it like a death-grip on a steering wheel of a car. However, letting go of an adverse emotion is going to enable you to release the stress of a given situation and manage your response to a negative scenario, and then, you won't feel like you need to respond to every little thing. Here are some steps that you can follow with that.

- A. Observe your feelings without judging them. Furthermore, see how the situation comes about.
- B. Say to yourself: "I am feeling this emotion. I won't feel the same way tomorrow or the next day."

C. Embrace your emotions. Instead of fighting off the negative feelings, we should embrace emotions as part of our humanity, because it will help you to have a better time at coping.

Example

Whenever you're feeling you need to let go of something, you release it so that you don't think about it anymore. For example, if you have a feeling of resentment against someone for passing you over and ignoring you one day at work and feel angry at that person, you're able to let go and forget about it when it happened. Even if a person does not tell you, he/she is sorry, you're able to release the feeling of resentment and keep going with your life. It helps you to live in complete freedom.

Self-care

Dealing with emotional cycles begins with taking care of yourself. You have to have a healthy body to feel well each day. Also, it is essential that you take care of your health because we are not guaranteed to have healthy bodies all the time. If we feel tired, sick, or hungry, our emotions can be negatively impacted. Physical effects on our body can provoke us to feelings of anger, anxiety, or depression. One example of an emotion that was recently added to the dictionary is "hangry," which is a combination of hungry and angry. The spelling is not off, because a person may be mad because they are hungry. It is evident that no one makes good decisions when tired and hungry.

Having good self-care is going to be an essential part of your routine, and it will impact how you feel in social situations. In the workplace, it will affect how productive you are, because if you feel good about yourself and your appearance, you will exude more confidence and project that assertiveness onto others. Having good hygiene, getting the proper exercise, and eating well will be ways that you can take care of yourself, and you will feel much better when you interact with others at the workplace.

Self-care will be especially important to you as a manager at the workplace, because you will be delegating tasks, holding meetings and conferences, and other jobs that demand a significant amount of your time and energy. Therefore, it is crucial that you find time to take care of yourself, because this will influence your emotions and how you behave and interact with others at the company.

Case Study

Amanda is a headhunter of a human resources company in Atlanta. She recently got promoted to senior manager at her company. She had to invest a lot of time and energy in her job at first that it became very stressful and challenging for her. For a while, however, she was not eating and was always stressed at work. Sometimes, she would work through lunch; she slept for 4 hours at night and did nothing but work even into the night. Amanda recognized her unhealthy attitudes toward work. It was affecting her emotions. She would get frustrated at work, swear, and yell when she didn't get her way.

Moreover, she would continuously feel stressed and anxious. In the middle of her second year, she decided she would stop working so hard and get her life together. She tried meditation and aromatherapy at home. She would also take long baths at home. Also, she developed a more positive work-life balance, which enabled her to be more successful and confident at work. Later, she would arrive at work each day eager for each new task. And when she had a dispute with anyone at work, she would control herself and respond in positive ways. It created a much friendlier and more relaxed working environment.

Be positive

Another strategy that you can incorporate into your emotional regulation is to be positive all the time. You should enjoy the beautiful emotions that you have and not dwell on the negative thoughts that you might experience. Let yourself smile and laugh even at difficult things. You should also learn to laugh at yourself whenever you make mistakes because everyone is prone to making an error here and there. To leverage your positive emotions, you need to find the time to enjoy positivity and surround yourself with others who will do the same. Try to counter all the negative thoughts you may be experiencing with positive ones. It will make a difference, and you will notice how you come across to others.

Many managers are quite critical of their subordinates and don't hesitate to point out all the mistakes in their employees' records of work. They tend to dwell on giving negative feedback to others, and this causes a significant amount of problems, because the workers may feel fearful or worried about their performance as a result of mistakes they have made. If a manager lashes out in anger, then this will impact the motivation of the worker and lead to employee dissatisfaction and discouragement. Therefore, as a manager, you need to find ways of looking on the bright side and control your negative response to the things that your employees are doing. By being positive and exuding that positivity, you can make a difference in transforming the work culture of your company. It will make for happy workers and managers.

Example

It is critical to stay positive whenever we are confronted with particularly challenging situations. Oscar was a manager of a Fortune 500 company in the human resources department. He always had a lot to do and seemed to have a never-ending list of things to do every day, but he struggled to complete all the items on his list. He became very discouraged by it. He thought, "I'm just no good and cannot do everything. I think I'm going to fail. I'm a failure to launch." One day, he was having coffee with his colleague and mentor named James and the two discussed how each one was doing after a long day. Oscar said, "I'm struggling with negativity. It seems to be welling up inside of me. Every time I go to my task manager on my computer, I start to have this surge of negativity, and it causes me to feel depressed and sad because I feel that I will not be able to accomplish all the tasks that are assigned to me. It's dreadful. What should I do, man?" James responded by saying, "Oscar, bro, you're going to have to practice positive thinking. It's so important that you find good things to say to yourself. You need to start by saying, 'I can do this. I am capable, talented, and smart. I'm just going through a rough patch right now.'" Oscar was relieved to hear this from his colleague and realized that he was too hard on himself and that he wasn't listening to an inner voice of affirmation and positivity. After that moment, Oscar started to affirm himself. He began to give himself compliments about his appearance and his ability, and he began to feel better. He realized that being positive would be vital to him reaching his goals and completing his daily tasks, so it worked.

Allow Yourself to Enjoy Life

Life is too short to be so serious and focus solely on work. As a manager, it is vital that you have a positive work-life balance and encourage your employees to do the same. Go to a movie every once in a while. Treat yourself to dinner at the newest cafe-restaurant. Hang out with your friends and family. Enjoy your life. It will encourage you to be balanced, and you can also model that for your employees. By leading a balanced life with finding room for work and play, you will also help with regulating your emotions and feel happier in the process.

In addition, you should foster this spirit of fun by inviting your colleagues and subordinates to a company dinner or outing, which can give your company a sense of conviviality and enable your company to have fun with a drink or meal. This will also help regulate the emotions by encouraging positive responses to situations. Not to mention, having a meal is a proven way to help relax a group of colleagues.

With the social aspect of enjoying life together, negative emotions will not overpower you, and you will feel the difference in many ways.

Case Study

To control his emotions, James had to do things to enjoy his life. He used to be a workaholic and work 60 hours per week and 12-hour days. However, lately, he has been timing himself and not overcommitting to the tasks he is doing. Instead, he is finding ways to have dinner with friends throughout the week, go to a movie, see a soccer game, and write in his journal. As a manager of a Fortune 500 company, he knows that he must have a cheerful attitude at work so that he can be the best boss to his employees. He is also aware of how balancing your life is essential to living a healthy lifestyle. Therefore, he strives to commit himself to no more than 9 hours at the office. He encouraged others at the office to do the same. James said, "When it's 6:00 pm, go home. Enjoy your family. Be with the ones you love. I don't want you to be workaholics and work until 8 or 9 at night. That is not healthy. I want you to enjoy your life." Work-life balance makes a big difference in how you can control your emotions and maintain stability in your health.

Worry Less

To avoid getting caught in the trap of a negative emotion that can disarm you, you should focus on the positive and practice uplifting self-talk that will enable you to get out of anxious or worrisome thought patterns. Admittedly, we have a lot to worry about in our lives, whether that is in finances, relationships, customers, or a number of other things. When you worry less about stuff, you will have less emotional responses that are negative to the various difficult emotions that we face.

Example

Yannick was a person who was a worrywart. He always seemed to have something to worry about all the time, and he especially got concerned during tax season and the time to pay his bills. He struggled with the finances of his small business. It was their first year in business, and things were going forward, but Yannick was struggling to pay off debts and bills that seemed to pile up endlessly. Because of this new business, Yannick was forced to think about money and how to operate his company seemingly all the time, and it was a real struggle to get through at different times. Yannick wanted to seek professional help for his emotional situation, so he saw his financial advisor who also did therapy sessions, which enabled him to get out all his worries about money and to feel good about everything. His financial advisor told him, "Yannick, you need to stop worrying about your financial future. Planning is everything. When you have everything planned out, you won't need to worry anymore about it. Everything will be settled. What I want you to do is stop worrying. Your emotional cycles get out of hand whenever you start worrying. You need to simply stop the thought and divert your thinking to your successful future." Yannick realized it would take time to train himself to not go in that direction of worrying about his business and financial future, but he stopped worrying and was able to reach his goals. After a year, he was able to stop worrying so much and lived a life full of joy and peace, because his financial advisor believed in him and his ability to overcome the hurdles that were in the way of his life. It was a success story.

Notice When Your Emotions Start to Get Out of Hand

When you start to feel the problematic emotions overflowing, you should respond to the situation. As we have suggested, you should journal about these experiences and write down all that you are feeling at a given time. Remember how you react to different situations and recall how you were able to solve different situations before. Then, you can correct your emotional response to things later on.

Example

An example of seeing when things are getting out of hand is Kelly. She was a hairstylist operating her own business in Central Square in Boston. She also managed the other hairstylists in this business. Kelly tended to complain a lot and to critique her stylists and their abilities and sometimes she would get angry and go off at them in her office whenever they made a mistake. She would always yell at them and show her anger to them in private, whenever the customers were not there. Little did she know, Kelly had an anger management problem, which had multiple causes. For one, she had broken up with her boyfriend who cheated on her for a long time and then told her. For another, she was resentful of her friends who were already married, and she was still single, so there was a lot of bitterness in her heart.

As Kelly learned emotional regulation from her mentor, she realized that she needed to stop herself before going off the edge. Whenever she felt she wanted to spill her emotions on others through her tirades about customers and difficulties, she had to stop herself before it got out of hand. Kelly became more self-aware as time went by and then she realized when she needed to stop herself from going off at people. So, when she felt she was about to get angry at someone, she would stop and sit in her office alone and give herself about 10-15 minutes to meditate in the silence and quietness of her heart. It helped things so much and then she was able to feel the difference in it.

Hit Your "Pause" Button and Stop Yourself

We all get furious over something that happens and yells or scream when something does not go our way. It is human nature. That said, one thing that you can do in practicing self-control is hitting your "pause" button. You stop in the middle of what you're doing. Observe what is around you and in your immediate surroundings. Take a deep breath and close your eyes before you respond to a given situation. Moreover, then, after this pause, you can return to what you are doing and can effectively manage the situation.

For any management situation, it is vital that you have a "pause" button to help you take a time-out before you get emotionally wrapped up in a situation and react negatively or regretfully. Exercising emotional self-control is an essential step to your developing as a person and manager of a company.

Case Study

Bill was a senior project manager at Apple Care products in San Diego, California. He was organized, helpful, and friendly. One thing that irked him was whenever his employees were late to a meeting. Once he got enraged and blew up in front of them and said how irresponsible and uncaring the employees were. After learning how to control his emotions from watching videos from seminars on emotions, he was able to learn how to manage himself and hit his pause button. Instead of lashing out at his late employees, he took the time to collect himself and then made a joke out of it to lighten the mood a bit. He then talked about the importance of punctuality. Later, he followed up with a company email that stressed the importance of being on time to meetings and that he was not going to let down on it. To motivate his employees, he chose the strategy of saying that he would make the meetings much shorter if the employees would come on-time. It worked and then the employees were happy and wanted to come on time. However, this happened as a result of emotional regulation and control, as well as influential people skills that motivated the employees to do the right thing and follow company instructions.

Conclusion

There are many different ways you can develop self-control in your emotions. Emotional regulation is one of the most important things you can do as a manager and as a person because the way you handle your feelings is going to speak volumes about your character and personality to others. If you're able to contain yourself and your feelings, rather than acting on emotional impulses, such as by yelling or throwing a temper tantrum, you will demonstrate a sense of maturity that will be a model to your employees. No one wants to work for the boss, who is moody and scares his subordinates into doing what they need to do. They want to work for someone approachable, friendly, and sensitive to the emotions. As we have mentioned above, emotional intelligence has a higher value over IQ, because when you connect with people, it has more meaning and significance than if you were to be smart and know all the answers. While having the brainpower makes a difference and is useful, it is more important that the manager has the interpersonal skills to resolve conflict, handle various difficult situations, and manage the emotions of the people around him or her.

We hope you have been able to note all the ways that you can exercise self-control in your workplace. We want to give you more space here below to reflect on what you have learned and put it into practice. Here are some more journal pages that will help you get started.

Notes:

Day 1: How are you feeling today?

_____

What happened today at work? Did anything upset you?

_____

Did you react to any situation in a particularly negative way today?

_____

If yes, how could you handle the situation differently in the future?

_____

Day 2: How are you feeling today?

_____

What happened today at work? Did anything upset you?

_____

Did you react to any situation in a particularly negative way today?

If yes, how could you handle the situation differently in the future?

Day 3: How are you feeling today?

What happened today at work? Did anything upset you?

Did you react to any situation in a particularly negative way today?

If yes, how could you handle the situation differently in the future?

Day 4: How are you feeling today?

What happened today at work? Did anything upset you?

Did you react to any situation in a particularly negative way today?

_____

If yes, how could you handle the situation differently in the future?

_____

Day 5: How are you feeling today?

_____

What happened today at work? Did anything upset you?

_____

Did you react to any situation in a particularly negative way today?

_____

If yes, how could you handle the situation differently in the future?

_____

Chapter 7: Week 3: Intro: Basics to Recognizing Emotions in Others

Welcome to Week 3! You're already well into the half of the program already and are prepared to tackle your next project, which is recognizing emotions in others.

Suppose that you and your spouse are having an argument at breakfast over who will do the household chores in the evening. Your wife or husband is furious and gets very angry over it. You can read it in their face. Immediately, you feel the sensation of it as you're about to walk out the front door. It is raining buckets outside, and you get out in the rain, and your dress or suit get caught out in it, and you get a massive stain on it. When you arrive at the subway station, there is a delay for the trains, because there was a runaway train on the tracks. So, you wait for 20 minutes. You realize you're going to be late for an important meeting where you're going to give a sales presentation about your company's signature product. You are anxious and nervous at this point. Once you arrive at the office, there is a fire drill, and all employees had to leave the building, so you have no time to prepare your PPT, which was supposed to go on the screen fifteen minutes ago... everyone goes back into the room. There is a state of dismay and discord among the people there. Your colleagues and employees are sitting in the meeting as you're giving the presentation. They are bored out of their minds and looking at their phones. You can read it on their faces that they are not buying into what you want them to know, so you feel quite disappointed with this. So, you go home and sulk with a bottle of wine.

This situation was an emotional day for you. First, it started with you recognizing your own emotions and respond to the stressors that were aggravating you. Then, you were able to read the cues of the people around you, while at the meeting. This is a sign of emotional recognition in others that you should take care to examine as you are becoming more aware of others' emotions.

Reading people's emotions is one of the most important things that you can do in understanding others and their reactions to different situations. The Mayer-Salovey-Caruso-Emotional-Intelligence-Test: MSCEIT Self-Development Workbook by Susan David and Jim Grant presents many different methods that a person can work with to regulate emotions and recognize emotions in others. It includes a chapter on emotions. Whenever you read others' emotions, you can pick up on cues that people are making with their body language and facial expressions, and it allows you to understand how a person is feeling.

Some have said that a lot of what we can pick up on about others is through nonverbal communication and often that is by looking at different expressions on people's faces to let us know how a person is feeling. In the MSCEIT Self-Development Workbook, there are several different passages on how to read people's facial expressions to let you know how a person is feeling at a given moment. Many decades of research have been given to studying facial expressions and have shown that 43 muscles in the face produce a given expression (Grant and David). These muscles can be connected to the different emotional expressions in people. One way that we can use facial recognition is by telling if someone is lying by their faces. It is a natural inclination that people have.

On the other hand, there are professionals at the FBI, who are trained in lie detection to spot fiction amid truth. Some people can read the emotions of others better than others, because of the way that a person has been raised. For example, they might have picked up on feelings of sadness, because they had had many traumatic experiences as a child of losing loved ones or pets. Therefore, they would be more apt to recognize the emotion of sadness in others.

Here below, we will look at different emotions, as they are presented in the workbook to give you a feel for how to do facial recognition in people.

Recognizing Emotions in a Person: The Basic Emotions

Happiness is an emotion that is shown in different ways. That said, a lot of it appears within a person's eye. It includes upturned corners of the mouth and a grin on the face. A happy expression on the face also has oblique eyebrows, and the edge of the lips is pulled straight down. The mouth also has a curved look. Often, with this expression, a person is looking down at another person. Sometimes, you can tell if a person's smile is a social smile to conform with rules of politeness or if they are genuine smiles. For example, when a person smiles with a social smile, the skin around the eyes will not wrinkle. Often, it takes a lot of practice to decipher if a smile is genuine or not. Some are easier to spot than others.

Example in Your Life

The way that you will be able to tell if someone is happy is by a genuine smile. For example, imagine you are the CEO of a company, and you are happy to give a promotion and pay raise to your employee. You have a big meeting, and you extend the offer to your employees and can immediately sense their excitement. The person lights up with joy, and their positive energy comes flying back at you. Their smile is infectious, and their voice is loud and responds with a resounding "yes! I will extend my contract! Thank you so much for this promotion!

It's fantastic!" When you experience this moment as a CEO, it will make you feel joyful and satisfied in your role of rewarding excellent work and providing your employees with valuable opportunities for advancement.

Sadness

Sadness is displayed on the face through a curving in of the eyebrows and upward toward the middle of the brow. The eyes are not concentrated and are looking out into space. An expression of sadness can quickly be taken for one of shame. It is not an expression that is easy to fake. You can even try to fake a sad face in the mirror, and you will find yourself unable to look at yourself without laughing. If you are not trained well, it will be quite tricky to look truly sad in the mirror. However, there are some emotional manipulators, who use tears as a way to fake sadness. Some people can do this, and force tears out of their eyes. It is essential for you to look at a person's eyebrows to find a genuine expression of sadness.

An example in Your Life

Imagine for a minute you have an employee, who is working for you and they recently lost someone special to them. Perhaps, they lost a grandfather, or even a mother or father. Their situation must deeply sadden them. If you have empathy for those who are hurting, then you will extend kindness to this situation. You will sense a person's sadness by the way they look you in the face, and you see the frown or low and downcast look.

Moreover, you will detect it. Once you do, you should do your best to help the person feel better. When you show empathy to someone who needs it, then you will be able to handle the pain along with the other person and share in the suffering of another. It's something that every manager needs to know how to do because it is a potent force that can connect two people through shared suffering and struggle. Empathy in this situation would probably only be genuinely achievable if you had gone through a similar situation, such as losing a loved one. However, when you can identify the emotion in another and offer some consolation such as "I'm sorry for your loss" or "I'm thinking of you," it can help another person feel a lot better about the situation. Just being there and saying nothing can help, because empty words can often hurt a person more than being silent.

Fear

Widened eyes usually indicate the underlying emotion of fear with the upper eyelids and the lower ones tense up. The eyebrows also come together and turn upward with the lips extending horizontally toward the ears. When a person is afraid, their eyes are not open wide like in a surprised look but rather the mouth is stretched out sideways. The lower eyelids also are pulled tight, and the whole face looks more tense than usual. In addition to the facial elements, fear also has several physiological factors that influence how we feel, including blood circulation to the legs that make us ready to run out the door.

An example in Your Life

Fear is an emotion that many people experience in their lives every day, and it is something that you should recognize in yourself, as well as in other people. Fear can easily cripple employees of different companies, who fear for losing their jobs due to some error that they make or due to cuts in funding that cause numerous layoffs. As a manager, you have to be sensitive to the emotions that your employees may be experiencing. Say, your employee makes some mistake in data entry that causes a problem and a person in Publication Quality Assurance (Pub Q/A) spots it. They also see that there is not only one mistake but many mistakes on the same form. This employee named Annie realizes her mistake and immediately displays a white face with shock from what she has done. Her mouth is open having realized what just happened and she is both fearful and surprised, a combination emotion. You see it and know how she is feeling at this time, so you try to console her and tell her to calm down. She is getting into panic mode. Her heart is racing, and her breathing is shallower and faster.

In this situation, it is best for you to find ways to console your employees. Let them know it was a simple mistake and that it can be fixed, but you should also warn them that it cannot happen again. Giving a warning is necessary for extending grace to the other person when they need to have a second chance. Having an emotional sensitivity to realize that everyone makes mistakes and to be kind to your employees will also help them in their emotional state to get better.

Anger

Anger is an emotion that can be recognized on the face relatively quickly. There are different degrees to which a person may become angry, due to frustration, indignation, or other factors. When a person is angry, their face will indicate a slight physical urge to propel forward at another. This makes a person feel threatened by the face of a person. The most obvious sign of anger is the narrowing of the eyes and a squinting face. This facial feature enables a person to focus on the target of their anger. In addition, anger has a variety of physiological effects including blood that flows to a person's arms.

An example in Your Life

Anger manifests itself in a variety of ways, but you will usually see it in the form of frustration with people that are unhappy about something. It can also be in the form of a complaint.

You can detect a person's anger by their tone of voice and looking mean and threatening. For example, you might have an employee, who is angry at the computer for being slow or not booting up properly. You see him banging on the desk, shouting curses at the computer such as "Come on, you piece of junk computer!" It is obvious when a person is experiencing an angry spell, and it is essential to be careful to handle it, as it can be quite aggressive as emotion and sometimes, people do not know how to control themselves. Therefore, exercising emotional sensitivity is a valuable skill to have when handling someone who is angry.

Let's look at a concrete example of an expression of anger within a corporate setting.

Say, one of your colleagues is late for work and is texting in meetings, and your boss notices it and gets angry at him or her. She becomes incensed that your colleague could be so rude and proceeds to have a shouting match with him or her at the coffee place of the office. She shuts the door to the place and continues to berate that person for a full five minutes. Everyone can hear it from the back of the office and are surprised at what's happening.

Why was she angry? Clearly, it was because the colleague had shown rudeness in tardiness and texting during a meeting. This escalated the problem and then she became utterly enraged by the situation and wanted to let it all out, so she proceeded to get into a shouting match. It didn't end well from that moment on.

Disgust

The emotion of disgust can be seen whenever there is wrinkling of the nose, the raising of the upper lip, and other factors. It often indicates when a person is not happy with a particular smell that they can sense. They will also turn their heads away from the situation. Disgust is an emotion that is too easily recognizable in a person.

An example in Your Life

The workplace can be a place of negativity and griping and complaining. Furthermore, you will notice people being disgusted by their boss's behavior and treatment of different people. For example, they might see their boss treat one of their employees to coffee for doing a good deed and then when they do a similar thing; they might get nothing. Special treatment and doing favors for others is something unfair and will make a person complain a lot. This expression would be disgust that a person would display because of the preferential treatment that is shown. Disgust is something that should be avoided in the workplace because it creates hostility and can put a rift in different kinds of relationships.

Surprise

Surprise is an emotion of instinct that a person will experience automatically when caught off guard. We are automatically trained to be alert to our surroundings all the time. Surprise typically lasts briefly and is a response to something unexpected. As it is a fight-or-flight emotion, it tends to propel a person forward. This emotion is a more complex emotion in that it can lead to other emotions. For example, if a person receives a letter informing them, they owe $2,000 to the government, they might be shocked and surprised and then consequently feel sad and disappointed. Another example might be if you received a tax refund in the mail that you weren't expecting, you might feel surprised and also happy and excited about that.

Typically, a surprise is indicated by a brief instinctual response and involves raising of the eyebrow and opening of the mouth. The eyes might be widened for a fraction of a second. There might also be horizontal wrinkles within a person's face. Surprise is something that does not last very long, so you have to be quick to see it.

An example in Your Life

Surprises come in all shapes and forms, but within the office, it could be an unexpected rush job that comes out of nowhere. Suddenly, you have to rush to complete a task that would have taken you twice as much time to do, but you have to do it immediately. Rush jobs tend to happen in publishing and editing businesses, where writers and editors must rush to complete an assignment. These are often high-stress positions that require the immediate attention of the worker. When a person gets a surprise rush job out of nowhere, they might hit the panic button, realizing that they have less time, or they might get excited and yell "Yahoo! I'm going to get double-time pay for this job!" Surprise rush jobs have a mixture of thrill (happiness) and fear (nervousness) because you experience the rush of adrenaline that hits you when you receive the request and accept it on the computer screen. But then immediately after, you think, "OMG, how am I going to complete this assignment on time! Shoot! I have two days to complete it. How the _____ am I going to do that?!" Surprises are quite exciting but also dreadful in the sense that they can lead to feelings of exasperation or fear immediately afterward.

Chapter 8: Week 4: Intro: Basics: Social Skill

You've done it! You've reached the last week of our course in emotional intelligence. Now we can talk about the previous part of the integration of this knowledge in your daily life. This week the main focus is after recognizing and understanding emotions in people and why they happen. In this chapter, we will talk about how to react the proper way to other people's feelings. We will talk about listening skills and give good examples of this. We also will discuss empathy and stress within the workplace. Finally, we will indicate to you the proper ways to react when angry, upset, and stressed.

Learning to React the Proper Way

Now that we have looked at all the different examples of emotions that you may recognize in the workplace environment, we can talk to you about the proper way to respond to these emotions. You should know when the right time is to react or ignore a situation because it is essential that you get the balance right whenever you are doing it. Often, people get into an emotional frenzy and react automatically without thinking and are unable to exercise self-control in playing down their emotions and then allow their emotions to take over their life. This creates a dangerous situation for anyone involved because once the emotions take over, anything is possible, and you might have a relationally disastrous consequence of the action taken.

As we have mentioned in Chapter 2, self-control is a crucial step to getting you to manage your emotions so that you can regulate your various emotional responses to a given situation. You should learn what it is that makes you angry and how you usually respond to the case so you can gauge what you need to do to address the same emotion the next time you have to deal with it.

Learning to react the proper way is going to involve you overcoming your pride and thinking that you know all things about the situation. Pride has too long caused the downfall of many men and women. Moreover, it can cause many problems in your life if you're not careful. Too many of our emotional responses come from a pride-based mentality that believes that a person knows everything and everyone else is stupid and wrong. Unfortunately, we think that way. We believe we are always right, and other people are wrong, and that is why we get into an emotional frenzy whenever we are disturbed by something that is bothering us. So, you should learn to exercise humility in all things.

Where does this humility come from? It comes from a place where you realize that your feelings are valid and that it is okay to feel the way you do but also that you might have something wrong in your assumptions, behavior, or other things within a situation. Developing humility will be an essential part of getting you into a place where you accept that you are not always right and that your assumptions and judgment may be clouded by wrong ideas that you should correct and modify your thought patterns and other things.

It will undoubtedly take you a while to fully adapt to new situations and to correct your actions, but step by step, you will be able to reach your goals so that you can do the right things and give the proper responses in situations that cause you stress.

Let's give an example in the workplace of reacting the proper way.

Let's say that you get an email from your boss that says she would like to see you tomorrow morning. No indication that it will be anything special, but then you might be wondering if it is serious and if there is something more that you need to do. Maybe you are in trouble? You might get fired. But you stop yourself from going there. If you went that direction, then you would immediately stop yourself and say, "you know what, I don't think that there is anything wrong in this situation. My boss just wants to see me. No problem here. Therefore, I am not going to worry about it."

You clearly responded well in this situation. While you could have gone off the deep end and started to worry and get anxious about a situation that perhaps had no grounds for worry in the first place. Instead, you decided to put the thought out of your mind and concluded that the situation required no immediate action other than to comply and go to the meeting.

Controlling your emotional response is going to take intentional training of your mind so that you won't go off the deep end and get yourself into relational troubles from responding in negative ways. When you react appropriately to a boss's request without going into a hypothetical struggle with your mind, then you will be more at peace with yourself and your emotions and be able to handle any stressful situation that you may be in. It will help you to do well at whatever it is that you do.

Developing Good Listening Skills

In the workplace, an essential thing that you need to acquire is good listening skills. It is crucial that you listen to others with attentiveness and understanding because that will make all the difference in building good relationships with others. Listening is a skill that is often overlooked and underestimated in our society because much is placed on a person's ability to speak well in front of others, but not enough attention is given to how we listen to others and give them our attention.

Listening is essential because we develop our sense of understanding of others' emotional needs and wants when we listen to what they have to say. Too much in our society makes us drown out the sounds of each other. We are on our phones all the time. Even on a coffee date with someone, we may be texting others at the same time or even take a call during a meeting with someone. So much that we do is just plain rude, especially in social situations. That said, we are also living in a society that is plagued by people who have ADHD, whether that be clinically diagnosed or not. Regardless, our attention is so short and limited, so we don't listen to people the way we should, and that gets us into a lot of trouble.

One way that we get into a lot of trouble is through the misunderstandings that we have as a result of not listening. It can be relationally destructive. Imagine that someone hears something that you said, and it was not meant to be offensive, but the other person heard something else, so it hurt their feelings. It can put a rift within a relationship and can cause anxiety and hurt on both ends of the spectrum.

Let's give an example of this in the workplace. Jacob and Jane are colleagues. They have a good working relationship, but sometimes they get into misunderstandings of communication, and it causes both of them stress and anxiety. Jane has given her concerns to Jacob, and yet he doesn't seem to listen to her and their communication together. He thinks everything is okay and that their relationship is good, but she insists that there is a problem and that it needs to be fixed. Jacob realizes that he is wrong and apologizes. He says, "Jane, I know I have not been listening to you, and it has caused you some emotional pain. I'm sorry about that. I realize that I am not listening to you. I am on my phone all the time, finishing up a task, or just simply not keeping my head on straight. That said, I'm genuinely sorry. Can we meet again on Friday to talk about the project?" Jane forgives Jacob for his blunders and seems to put it behind her. She responds with: "Sure, Jacob. No problem. I understand you're busy. However, you also need to learn to listen to others, because that will help you to do better."

Jacob was a jerk to Jane. He was missing meetings, not communicating properly, and causing great frustration in the working relationship. But as soon as Jane confronted him, he was able to hone up to his mistake and made a difference in his action, which was quite positive and enjoyable. Therefore, he was able to make adjustments in his habits and acts which make a difference to his life.

Listening is an essential skill in communication because it shows a vested interest in someone else. When you listen to someone, you're showing the proper respect and honor that a person deserves to have. Playing on your phone, texting another person, or even taking a call during an important meeting is blatantly disrespectful to a person's time and is also going to cause emotional difficulties between persons. Therefore, it is vital that you find ways to listen to others and show them the respect they deserve because otherwise, you are showing dishonor to them and it is absolutely ridiculous. It is vital that you do this and that you are careful to do all things well.

The people that listen well are those who are typically reserved and don't like to talk too much with others. Introverts, in general, seem to fit this type of profile. People who listen more than they talk are the ones that do the best with this type of task and can provide the kind of emotional stability that is needed within a relationship. Introverts are people that are not necessarily unsocial, but instead, they adapt themselves to social situations so that they can listen to others and give an ear to hearing from others. They are emotionally sensitive in many cases and can be good listeners to hear you out whenever you're having emotional difficulties. Extroverts can be good listeners too, but often, they are so wrapped up with what they have to say that they don't take the time and energy to listen to what another person is saying. While the interlocutor is talking, extroverts can concentrate so much on what they have to respond to that they forget how another person is talking to them and this causes disgrace to them. It is vital that you find ways to help others by listening to them and caring for their needs before your own. Thus, an extrovert can learn a lot from an introvert by learning how to withhold their thoughts until listening to what another person has to say because that shows respect and care. It also demonstrates a great deal of emotional maturity that is necessary.

Let's look at another example of workplace listening that is crucial to your success in a company.

Sam was a very enthusiastic worker and was full of questions that he wanted to know everything there was to know about his job, so he would intervene whenever he wanted. At a meeting with his coworkers, he was always the one to ask questions. While everyone sat there and were mindlessly on their phones without looking up at the speaker, he was taking notes and actively seeking answers to his inquisitive questions on the topic of the day, which was Python. Most other people in the room were not interested and were showing that they didn't care about the speaker, who had come from New York for this meeting. Sam demonstrated a great deal of maturity to listen to the speaker and ask good questions of him during the meeting, which was essential to help the speaker feel welcome and valued.

After the meeting, the speaker had a coffee with Sam. They went to a local Starbucks and engaged in deep conversation together. It was great, and they became good friends and talked about Python in depth. Furthermore, it all started with Sam and his excellent listening skills at the meeting at his company. He showed a vested interest in the speaker and then went out for coffee with him. He practiced his listening skills and asked a lot of questions and the speaker developed a lot of respect for Sam. In the end, it led to the development of a relationship and the two shared each other's business cards.

What can we learn from Sam?

Sam was an active listener and showed interest in someone else by developing a list of questions that would help him express his interest in the other person. He demonstrated a great deal of respect to others, even when other people showed a disinterest, rudeness, and attention-deficit behavior. In contrast, he was an engaged listener and was willing to have a conversation with the speaker after the meeting, because he wanted to get to know him more. Active listening is an important skill that helps bring people together and allows relationships to flourish and improve over time. If one person is doing all the talking and the other person is doing a lot of listening, it can be a bit too much to handle. But the thing is, we have to listen as well as speak and do a lot of give-and-take in situations. To be a good listener, we need to ask good questions, and that is what Sam teaches us. The power behind being a good listener is how to ask questions and follow up with questions that respond to what a person is saying to you. If we have the right questions, we will be able to engage with the other person and activate their knowledge of the topic at hand.

What are some good questions to ask another person?

One of the critical aspects of asking good questions is a curious attitude that listens carefully to what others have to say. So, you need to ask the right kind of questions. You shouldn't ask simple yes or no questions that demand no other response other than "yes" or "no." This will not activate prior background knowledge that is useful to help cue a person into making their response. Instead, you should use responses that include questions such as the following:

- Who, What, When, Where, or Why: These are specific kinds of questions that demand more thoughtful responses other than "yes" or "no," and require more reflection and preparation from the person. These kinds of questions are specific to a type of presentation that you do and will help you to activate the background knowledge of a person, as they are speaking to you. As a prompt, these questions will provide the speaker with the cues that they need to describe something.
- Also, make use of "How?" The question of "how" will help the speaker reflect on how something is done and will require more thought or consideration but enable a person to respond to your question appropriately.
- Ask follow-up questions. Rather than leaving your questions to open-ended or yes or no questions, it is

vital that you prepare a list (in your head) of follow-up questions, which will be helpful to get you to listen to what others have to say. It will also demonstrate that you are listening to what another person has to say.

- Avoid asking the question: "what do you think about this?" This question is too general and vague and does nothing to activate the background knowledge of another person. It can also cause another person's stress to think of something to say in response to what another person has prepared to say.
- When listening to another person as they are answering you, don't think of what you are going to say. Instead, think of what kind of follow-up question would go with the answer that the other person is providing you. This will demonstrate that you are interested in them and that you want to know more about what they think about different things.
- Don't change the subject when you feel that you are not interested! You may be tempted to change the subject when you don't feel interested in what another person has to say, but if you change the subject too soon, it is dismissive to another person and can be quite offensive to them.

One of the visible signs that you are interested in a person is by the questions that you ask that person. If you don't ask enough questions or don't respond to what another person has to say, it shows that you weren't actually listening to what the other person had to say. It is rude and disrespectful. That said, when you take the time to ask questions, respond directly to what another person has to say, and engage in the topic that a person gives to you, then you will show that you care for the other person and his or her interests and all will be well within the relationship.

Genuine Empathy

As we have mentioned above, one of the critical aspects to emotional intelligence is the ability to empathize with another person, to honestly "feel" what another person is feeling and understand where they are coming from, because that brings you into a relationship with another person and will enable you to have a good relationship with others. The way to relate to another's emotions is to show empathy to him or her. That can be done by showing a person you care about, but it is also through identifying with the struggles that a person is facing. It takes a step of rejoicing with a person who is celebrating and weeping or mourning with a person who is doing the same. You take all the steps that will enable you to enjoy the success of others and then understand and grieve with another person who is going through a difficult time. This is a crucial part of your emotional intelligence because you have to show that you can understand their feelings and be there with them through it. Let's give some examples of how you can rejoice with another and share in the suffering of another, which helps you to exercise emotional empathy in the workplace.

Understanding Stress

Stress is a cause of anxiety in workplaces today, and it causes people to have hard times. Work-related stress causes more people to be absent from work due to illness and also causes people to have relational difficulties. However, when people can work together amid stressful situations, they can collaborate and solve problems in tandem. Stress causes people to be relationally distant from each other; however, when people come together to solve their problems, they realize that it is easier than before to resolve situations because two or three are better than one.

Within the workplace, there are several stress factors, including finances, client expectations, job demands, and management expectations. Managing this level of stress requires a great deal of skill from the worker. He or she must be emotionally mature to handle different stressors because they can cause emotional discouragement, depression, or anxiety. With empathy, workers can understand each other and the factors that cause them stress and then they can de-stress from their work together. This often happens after work at company dinners, or out having drinks with co-workers. But it can also occur over coffee, a cigarette break, or in other ways too.

It is essential to understand how you relate to stress every day and how you react to it. Often, when you have coworkers who know what you're going through, they can help provide emotional support through the difficulty and then you can handle future situations. Finding ways to handle stress is something that requires collaboration, not just individual therapy. Group therapy has had proven benefits that enable a person to manage symptoms of their work-related anxiety effectively. Let's talk about Amy and Emma.

Example

Amy and Emma are both nurses, and they work at a hospital in Bristol, Tennessee. They work long hours and usually twelve-hour shifts. This causes their bodies a lot of physical and mental stress, because they have to be on their feet all the time, take care of the patients, witness traumatic situations, including deaths, help patients use the bathroom, and provide support to their patients. This is a very challenging situation to continually be in.

Consequently, Amy and Emma provide support to each other. They help each other throughout the day. Sometimes, they send texts to one another that gently encourage one another. Although they don't work at the same time, they try to provide emotional support to one another. On Saturdays, they meet for coffee and lunch and provide talk therapy to de-stress and discuss the week's happenings. It helps them to feel better about themselves and to encourage each other to face the challenges that they have as nurses. Being a nurse is one of the most challenging, underappreciated, and noble professions in the medical field. Nurses provide care to the world's sick, dying, and aging population. They are the heroes of the medical world and need to have the mental capacity to handle all of the traumatic and stressful situations that they continually have to deal with because they suffer alongside the patients.

Additionally, they must have empathy for their patients, to do an excellent job in treating them for the various illnesses that they have. Through the variety of experiences that they have with patients, they develop the emotional maturity and empathy that is crucial to aiding patients who are suffering and their families and loved ones. However, they also need to have emotional support themselves and may need to have talk therapy with friends, therapists, counselors, or mentors.

How to Deal with Complaints: Is it Valid or Invalid Complaining?

Complaining is an aspect that always comes with the territory with workspaces. There are always going to be complainers who are loud and obnoxious in the workplace. You have to learn how to deal with them. One of the best ways to deal with them is to avoid them and not talk to them. If you have people who are complaining, you should try to avoid being with them, because their constant negativity is going to affect you and your overall morale. You could also try ignoring it and not talking to the other person, who is active in complaining within a situation. If it is valid complaining and it is about a justice issue or something that is not right, then it is best to talk privately with a supervisor or write an email to that person to address the situation. Gossiping in the office with other coworkers is usually counterproductive and creates an atmosphere of hostility and discomfort for everyone. If you have a valid complaint, you should voice it, but you should do something about it and talk to your supervisor about it. You shouldn't simply gossip with your colleagues and talk about it negatively. Instead, you should be proactive in doing something about it. This action shows initiative and responsibility, which are necessary to accomplish new things in different environments.

If you have someone who is complaining and you have to deal with it directly, it's best to just change the subject and talk about something else that is more productive and positive. Also, keeping a positive tone is going to help others to experience more joy in their lives. When you can give a positive spin to something, then you can help others to see life on the brighter side, and you can transform your environment into a positive one.

How to Create a Positive Atmosphere

This brings us to our next point: how to create a positive atmosphere. The way to create a positive environment is to be positive yourself. When you are confronted with a negative situation, you should counter it with a positive. For example, when a person comes to you and says, "See, Kelly, that shitface manager Jennifer was causing so much of a stir at the meeting. She was telling everyone how badly they did on the recent collaborative assignment. I hate her. She is always so negative. I want her to bust her butt on something," you can counter this with a positive. You could say: "Nelly, I understand your point of view, but you should understand how frustrated she was feeling. Jennifer was also having a bad day because her car broke down and she had to walk for a whole hour to get to work. Not only that but her purse got stolen while she was on a coffee break. You have to understand she was having a shitty day and therefore, you shouldn't judge her for it." What you did was that you created an environment of empathy for this person. You realized that your friend Nelly was complaining about her supervisor and that she was incensed at what the supervisor had done. However, you were seeing things from the supervisor's perspective and empathize. Also, you told her not to judge her. So, you were effectively negating the negativity of your colleague and making it into a positive one. You could say to Nelly, "You know, Nelly, we all have bad days. It causes us to act out in ways we previously wouldn't. It's going to be okay. We have to understand each other and forgive others."

Positivity involves emotional empathy and understanding, but it also consists of looking on the bright side of things so that you can get things done more effectively. For example, say that your boss gives you a 15,000-word report that you have to do. You could feel bad about it and say, "Gah! This is terrible. I don't want to do this. It's horrible." Alternatively, you could say, "let's do this thing. It's going to be great. I'm going to learn a lot from it. Let's work together on this project, and we will do an amazing job!" Having a positive, upbeat personality is going to enable you to be a great changer in your environment because you can create that positive vibe that others will experience, and they will want to be around you more because you infuse the atmosphere with positivity. That will also be a motivating factor in getting your colleagues to produce genuinely wonderful work. It will make your colleagues want to go to work and do all the things that they have to do.

You should realize that you have more control in the kind of environment that you're creating with a positive or negative attitude. If you are always positive, you will undoubtedly cause others to feel the same way. When you are encouraging, you can build others up, and it will create a fantastic environment for you and your colleagues at the workplace. That said, if you are negative all the time, it will bring others down and build a stressed and depressed working environment, which will cause others to suffer and may make you feel better, but at the expense of others. Schadenfreude is real, and yet it is something that does not give you pure joy. Instead, it causes other people to suffer. Negativity, while also powerful, cannot win in the end, because positive feelings are so infectious that they light up a whole office space. When everyone is happy, then the entire office is, and people are prosperous in their work. Moreover, the entire company will be able to produce fantastic work that pays well. Managers will pay their employees what they're worth, and workers will do their jobs well because they feel respected and valued. And everyone will be positive because things are going swimmingly well.

How to Give the Correct Guidance

In mentoring relationships at the workplace, it is a great thing to be relational and emotionally aware of what someone is going through in a work placement adjustment. Say, you are a manager, and you have a mentee who is new to the company for the first time. Her name is Nicole, and she is quite nervous and unsure of herself. She doesn't know all the rules and has to learn everything from scratch. However, you are there with her to adjust to the new situation because you have the empathy to understand where she is coming from because you have also had similar experiences. Using your emotional intelligence and experience, you can effectively guide her in the direction she needs to go. When you see that she is down on her luck for doing something wrong, you can come to her and gently tell her, "it's okay. Keep your head up. You will get better with time. This is the first time you've done it. You can do better next time." You have to be encouraging of your mentee and to provide the guidance that will help her to get back up and keep going.

Emotional intelligence is going to help you to relate to your subordinates and colleagues and enable you to connect to others around you, which will help you to be a better manager of others. When you can see where others have been and are aware that you had been in the same situation, for example, as an intern or administrative assistant, then you will be able to empathize with them and provide them with the right kind of guidance, to assist them emotionally and professionally. This will significantly improve working relationships with others, as well.

When to Get Mad? When Not to Get Mad? How to Get Mad in a Civilized and Productive Way?

Being emotionally sensitive is going to help you to avoid getting too angry at work and will help you to do well at managing others and be a better manager. When you know how to control your emotions, then you can do your best to help others to achieve their dreams. If you don't have enough emotional control, then you will not know how to manage others, and they will resent or hate you for it. You will be the target of your subordinates' judgment and mockery. Therefore, exercising self-control will be crucial in this matter. If you are angry, you should be in a situation where there is a legitimate reason to be angry. For example, if you find that your subordinates are cheating on their timesheet or if they are doing a sloppy job or taking too long breaks, you should confront them about it and express your displeasure with what they are doing. They are doing a terrible job and something reprehensible, deserving of disciplinary action. It is crucial that you find ways of getting your colleague's attention in a way that lets them know that what they are doing is wrong and needs to be done away with.

On the other hand, getting angry at someone for no reason can cause rifts in relationships that can cause a lot of problems at the office. Thus, it is vital that you get your act together and show restraint and not get angry at the smaller things that don't matter but to let things go. This will make things a lot better for you and your colleagues at work.

Conclusion

As we have talked about, it takes empathy, listening skills, and the ability to relate to others to be better at relationships. It is vital that you develop these interpersonal skills because they are indispensable to your professional life. They will make your company a place that is worth working for with happy workers and supervisors. That's the best.

Day 1: Did I react correctly to other people´s emotions?

_____

Did I let pride get into the way?

_____

Did I genially listen? If not, what happened to me so I got distracted?

_____

Did I show empathy? Did I ask the right questions? What can I do better?

_____

Did I show empathy? Did I ask the right questions? What can I do better?

_____

Did people complain to me? Was this valid or invalid? Did I react properly?

_____

Did I get mad or angry? Did I show my emotions in a good way or a bad way? What should I do different the next time?

_____

Day 2: Did I react correctly to other people´s emotions?

_____

Did I let pride get into the way?

_____

Did I genially listen? If not, what happened to me so I got distracted?

_____

Did I show empathy? Did I ask the right questions? What can I do better?

_____

Did I show empathy? Did I ask the right questions? What can I do better?

_____

Did people complain to me? Was this valid or invalid? Did I react properly?

_____

Did I get mad or angry? Did I show my emotions in a good way or a bad way? What should I do different the next time?

_____

Day 3: Did I react correctly to other people´s emotions?

_____

Did I let pride get into the way?

_____

Did I genially listen? If not, what happened to me so I got distracted?

_____

Did I show empathy? Did I ask the right questions? What can I do better?

_____

Did I show empathy? Did I ask the right questions? What can I do better?

_____

Did people complain to me? Was this valid or invalid? Did I react properly?

_____

Did I get mad or angry? Did I show my emotions in a good way or a bad way? What should I do different the next time?

_____

Notes:

Day 4: Did I react correctly to other people´s emotions?

_____

Did I let pride get into the way?

_____

Did I genially listen? If not, what happened to me so I got distracted?

_____

Did I show empathy? Did I ask the right questions? What can I do better?

_____

Did I show empathy? Did I ask the right questions? What can I do better?

_____

Did people complain to me? Was this valid or invalid? Did I react properly?

_____

Did I get mad or angry? Did I show my emotions in a good way or a bad way? What should I do different the next time?

_____

Day 5: Did I react correctly to other people´s emotions?

_____

Did I let pride get into the way?

_____

Did I genially listen? If not, what happened to me so I got distracted?

_____

Did I show empathy? Did I ask the right questions? What can I do better?

_____

Did I show empathy? Did I ask the right questions? What can I do better?

_____

Did people complain to me? Was this valid or invalid? Did I react properly?

_____

Did I get mad or angry? Did I show my emotions in a good way or a bad way? What should I do different the next time?

_____

Conclusion

As you have seen from this book, emotion regulation plays a big part in getting you to improve your emotional intelligence is by developing self-awareness and monitoring, which enables you to see how your emotions work. By exercising self-control, you can regulate your feelings constructively and healthily. You're able to get out all the negative emotions and continue to produce positive emotions, which will naturally be infectious and helpful to others. Emotions are powerful, and they influence others in many different ways, especially the "feelers" from the Myers Brigg Type Indicator. Some people feel more intensely than others.

As a manager of a company, your responsibility is to take care of your employees, and you have to be sensitive to their needs and emotional expressions. Many times, colleagues and subordinates will get frustrated and complain when times are difficult and when work is tedious and taxing. The manager needs to address the needs of his or her employees to make them happy because a happy employee makes a happy company. It is essential to gauge the emotional level of the employees within a company because you want to create an upbeat and enthusiastic atmosphere for your employees. They should want to go to work and not dread having a case of the Mondays. You want to make work exciting, enjoyable, and profitable for your workers because then they can produce the best products for your company.

We have been able to walk you through a four-week plan of monitoring of emotions within your company. We hope you have taken careful notes in the journal and notes pages that we have created for you. Emotional control and regulation will enable you to understand people within your company and their unique personalities. It gives you a taste of how to relate to others and practice intuitive social skills. Therefore, having high emotional intelligence (EQ) will allow you to make good relationships with others in ways that you didn't before. It is important to develop people skills for any vocation or job but especially for the role of the manager in a company. You have to learn how to relate to all of your employees and treat them with respect and care. Being sensitive to their emotions will give you a quality of compassion that they can identify. Moreover, the employees will respect you more if you connect with them on a relational and emotional level.

With your knowledge of emotional intelligence, we hope you can take this information and form the best relationships with your colleagues, clients, and employees. You will receive high ratings from all the people you work with and be truly successful in achieving great things if you are more emotionally sensitive. We can guarantee that people will like you more and will respect you for what you're able to see in them, a person who is worthy of honor and respect. Finally, you can achieve whatever you set out to do because when you are people-centered and oriented around others, you will find complete happiness, joy, and satisfaction in your job and company.

Part 2: NLP for Leadership

Leverage NLP to Develop the Same Psychology and Skills as the Exceptional Leaders for Better Decision-making, a Clear Vision, More Courage and Self-leadership

Introduction

When you finally get a promotion into that new manager's office, you move in there with the excitement and expectations of a very fulfilled and decorated employee. However, once you settle in, you realize that you underestimated the challenges of being responsible for the productivity of not just yourself but everyone in your department as well. You are not alone in this though. Every leader charged with the supervision of a group of junior employees and delivering certain company goals will invariably find themselves facing a myriad of challenges in this quest. As you settle into your new office, you will have to adjust to a very different job description, fulfilling managerial rather than technical functions. And while you are at it, you can expect to face a whole new lineup of obstacles.

Problem statement

The following are some of the main problems new managers face in establishing their leadership.

- Not only do you have to work hard to be a better manager for your employer, but you also have to set an example for every other employee who looks up to you for guidance. You cannot do this with the same mentality you used to get there. Moreover, you will find that adapting to this demanding task can be very challenging. Not only must you ensure that the team works seamlessly, but you must also motivate every employee to work at his or her best to get there.

- Difficulty dealing with stress; a position comes with a corresponding amount of stress. The relationship between leadership and stress is directly proportional, which means that the more senior your position, the more stress you can expect to have to deal with. Managing your stress levels will turn out to be a critical aspect of your managerial career. At one point, you will just have to deal with the fact that popping Xanax does not really help you overcome your stress.
- Getting people on board with your vision; you are the kind of manager who creates a vision and mission statement for the department as soon as you take charge. You have presented the ideal scenario to work towards, a plan you think makes absolute sense and one that you feel will motivate your team to achieve goals like they never did before. Except for one problem, you cannot get everyone to get on board with your vision. What do you do at times like these?
- Decision making is another problem that many managers face. In a stressful environment, with every decision you make carrying stakes so high they frighten you, it is a challenge to think clearly enough to make

the decisions you need to make in the time you will be required to make them.

- As the manager, you are supposed to be the self-assured one. Everyone expects you to be the man or woman who makes tough choices and faces the consequences without blinking. So, what do you do when you feel your confidence slipping? Lack of confidence and self-esteem can be caused by many things: previous failures, problems in your personal life, deep-seated insecurities, and the fear of failure after setting huge goals for the department. Yet you are expected, as the leader of the group, to roll up your sleeves and lead the charge every single day. If you freeze up, the whole group freezes up and the momentum is lost.
- Communication skills are another area in which many managers struggle. Acquiring high competency in all forms of communication means that you can convince your team to believe in your vision and to apply their energies to the accomplishment of your goals. Decision making also requires the proper communication and deliberation of thoughts until you settle on the best one. Many managers have trouble communicating internally and with other people.

Solution

The solution to all these problems can be found in Neuro-Linguistic Programming (NLP). NLP is equivalent to learning the language of the mind. NLP is based on the premise that you can train your brain to adopt certain attitudes that will in turn empower you to achieve personal goals and objectives. Therefore, the things we say and the language we use to say to them work together with our thoughts to shape the reality in which we live.

This concept is referred to as the map of the world within NLP. More specifically, it refers to the perception of the world that you have created for yourself. Once you understand that you create your own perception of the world around you and that your perception of the world around you influences your reality, then you will be one step closer to arriving at the solution for all the problems stated above.

That is right; NLP is not something you get overnight. NLP is a process that starts with the recognition that you have more control over your own life and the things that happen around you than you previously thought and ends with actually gaining this control. In this book, we will get into the more minute details of NLP practices. We will also touch on the different ways that you can adopt NLP routines to improve your life in profound ways.

Albert Einstein famously said: "Everything is energy...match the frequency of what you want by your actions and you will automatically acquire it... it is pure physics." And it really is that simple. As soon as you have adopted the belief and action systems of the people who already have what you desire most, you will transform yourself into one of those people who have it and exhibit the habits you want to have by default.

By this logic, instead of transforming yourself into someone who is able to deal with stress, you simply transform into a person who deals perfectly with stress. The problem goes away completely and your transformation is almost effortless. It is the simple yet profound difference between "I'll believe it when I see it" and "If you believe it you will see it."

Credible evidence

Despite claims to the contrary, NLP has produced very tangible results in some of the most famous business, political, sports, and entertainment personalities. Because NLP challenges us to go out of our way to pursue excellence, the best leaders in the world are invariably the best examples of how using this strategy can bring success and immense personal development.

No single man better exemplifies this reality better than Sir Richard Branson, the founder of the Virgin Group of Companies. He has been quoted saying, "Dream big...set yourself impossible challenges...you will have to grow to catch up with them." This is perhaps the most succinct summarization of NLP. As stated above, it proposes that we can achieve the loftiest of goals if only we are willing to dare. Our brains can bridge the gap between our current abilities and our aims to grant us whatever we wish for.

In Sir Richard Branson's case, he started by overcoming dyslexia at a young age. Branson started Virgin Records, his first company, at the age of 20. He grew it rapidly and ultimately sold it for half a billion pounds just 20 years later. It was a painful decision that he had to make, but one that served him well, enabling him to start Virgin Galactic, the space travel company that is set to take the world by storm by offering commercial space travel. Here, he demonstrated a key quality of NLP by sacrificing something he valued for the chance to realize his goal. As much as you may want to use NLP to advance yourself, you must be ready and willing to pay the price.

Another instance where Richard Branson employed the concepts of neuro-linguistic programming was when he started Virgin Airways. He was stranded on his way to the Virgin Islands for a vacation with all flights canceled when he chartered a plane, solicited for customers among his fellow stranded travelers, and made it to his destination in time at no extra cost. This can-do mindset opened his eyes to the opportunities that existed in the travel business. He has since established numerous ventures in air, rail, and water transport, adding to his impressive pool of business holdings.

The benefits of NLP

Leaders who use NLP for self-development can attest to the numerous benefits it brings. These benefits include:

- Better decision making; NLP enables you to become more integrated with your thinking, which means that you are more likely to detect visual and kinesthetic (body language) tells in other people when taking in information. This heightened sensing ability increases your decision-making capabilities and makes you a better leader.
- Increased efficiency; the enhanced sensing and decision-making capabilities generated from neuro-linguistic programming empower you as a leader to streamline their work process. This means that when you use NLP, you are more likely to increase your own efficiency and that of your subordinates after some time.
- Higher productivity; increased decision making, and efficiency mean that you will be able to get more work done with fewer resources.

- Better communication skills; in essence, NLP is a way of thought that enhances communication for personal development. The first aspect of communication that receives a boost with NLP is internal. This empowers you to model the skills of the best leaders in your sector for your own success to manifest.
- Better vision; the first thing that you need to do on your journey to excellence using NLP is to clearly define your vision. This gives you the impetus to program your behavior in a way that makes it easier to achieve your personal goals. You cannot program your mind to succeed if you don't have a clear vision of where you want to go.
- Better influence and motivation skills; using NLP, you will learn to persuade your subordinates to act in a certain way. This means that you can influence their behavior in a way that supports your own goals. However, the skills you learn with NLP are altruistic, which means that your influence will be positive, and it will motivate the employees to work towards excellence for their own benefit as well as yours.
- Higher intrinsic motivation; NLP does not just motivate you to achieve your goals. It motivates you to become the person who is capable of

achieving the goals you have set for yourself. It may seem inconsequential, but this intrinsic motivation means everything. With intrinsic motivation, you will be equipped with the tools to continue trying even in the face of failure—something a lot of people struggle with.

- Better stress management; the reason why the most successful leaders manage to push forward with their dreams despite facing failure is that they embrace failure as part of their success. In a similar way, NLP teaches you to embrace challenges in your quest for success. When you believe in yourself and you know that you will succeed despite the challenges you face, nothing can stress you out.
- Easier to disconnect and relax; NLP is therapeutic in nature. This means that you can disconnect from the stresses of life and unwind, recharging your mental energies for when you immerse yourself back into the rigors of pursuing success.

How do I know this? I have studied some of the best NLP practitioners of today for a long time—that's how. Tony Robbins uses NLP. He is one of the most successful business strategists and authors on Wall Street. Another prominent NLP practitioner is Eben Pegan. He is a multimillionaire who has taught numerous business leaders how to make money and sold hundreds of millions worth of products in practically every industry as a business leader himself. His specialty is using the principles of NLP to make products that connect with customers' feelings. Stefan James Pylarinos has adopted NLP to start a very successful career teaching other people to master their lives using NLP principles.

With such practical solutions available, why should you waste any more of your time and energy struggling to establish yourself as a leader? By learning a few simple NLP techniques, you can change both your life and your career dramatically. Not only will NLP improve your quality of life and ability to lead, but it will also empower you to enhance the lives of people around you for even greater productivity. In the words of Abraham Lincoln, the best time to prepare for the responsibilities of tomorrow is today. Give NLP a shot. I can promise that you will never live to regret it.

Chapter 1: NLP Explained

It is effective and it has been used by some of the most successful world leaders to attain massive success, but what exactly is NLP? In this chapter, we will cover the history and show you how leaders used the concepts attributed to NLP long before it was called NLP.

Neuro-linguistic programming

Neuro-linguistic programming is a style of using enhanced communication to nurture interactions with other people by combining the mind, the body, and our emotions. It is used to put us in a place where we can work smart and achieve more success. Another definition of NLP, one used by some of the greatest NLP practitioners, is "the study of excellence and the art of change." This is because NLP is concerned mostly with the enhancement of our own abilities to achieve success by studying and modeling our behavior after people who have already achieved success.

In practice, NLP combines the three scientific fields of neurology, linguistics, and programming. In neurology, the mind is the central processing unit of our brain. Everything that happens around us and to us is filtered into the conscious parts of our mind for us to experience through our minds. By understanding neural connections, you will be able to understand your own perception of the world and work to improve it for more success. The only way we can ever achieve success is by working towards it the right way. If your mind is not in the right position, you could spend years working towards success and never get there. Hindrances like self-doubt, fear of failure, and procrastination are the self-sabotaging tools that the unprepared mind uses to keep us from attaining victory.

The second aspect of NLP is, of course, language. Language encompasses everything from the way we think to the way we communicate our thoughts, both to ourselves and to others. More importantly, the linguistics part of NLP allows us to understand the language of the mind and overcome its weaknesses. Sometimes success is elusive because our minds are not aligned to the right position to acquire it. Understanding the language of the brain allows us to manipulate the brain using programming techniques. Therefore, the linguistic aspect of NLP bridges the gap between our minds and reality and empowers us to program ourselves into success.

NLP works only because we have the power to talk ourselves into succeeding. The way we do this is by brainwashing ourselves with the mindset of successful people. The programming aspect of NLP carries all the power of success. In essence, it teaches us that we can achieve any level of success as long as we can train our minds to think in a particular way. Want to succeed in business? Train your brain to think like a successful businessman. Want to lead your division to great new heights and improve your profile within the company? Train your brain to follow in the footsteps of a great business leader like Jack Welch. As long as you know the destination, you can teach your mind how to get you there.

By combining these three fields, we get neuro-linguistic programming. When you consider how hard it is to change behavior—if it were not so, we would not have such a thing as alcoholics or drug addicts—you can appreciate the power of NLP. It changes the way we think, addressing the reasons why we do the things we do to bring about change. This is the simplest definition of NLP; it is getting a user's manual for your own brain. This means that when you learn to use NLP, you discover ways through which you can make your mind work in a certain way to generate a particular outcome.

NLP can also be defined as a system of tools and techniques that you manipulate to bring about your own success. With NLP, you learn to adopt the right attitude to achieve your goals. The techniques you adopt are aimed right at the subconscious mind, positioning it so that success comes almost automatically.

To sound less technical, NLP gives you a shortcut straight to your subconscious and allows you to place it in the right position to attract success into your life. This means that you condition your mind in such a way that, instead of sabotaging your efforts (which is very common when you have set lofty goals) it goes out of its way to foster your success. Your brain thus becomes the greatest asset in your pursuit of success.

Modeling

Within NLP, modeling is the process through which we adopt strategies, beliefs, language, and behavior from other people. We do this to model our own character to the successful people we look up to. For example, if you admire the work and life of Elon Musk, you can study and enumerate his behaviors, beliefs, and way of thinking.

If you model your behavior properly to a role model, you will find yourself systematically getting the same outcomes when you do something. Modeling allows you to automatically integrate a master's personality into your own. Because you engage in a critical analysis of a role model's behavior, you will often discover aspects of their personality that play a huge part in their success that even they are not aware of. You can then apply that aspect to your own work in a more pointed manner and attain massive success.

The process of modeling starts with suspending your own beliefs. This allows you to take up the mental models of the other person, starting with the psychology, beliefs, and strategies. After successfully integrating them into your own life, you will notice that your old beliefs, strategies, and psychology will start to manifest. You can never adopt another person's mental models without adding your own touch to them. This is the beauty of modeling. All you need to integrate a proven winning mentality into your life is to purposefully model your behavior to someone who has already succeeded.

Representation systems

The way we look at the world depends in a big way on the notions we hold of it. You could spend years living in a city and believing something about it based on the things that happen around you. But if you could move to a high point and view the entire city, your view of it would change dramatically.

For example, you could spend an eternity in a closed room that grows gradually stuffy, but because your senses adjust to the air within, you will not notice it until someone points it out or you walk out of the room and walk back. The same is true for a fresh room; you won't realize that a fruity-fresh room is fruity fresh until you experience different.

In the same way, we interpret information about events that happen around us based on previous experiences and the notions we have created about them. The processing of information takes place at the conscious and unconscious levels and impacts in a huge way on the way we do things.

With NLP, we focus on disrupting interpretations that were improperly formed but that nonetheless affect the way we do things. Representation systems can also be great predictors of sensory preference, a useful tool for persuasion. For example, someone who communicates using visual descriptions like "see" would be better suited to visual presentations. The same goes for people who "feel"—appeal to their emotions—and those who "think" more—use logical language.

Practical techniques of NLP

Now let us get technical and look at the specific concepts that make up neuro-linguistic programming.

Anchoring

We are always making connections between the things we hear, see, and feel and events. For example, if you set a particular song as your alarm and it is the first thing you hear once you wake up, your brain will make an association with it. This connection is even stronger when you are in an emotional state. This is because a connection is made between the specific stimulus and a very specific feeling.

In NLP, these associations are called anchors. They are created using touch, sight, and sound. More importantly, NLP teaches us how to deliberately trigger a certain emotion using these anchors. For example, listening to your alarm song in the middle of the day will most probably make you anxious and alert.

To successfully create anchors from the things we encounter, you must detect the emotions associated with every stimulus of touch, sound, and sight. That is why your workspace should be personalized. From a picture of your family, pet, or your graduation, we all need something to remind us why we give our work everything we've got. Your anchor will help you to find and keep your focus on the most important thing.

Future pacing

Future pacing is used in two ways. First and foremost, future pacing is used to gauge the effectiveness of an NLP intervention. If after an intervention someone reacts to a future prospect the same way they reacted to it before getting it, then the intervention hasn't been successful. An intervention is said to have been successful when the person reacts as desired to triggers.

In the second application of future pacing, "what-if" scenarios are painted with the intention of embedding change into the psyche. To a large extent, the mind is incapable of telling apart visualized and real events, which means that reactions are usually the same whether stimuli are real or simulated.

Visualization is one of the most important techniques in NLP. In particular, positive visualization plays a big part in motivating people to action. Sometimes, visualizing something you find hard to do as having already happened can help you in actually getting it done. This is especially true for those situations when you find yourself procrastinating.

And when making a choice between two things, visualizing each one of them as the reality and gauging your reaction to it can help you to figure out the best choice.

Swish

Every thought comes with an attached emotion, just like every memory does. The swish pattern is a model of thought that advocates swapping the emotions associated with a bad thought with the one you have regarding a good memory. The swish technique works because our minds are easily deceived and can be made to feel a certain way with the right stimuli, genuine or simulated.

More importantly, what this means is that you have it within your power to change how you feel about that scary interview from anxious and terrified to confident and self-assured. All you need to do is bring to mind a previous experience when you felt good and swap the memory picture of the event with the one that comes to mind when you think about the thing that terrifies you. When at last the event does transpire, you will find yourself looking forward to it and actually being confident and self-assured.

Reframing

Every event takes on a very different meaning when looked at using a different frame. For example, a horrible event that you can't see a way out of right now might be funny when considered in the long term. Reframing occurs in a few distinct ways:

Context; this entails looking at a bad situation and finding a positive spin to focus on instead. Failed the midterm? At least there's the final exam to make up for it. Failed the final exam too? Well, it is an average of annual performance that matters. Does annual performance suck? At least you're still alive…See, anything can be spun positively when the context is adjusted.

Content; NLP presumes that everything people do is motivated by positive intentions. If you want to live positively, finding and nurturing that good intention in everyone can be very important.

Well-formed outcome

Instead of setting a goal that you will reach and settle on, NLP suggests creating a well-formed outcome that will force you to continue working at something even after getting there. This is the standard way of setting goals in NLP. To do this, we break down the goal into smaller parts. For example, a goal like "I want my business to outdo the rest of the industry this year" breaks down into smaller objectives like "I want to win over more customers from my competitors" and "I want to be more efficient than my competitors." These goals will push you to keep working because they are a work in progress.

Ecology

The ecology technique teaches that you must look at the consequences that the pursuit and attainment of the well-formed outcome will have on your life from every angle. This enables you to prepare for the changes that will come and sacrifices you will have to make to accommodate them.

Parts integration

The parts integration technique seeks to harmonize the different pieces of ourselves that are usually in conflict arising from the different beliefs and perceptions that we hold. Integrating all parts of our psyche allows us to quell the internal conflict that often hinders our ability to achieve the goals we set for ourselves.

VKD

VKD is an abbreviation for Visual Kinesthetic Dissociation. VKD is aimed at eliminating bad feelings we have about past events. A common strategy of VKD therapy is to replay a traumatic event over and over again in a dissociated state until we no longer react badly to it. Visual triggers like pictures and film are used to trigger the bad feelings and then positive reinforcement is used to enable one to overcome them.

Metaphor

NLP trainers use metaphors to connect with the unconscious mind of their clients. Metaphors are given in three different types: shallow, deep, and embedded. While shallow metaphors are simple, comprised of comparisons or similes, deep metaphors have multilayered meanings that give the trainer deeper access to the client's source code for behaviors.

Embedded metaphors, on the other hand, contains a number of metaphors that have been linked together. Stories have given in an embedded metaphor often don't make sense, which means that the trainer is in a better position to manipulate the client's subconscious mind for improved learning and healing.

Metaphors create mind shifts because they imply relationships and force the client to fill in the blanks. This allows for new interpretations and insights.

State management

The emotional states we find ourselves in at a particular time have a huge impact on the ability we have to do things. When you are emotionally balanced, you will be more likely to focus on the job than when your mind is in chaos. As such, it is important that we maintain the state that is most conducive to the attainment of a goal. This entails managing relationships, setting a schedule, and reinforcing positive behavior.

Covert hypnosis

Any time you do something unconsciously, you are essentially in a trance. This includes automatic body functions like breathing, blinking, etc. At other times, we do things without being actively involved. Like when you drive home but don't really pay attention to the road because you have made the trip thousands of times or tuning a boring colleague out when he or she prattles on. The unconscious mind takes over in these situations, putting us in a state of semi-hypnosis.

Covert hypnosis in management is mainly used to satisfy the embedded desires of employees by making the job have a deep personal meaning. This way, the worker finds their job deeply satisfying and meaningful and you as the manager get better results from your committed workers. Any time unconscious emotions are appealed to, people react positively. It is hypnotic in that you get them to do what you want, and it is covert in that they actually do want to do what you want them to do. However, you must be careful with this particular technique. There will always be the accompanying temptation to misuse it for selfish ends.

Internal maps of the world

We touched lightly on the internal maps of the world in the introduction. In this section, we shall delve into the topic in more detail. How exactly does your internal map of the world affect your success?

The internal map of the world is what forms when the mind/body blends together with the things we say, or language. This is something that will always happen eventually as long as we are actively interpreting the world around us and forming some understanding of it. Therefore, the view we hold of the world often plays the greatest part in determining how we act, the things we believe are possible, and the goals we set.

The internal map of the world is the expression of not just our current perception of what the world around us looks like but also the perception we have of the future and possibilities for success. As such, just like in the real world, your internal map of the world determines the jurisdiction you perceive yourself as having. If you think you have a very limited role to play in attaining success in your career or any other aspect of your life, then your internal map of the world is probably tiny and limiting. You cannot see how you would be able to push the borders and come into a greater state of being: owning more, achieving more, and being more.

Your map of the world determines how you feel about yourself and the world. It also plays a part in your day-to-day actions. If your current map is impoverished, you will experience insurmountable problems in your quest for success. If your mental map is abundant, your life will reflect this.

The good thing about the map of the world is that you can change it. With NLP, you can shift your perception of the world from impoverished and limited to abundant and unlimited. You can get the motivation to wage war on limitations and expand your borders outwards. Because only you have the power to mark the territory you occupy, you can redraw the map to make it as big as you want.

A limited view of the map of the world is that it is the way we perceive the world. Looking at it broadly, however, you can draw endless meanings from it. Adding to the idea that you create your own map according to your own personal desires, we can add that your stability and ability to maintain the highest ideals or state of being depends, like in a real-life country, on the neighboring countries. The people you surround yourself with can either empower you to achieve more (expand your borders) or hinder you from succeeding (infringe on your territory).

To change a destructive internal map of the world, you need only modify or change patterns of belief and behavior with useful ones. But first, you must change the internal representation of your map of the world to increase behavioral flexibility.

The history of NLP

NLP was created by John Grinder and Richard Bandler in the early 1970s. The two authors built their concept on the model of self-realization created by Abraham Maslow in the 1940s and modeled it around the work of world-famous psychotherapists of the time. Initially, the aim of their model was to determine what made their admired therapists special and how they could transfer this specialness to other people.

From the time Grinder and Bandler formed it, NLP has gone through a few transformations. Prominent among them are NLPure, NLPt, NLPeace, and NLPsych.

NLPure

NLPure is the original NLP that was started by John Grinder and Richard Bandler. Its main focus was success and enthusiasm. The founders were joined in advocating success and enthusiasm through neuro-linguistic programming by numerous other scholars. This paved the way for the growth of NLP, with speakers teaching enormous groups of people the benefits of NLP through seminars.

NLPt

In the 80s, health and the joy of living gained more appreciation among proponents of NLP at the same time that applications in psychotherapy spread. The widespread acceptance of NLPt led to the creation of associations like the European Association of Neuro-Linguistic Psychotherapy (EANLPt).

NLPeace

At the turn of the century, people started to apply NLP to spirituality and created the third wave of NLP. More and more people were now seeking to use NLP to improve their meaning of life. Applications for general improvement also went up at around this time.

NLPsych

NLPsych is the most recent improvement in NLP. Suggested after a 2006 study of the application of NLP, it substitutes programming with psychology and requires NLP practitioners to be trained in psychology. More than any other version of NLP, NLPsych relies on scientific methods. The increased reliance on scientific methods also helps to change the narrative that NLP is a pseudoscience, a claim that has dogged it since its inception.

NLP in leadership

NLP was practiced by some of the most popular world leaders long before it was even invented. To prove this point, we will discuss the five universal qualities of a good leader and demonstrate how they fall in line with the concepts of neuro-linguistic programming.

Self-restraint

Leaders are often faced with extremely stressful situations. The best trial of the mettle of a leader is their temperament in times of crisis. NLP holds the idea that with self-reflection, we can work past emotional triggers of anger and develop a more withstanding type of patience that will help us weather any adversity that comes in life. A leader like Harry Truman, who led the world calmly through the cold war, is a textbook study on NLP leadership concepts.

Leading by example

Pretty much any successful leader has led by inspiring their followers to do something they would normally balk at doing, simply because the leader himself was willing to lead by example. Vision- setting and selling your vision to your followers is one of the most important facets of NLP training.

Learning from mistakes

Leaders are not made when things are going well; they are made when everything is going horribly wrong. It is also believed that you are not a leader until you have failed because failure is the biggest, most challenging test any leader faces. Notably, every prominent leader from Nelson Mandela to Franklin Roosevelt to Richard Branson and Albert Einstein—both of whom overcame dyslexia and went on to achieve great success in their respective fields—proves that challenges make a good leader.

NLP teaches us to be bold while taking calculated risks. Mistakes are a part of life and we need not worry about making them. Rather, we should learn from them. Leaders were doing this even before Richard Bandler and John Grinder conceptualized their NLP model.

Proper communication

Leaders use communication tools to cultivate loyalty and motivate action from their followers. NLP also teaches us to develop our self-awareness tools and enforce positive behavior from employees.

Emotional intelligence

NLP is essentially a study in emotional intelligence. We learn to identify our own emotions and the emotions of our subordinates as well as how we can capitalize on both for more productivity. The world's most successful leaders display a common quality of extremely high emotional intelligence. They are able to detect the emotions of their followers and position themselves in such a way that they harness them for the greater good.

The current status of NLP

Today, NLP is taught by hundreds of thousands of coaches and thousands of books have been written about it over time. The people who use NLP are able to replicate the success of other, more successful people to achieve success in their own lives. The main reason why people are drawn to NLP is that it works in such profound ways. Coincidentally, it is for the same reason that many people doubt its effectiveness, even without first having tried it out.

Even with maestros like Tony Robbins (who learned NLP directly from Grinder) screaming the benefits of NLP from the biggest stages in the world, the opposition to NLP remains. In the meantime, the people who practice it succeed and even many of those who don't consciously practice it will match the strategies taught by NLP coaches. One of the reasons why NLP faces so much opposition is that it has been commercialized to a greater extent than other psychological models of the 20th century. In spite of the opposition, studies have increasingly shown that people who use NLP find success a lot more frequently than any other group.

All in all, NLP practitioners have created exceptionally powerful tools for the improvement of communication and neural processes over the years that are still paying off to date. Applications include in the fields of psychotherapy, education, leadership, counseling, and creativity. And even though the scientific proof for NLP is still lacking, the relationship between mind, communication, and reality are widely accepted.

Applications of NLP Techniques

Neuro-linguistic programming has numerous applications. This is because NLP techniques are incredibly powerful tools when applied to real-life situations. They are capable of empowering profound change. However, the power of NLP is directly proportional to the ardor of the person applying them. In this section, we look at some common NLP applications.

Personal development

NLP is essentially a self-development tool. Through NLP, we learn to reflect on our own actions, build confidence, and communicate effectively. More importantly, NLP teaches us the surest way we can go about achieving personal goals—modeling our behavior after that of someone more successful. This is a surefire way of attaining your potential and the reason why men like Tony Robbins have achieved the success they have achieved to date.

From the actions of business leaders like Richard Branson, Elon Musk, and many more, we also learn the concepts of aiming for the sky even when our current skills do not match up. Using the concepts of NLP, as long as you want it badly enough, your mind can always find a way to get you there.

Achieve goals

Neuro-linguistic programming has also been applied in the workplace to empower leaders to achieve work-related goals. By applying the concepts used by the most successful of business leaders at the workplace, you will meet and exceed workplace goals, increase the productivity of your department, and guarantee your progression up the corporate ladder.

Therapy

NLP has also been used in the treatment of psychological disorders. For example, people with anxiety, depression, and low confidence (low self-esteem issues) can apply NLP to find relief.

In the rest of this book, we will focus on the ways through which you can use NLP in your workplace to improve your management skills. This is an important subject of discussion seeing as you will be expected to provide leadership for subordinates, have a vision for the group, and figure out a way to get there. And unlike senior management positions in a company, lower-level managers are judged more by the results of their own work, i.e., the results posted in their division or department. If something happens that prevents you and your team from achieving your goal, the responsibility lies with you and you only.

So, read on to discover how you can apply the techniques of NLP discussed in this chapter to different aspects of your job as a manager. These include vision setting, decision making and problem-solving, time management, communication and negotiation, stress management, and motivation.

Chapter 2: Vision

A clear vision and mission statement is indispensable when you are leading a group of people. It is what creates a strong foundation for you as you tackle the difficulties that come along the way to success. When your career is guided by a clear-cut vision, you will always have something to consult when making those difficult decisions and answering unexpected questions. It also means that you will be less likely to fall for distractions that come along the way. In this chapter, we will talk about vision setting and pursuing with NLP.

The most effective NLP technique for setting and selling your vision is future pacing. It has been used by legendary leaders, especially in the political field, to great effect. In the current age, few leaders stand out as having sold their vision to the public more than Martin Luther King, Junior. His "I have a dream" speech electrified a nation to action and ultimately brought civil rights to millions of Americans.

But arguably more effective in employing future pacing was the forty-fourth President of the United States, Barack Obama. In his 2004 Democratic Convention speech, the hitherto unheard-of senator from the tiny state of Hawaii rose to overnight eminence by leading the American public to visualize a rosy future with his "Yes We Can" speech. Four years later, he moved into the most prestigious office in the world— the White House. All this because he had a vision and was able to make others believe in it.

The reason why a vision holds such great sway over people's emotions is that there is the perception that it is the only part of the time that we can affect today. The past is already gone, and the present is the product of what we did in the past. Only the future remains open for exploration. If you can manage to create the best idea of a future, selling it to your employees will be easy enough as long as you take their needs and desires into account.

Benefits

And on a personal level, you can expect to witness the following benefits.

Improved self-confidence

As we mentioned above, a vision statement takes into account everything you want to achieve and compresses it in a way that is easy to reference. When creating a vision, you first determine the ideal destination you would like to get to. You think one year, two years, five years, or more into the future and define the goals you would like to have already achieved. The goals allow you to focus your energies on the things that will propel you towards your ideal future. With focused energy comes increased efficiency and with it, more results and confidence in your own abilities.

Moreover, as you deliberate on your future for the purpose of goal setting, you will notice that it is easy to indulge your more ambitious tendencies. After all, it is in the future and everything is possible. But once you set the goals and break them down to the present where a simple task is what sets you on the path to the main vision, you will realize that it is very possible to attain the lofty goal you set. You sure will get a bump of self-confidence then.

A leader is only as good as the people he leads allows him or her to be. A common goal is one of the most rejuvenating incentives in the workplace, but it is also true that people are more motivated when the goal they pursue as a team is even bigger. So, when your employees believe in your vision, they will work even harder to bring about its actualization. The dedication of your employees (and the success it will undoubtedly bring about) will leave you feeling more confident and self-assured than you have felt in ages.

Reduces stress

Leadership is a very stressful career. The responsibilities are greater, accountability is to a higher authority, and you will be granted very limited room for mistakes. You will definitely feel the pressure of your new position more. Managing the pressure can get especially stressful. If you are not careful, the stress could get to you and drastically affect your ability to deliver. This is where a vision and the ability to visualize the future come in handy.

First off, a vision reduces your stress levels by giving you something to focus on. The goal becomes your worth to the senior managers, your employees, and the customers. If it is a good enough goal, your singular dedication to its attainment will leave you feeling empowered and driven. Even when failure crosses your path, you can shrug it off and carry on.

Now, when pursuing a vision with NLP strategies, you have another advantage that other people do not have. You can visualize the future. Visualization is a powerful motivation tool that will transport you to a magical world of blissful achievement in your most stressful situations, remind you why you are doing what you are doing, and leave you feeling more positive than ever. Moreover, when you can visualize yourself having already achieved something, your belief in your ability to attain it increases and you feel less pressure to be perfect.

Improves thinking and decision making

Roughly 80% of what you will be doing in your new job will involve thinking. You will get a lot of questions for which you cannot produce a direct answer each and every day. You will be called in to solve huge problems and be asked to make a choice between two impossible situations so often you will not believe it. This is a lot of mental activity. If you are not careful, it could easily overwhelm you.

But when you come up with a defined vision, your thinking will be compartmentalized based on its contribution to the ultimate realization of your goals. Every question posed, every decision and every problem will be answered the same way—using the checklist of your vision. The more you prioritize the vision in your work, the more passionate you will become about it. More passion increases your chances of actually accomplishing what you set out to accomplish in your vision.

In 1990, Microsoft was facing a dilemma in regard to its strategic relationship with leading computer manufacturer IBM. Started ten years prior, the relationship had been vital in the quest of Microsoft to become the best software company in the world. Behind this vision was a young man named Bill Gates. He had navigated the murky waters of software publishing from the onset and proven himself to be a ferocious leader. The vision of a world-dominating Microsoft had originated with Gates. His partner Paul Allen was more content making software that conquering the world.

Cutting ties with IBM was a decision unlike any other Gates, or few other men, had ever made. It would be akin to jumping off a ship with nothing more than a sailboat in the middle of the ocean. Will the fuel last you to shore? Will you be able to navigate? Is it even a good idea?? Well, for Bill Gates, the way to answer that question was simplified by his NLP-like thinking. He had a great vision, one that IBM was, as of 1990, frustrating. As much as the decision looked like a terrible idea at the time, he made it without flinching. And his company emerged even stronger from the ordeal.

Removes complexity

Have you ever been so worried about a seemingly huge problem, only to find the decision about how to solve it really easy? You see, this is a common trick our brain uses when it is anxious—it magnifies a small problem. Evolutionarily speaking, this means that we take seriously things like cold weather and avoid coming down with a cold. On the job, you will find yourself feeling better about firing an underperforming employee if you consider that it will free him or her up to find a better place of work and enable you to hire a better-suited employee. When you look at the bigger picture, you go back to the core foundation and consider them more wholesomely. The result, you will find, is that the answer always becomes clearer.

As I said, the best visions can usually be summarized using simple phrases. This condensation removes the complexity and ambiguity and points you in the right direction. Whether you are answering questions, making decisions, or solving complex problems, you can arrive at a solution faster when you get down to the basics. Ask pointed questions. Find out the crux of the matter. Have a clear idea of what is in question and then you can endeavor to find a solution. And as usual, the only viable solution is one that helps you to realize your vision.

The SMART vision

Future pacing using NLP follows a very simple and very universal tactic- the SMART approach. Specific goals are easier to make but surprisingly hard to implement. Think of a vague goal such as, "Be the best department in the company." Unless your company holds an annual gala where it awards the best department in the company, this is too subjective a goal. You can claim to be the best because you have a margarita machine in the office on Friday, but that is neither here nor there. Specific goals are also measurable. For example, growth in sales volumes quarter to quarter, profit levels, and ROI. These are quantifiable units that you can objectively track.

It is very tempting to set goals that are so wildly out of reach that they become untenable. This will derail your vision. Achievable goals are easier to reach because it is within our power to attain them. I am not saying that you should not aim high. Just know your limitations and keep your goals within them. This is also why the next quality of a SMART goal is realistic. The attainment of the goal must not be so out of the ordinary that it requires a miracle. It is much better to shoot within your capabilities and actually win than to aim for the improbable and lose.

Finally, a smart vision should be timed. Using NLP, setting a timeline for goals follows a very specific process. It entails thinking about something that will happen in a few hours' time, tomorrow, next week, next month, in the next year, the next two years, and so on and so forth. The things you think about will usually come from the same direction. Moreover, you will realize that the ideas generated by your mind are either spontaneous or there is a tug-of-war before you settle on an idea.

Within that tug-of-war is the ideal goal to aim for and another, either higher or lower, that your biased mind is trying to push through. If you are more ambitious, the alternative will be far above what your subconscious knows is attainable. Through focused timeline thinking, you can uncover from the deepest parts of your brain the limits of your abilities and strive to set goals by them.

How to create a vision

Martin Luther King, Jr., and Barack Obama shared their visions with the American public to great rewards. Analyzing these two visionary leaders, one tactic stands out far above the rest. Their visions are best summarized in a few words. "Yes we can" and "I have a dream" are both slogans that represented a broader vision, but with time they came to be the vision. When selling your own vision, you should keep in mind that humans are associative in nature. If you can compress your vision into a few words, your followers will subscribe more wholeheartedly to the core ideals.

Okay, so a vision is clearly very important. It creates clarity where confusion hitherto existed and plots a clear path to the future. But how exactly do you come up with one? And how do you put it into action? In this section, we will look at the most effective NLP exercises to practice and execute in relation to future pacing and setting a vision for you and your department.

Discover

Creating a vision is all about plotting a path to the attainment of your goals. On a personal level, you simply reach into your heart and find your purpose in life, then come up with a way to get there. As a leader, you will be responsible for the attainment of the dreams of all your employees, the company, and your customers. You must be very clear about what you are aiming for. This is why the first process is discovery. In discovery, you ask yourself a few questions:

- What are the most valuable things to (1) the customer, (2) my subordinates, and (3) my bosses?

If you can find the answer to this question, you will have in your hands the tools you need to reconcile the different demands of your job into a single aim. By visualizing, you can brainstorm ways through which you will manage to satisfy everyone who relies on you for leadership.

- What is your resource endowment?

Your ability to do anything is always restricted by the resources you have to accomplish it. This goes for time, money, and more importantly, goodwill. Whatever vision you come up with will govern your actions into the foreseeable future, so you must be really sure before you embark on the journey.

Find your heroes

NLP owes a big part of its power to motivate people to succeed in the techniques of modeling. While creating a vision, you must take advantage of modeling and find inspirational figures who have been at your position and worked their way to so much greater success. These role models become your heroes and heroines and you model your vision—at least in part—to their behavior.

There are not many celebrity business leaders who rose to prominence through employment, but the few outstanding ones left a mark in their companies and entire industries. Lee Iacocca is one such leader. He employed NLP concepts like rapport building and future pacing to lead two of the world's biggest automotive companies. At Ford, he rose up the ranks from a lowly sales manager to CEO. At Chrysler, he rescued an American icon from bankruptcy. The outstanding quality of Iacocca's management career is that he always had a vision. Some of the most successful cars at Ford, like the Mustang, were developed under his leadership. And at Chrysler, he orchestrated the acquisition of the American Motor Corporation simply to bequeath the highly profitable Jeep model to the company.

Dream

After discovering the thing your dependents value most and the resources you have to achieve them, you have to commit to a particular course of action. Using NLP, the ideal way to set a dream is by closing your eyes and transporting yourself into the future. Here, keeping the facts you acquired in discovery, you envision a world where you have already achieved them.

Immersion helps you to discover specific details about your vision that will enable you to tackle future questions and problems with conviction. This step of the vision setting is akin to meditation, whereby you follow the initial train of thought (the dream) and then let it transport you to a make-believe world where your vision has come to life. You will obviously be biased, thinking about the common complaints you get at work, problems you encounter, and challenges that face you. But here is the key; as you envision a world in which these problems are nonexistent or you have prevailed over them, your mind will become enlightened to find ways of solving them so that your goals are indeed achieved.

Conscious dreaming can either be guided using covert hypnotism or you could do it alone. Either way, it helps your mind conceive a world of success which motivates you to work towards it. And with a team, you can do this even more effectively because you will call every employee to share their dreams, right down to the specific ways they think you can attain them as a team. The advantage here is that an employee working in IT is in a better position to imagine the future of IT, and the same with accounts, sales, and every other division.

Design

As you dream up a new world where you are achieving your goals, focus on the most important things. You must work towards the most compelling vision, not the easiest one. It is very important that you make the vision achievable because unrealistic dreams are very often unachievable. In fact, an unreal objective is one of the leading causes of procrastination.

And having figured out a compelling vision, the next thing is to find out what you need to do to achieve it. This means you research and educate yourself on the process of achieving whatever it is that you want to be. Along with the skills you must learn to be in a position to achieve the dream, find other people who can lend a hand.

When designing a vision for your department, selling your employees and employers on the idea is imperative. The employees will play a huge part in the actualization of the vision and your employer will provide you with the resources and the goodwill to pursue it. The worst mistake you can make at this point is to think that you can do it all by yourself. Teamwork is the key.

Destiny

The last process of crafting a vision is defining it in a succinct and direct manner. Here, you write down all the vision and mission statements that make up your dream. You must be sure to write the vision statement in a positive and affirmative tone. It should also be provocative enough that everyone involved in the quest to achieve it will be motivated to work.

After reading through it to make sure that it is what you want, apply yourself to the vision and don't give in until you realize it.

Chapter 3: Thinking, problem-solving and decision making

I have said this before and I will say it again. The most important job description of a manager is thinking. Improving your ability to think, problem-solve, and make decisions can be a huge boost to your career. On the thinking front, the most crucial advantage of clarity empowers you to spot opportunities. Superior decision-making capabilities mean that you can do what you need to do to take advantage of the opportunities.

Problem-solving is another important skill for managers. It comes in handy when you are facing a crisis at work, improving service delivery, or arbitrating disagreements between your subordinates, among other applications. In this chapter, we will look at different ways to use NLP to improve your thinking, problem-solving, and decision-making skills.

Thinking

To become a good business leader, you must be capable of higher-order thinking. Only in the military and disciplined forces can you possibly scrape through without being equipped with the best thinking capabilities. But even military leaders have to be good tacticians, and creating good tactics requires that you have a good brain on your shoulders and the ability to use it.

There are two main styles of thinking: creative and critical. A good leader combines elements of both to come up with unique, well-thought-out solutions to business problems. If you want to become a good leader, then you must start by fixing the way you think. You must be aware of the mental models that are responsible for your actions, understand the conscious and unconscious mind and how the two affect your life, know the right questions to ask, understand associations, and recognize the shortcomings that exist in your thought process.

Mental Models

Mental models are the ways we analyze and understand the world. Mental models are often based on basic principles that we use to simplify complex events that happen all around us. Mental models are often limited and stereotypical, but we can adjust them by objectively analyzing new information rather than relying on our old stereotypes. And because mental models inform every single decision we make, we should be careful to moderate the sort of thinking that governs our thinking. In this section, we will look at some of the mental models that hinder our progress as leaders.

For example, if you micromanage your employees, this is because you have a jack-of-all-trades mental model. You only trust in yourself to get things done, which could turn out to be a huge burden. Even if there is evidence to support your assumption that you get things done more effectively than your subordinates, continuing down micromanagement lane will lead you to overwork, burnout, and mess-ups. Delegating is an even greater mark of a good leader because it means you have put together a team you can trust. It also frees your mind up to think about the more important things like the long-term strategy of your division.

Another destructive mental model that you may be laboring under is perfectionism. As much as you must always strive for excellence, chasing perfection will leave you exhausted and anxious. What's more, you will probably never get to the point of utmost satisfaction with your achievements, which is crucial for motivation and inspiration.

Snap decision making is a mental model that very often comes disguised as an aptitude. People who do it often believe that it is a strength to exploit and be proud of. But it is anything but and could, in fact, be derailing your career advancement. When you make snap decisions, you fail to take the time to consider the consequences of doing something. This could have disastrous implications not just for you but for the company and your employees. Snap decision making also means that you expose yourself to subliminal and deliberate manipulation.

To make it from a regular employee to manager takes a lot of hard work and hours of routine work. The more you get done, the greater the rewards you reap. This tends to program our minds in a certain way, leaving most of our minds modeled to believe that productivity can only be achieved by working long and grueling hours. This could not be further from the truth as a leader. Your job in this new capacity is to govern, which includes organizing your team based on the competency of each member. If you have created the mental model of working late into the night, neglecting your work-life balance, and sleeping a few hours every night, you must realize that this simply won't cut it. Leadership is a whole new ballgame and you must upgrade your skills to make it.

The other mental model most business leaders create for themselves is the superman complex. Managers with this mental model live under the assumption that they don't need anyone to help them perform their duties. While admirable, you must learn to tame the inclination to take the blame for everything that goes wrong (or right) in your department.

Instead of using these negative mental models, you should instead copy the thinking style of leaders like Ray Dalio, a man who has used second-order thinking perfectly to establish a very successful career in stock market investing. Thinking about consequences to the second, third, and fourth-order means that nothing will ever find you unawares and that you will always be a few steps ahead.

The conscious and unconscious mind

What is stopping you from adapting to your new role as a manager? Most people will answer this question by citing external causes that are completely out of their direct control. This is the wrong approach. For a better understanding of how you can use your mind to understand and influence your internal world, you will have to use NLP. With NLP, our mind influences our thinking on two levels: the conscious and the unconscious.

Conscious thought is done deliberately. The concept is simple; for a positive impact on your inner thoughts, you will have to think positively. It is quite effective and is widely used around the world to affect constructive actions.

However, the conscious mind is limited by its capacity to retain information. At best, we are able to follow nine simultaneous bits of information. Just think about it. Do you even memorize your phone number (or any phone number) ten digits at a time? No, you do it three or four digits at a time because this information is far easier to collect, store, and recall. Sleight-of-hand magicians and other tricksters also use their knowledge of the limitations of the conscious mind to trick their audiences.

As a manager, your diary will be filled with important meetings, interviews, and business functions. Your chances of excelling at these activities depend on your ability to absorb and retain massive amounts of data and keep it at your fingertips, the agenda for a staff meeting, for example, including the exact agenda that carries an important issue you intend to raise. All this information will be stored in your conscious mind.

The unconscious mind, on the other hand, is the store of information that we don't need at this exact moment. In addition to the nine bits of information you hold at the fore of your mind, there is a whole lot of information that you are not consciously aware of. If you can manage to unlock this part of your mind, you will unlock a massive bank of information, some of which you wouldn't even be aware of holding. In one study, anesthetized patients remembered word for word the conversations that went on around them while they were being operated on.

Even though you will hardly ever be aware of it, your unconscious controls every aspect of your life. It also responds to all external stimuli without any prompting whatsoever. So, even if your conscious mind sees success in a straightforward situation but your unconscious mind is prompted by some random stimuli to go negative, you will somehow wind up sabotaging yourself.

NLP intervenes in this kind of a situation to create congruence. Congruence means that you have aligned your brain and your actions with positive thoughts and commit totally to the achievement of the desired outcome. In the event that you are finding it hard to focus on positive thoughts, you can recall the positive events of your past and use them to motivate yourself when negativity interferes with current actions. With 10 billion neurons in our brains, the possible connections we can make in our minds are infinite. Only when we don't utilize the brain to the maximum do we limit ourselves in life.

NLP Exercise—Circles of excellence

To create a resourceful state of mind and body any time you need it, perform the following time-proven exercise.

1. Stand at a point with six feet of space ahead of it.
2. In your mind, draw a circle on this floor. Make the circle as visually attractive as you'd like.
3. Think of an encouraging phrase like "Yes I Can," "I Can Do It," or "I Am Success" that motivates you.
4. Think of one time when you exceeded your highest expectations and go back to that time. Try to recall it as vividly as possible, including the smells, tastes, or colors associated with the memory.

5. Let this memory fill you up, then say your phrase out loud, take a deep breath, and step inside the circle.

6. Inside the circle, give yourself up to the memory, taking the time to enjoy the sensation of excelling.

7. Now think about the situation you are about to face and see yourself excelling beyond your wildest dream. Let the confidence of your past victory fill you up.

You are set to go and conquer the world!

Logical fallacies

Few things hamper success more than shortcomings in thinking. In logical fallacies, false ideas created from flawed opinions and personal biases get in the way of sound thinking. It is very important to learn how to argue or reason without resorting to unsound arguments and also to have the ability to spot fallacies in other people's opinions. Let's look at logical fallacies in short, shall we?

You see, there are several types of them, and all differ from each other in various ways. First off, there are formal and informal fallacies. Formal fallacies are also called deductive because they entail a clear-cut error in inferring a conclusion from a reasonable argument. A reasonable argument contains a premise, evidence, and a conclusion. For example:

All scientists are curious

Bill is a scientist.

Therefore, Bill must be curious.

Let us look at the argument above from a different angle.

All scientists are curious.

Bill is curious

Therefore, Bill must be a scientist.

This constitutes a deductive fallacy based on the fact that we used the evidence of being (curiosity) rather than the state of being (a scientist) to make our conclusion.

Informal fallacies are inductive in nature. They support the conclusion but they are not necessarily completely true. You can only be sure of the accuracy of a conclusion to a limited level of certainty. For example, the following argument would have been correct in 1958 but incorrect in 1959.

The coast of Alaska has never been hit by a tornado.

Therefore, the coast of Alaska will not be hit by a tornado this year.

Errors in reasoning can either be logical or factual. If you take a valid argument and make the wrong conclusion based on the wrong evidence presented, you will technically be right (logically) but wrong because you can't make a valid conclusion from the wrong information.

Using metaphors in NLP, you can perform exercises to improve your ability to detect fallacies. Metaphors help by training your brain to find the meaning hidden behind cleverly worded statements. You can also use your knowledge of logical fallacies to detect when someone is trying to hide something from you or influence your decision in a certain direction.

The "why" model

The whole point of being a leader is to inspire your employees to want to do what you want them to do. This is the definition of true power: making people want to bend to your will. This power is held in high regard because one, it is hard to wield it, and two, it is altruistic in nature. People are self-serving. The only way they would want to bend to anyone else's will is if they stand to benefit from it. The "why" model is the best strategy of thinking as a leader because it teaches you to wield this power.

With the "why" model, you will have to communicate your message precisely and articulately. You show your employees reasons why your vision is the best way forward for them and the company and in this way enforce their inner purpose and align it with your own. Few people can do something without a clear justification. You don't need people who do whatever you ask without asking why. In most cases, these people will do nothing at all unless you push them.

The "why" model was adopted into NLP during the NLPt era, which was also the time when psychotherapy was rising in prominence as a valid treatment for psychological issues. Its use on a personal level entails asking the question of why for every out-of-the-ordinary behavior till you reach the root cause. This is the one true way to resolve deep-seated issues and free yourself from self-sabotage.

Pavlovian Association

The Pavlovian Association Theory simply reiterates the concept we stated at the beginning, that thoughts and memories have sensory associations. This theory of thought is as much a strategy to employ in motivating yourself as it is a cautionary tale. You see, Ivan Pavlov (author of the Pavlovian association theory) conducted experiments that showed that human beings are extremely susceptible to classical conditioning. We create biological and mental associations at both the conscious and unconscious levels. Being aware of the associations you have made over the years means that you can free yourself from possible manipulation. On the other hand, you can exploit habits you already have to create new ones by creating associations.

Cognitive dissonance

Cognitive dissonance exists when people act contrary to their values, ideals, or beliefs. To make the actions logically palatable, we form new standards to fit them. A cognitive dissonance is a form of fallacy, except that it is internal and instead of changing the behavior to match the principle, we twist the principle around to accommodate our own failings. With NLP, we use mental maps to open the lid on our own unreasonable behavior and thus ensure that our beliefs and actions align.

The swish technique for negative thoughts

The swish technique is specially crafted to help us overcome irrational negative thoughts. We do this by changing the direction of our thoughts away from negativity and into positive territory. The swish technique is especially suited for this role because it leaves a trail for all our thoughts to follow, meaning that changing the direction of one negative thought from negative to positive induces all other thoughts we have to follow the same pattern.

The swish pattern cleans negative thoughts through the following process:

1. Detect a negative or unwanted thought and the bad feeling it stirs up

2. Separate the bad feeling from the thought-through focus. You might need to close your eyes or hum a funny lullaby here.

3. Search your mind for a replacement thought and shift your conscious mind from the negative feeling to the new positive thought.

4. Realize that you don't need to do anything because the negative thought has already been banished.

Problem-solving

As a common employee, you learned to pass the buck over to your manager. He or she was there to handle any unforeseen difficulties and smooth things over for you to do your job. Well, you are now the manager and it falls on you to bail out everyone who works under you. And when you form an audacious dream, you can expect to solve even more problems because there will be more difficulties arising. You can either look at problems as hindrances to your progress or as stepping-stones to a higher stage. All the successful business leaders of today (and ever) have followed the latter path, so that's what we will discuss in this section.

Adapting to your new role can be a problem in and of itself. When you are faced with an unfavorable situation, the mind perceives danger and activates the fight-or-flight instinct. When your body prepares for an emergency, blood stops flowing to the brain and is instead directed to motion muscles and organs. If you have ever been faced by a problem only to find a perfect solution long after the crisis has passed, this is probably because you made a decision in an instant of fight-or-flight adrenaline, and your brain was not fully powered to evaluate the options.

Thinking backwards

When you are faced with a problem, you will probably feel that your vision is challenged and your chances at future success are dimmed. This is especially true when you are following a strict timeline. A small problem could have serious repercussions down the line. Thinking about the future is a great idea at all times, except when you are trying to solve a problem. At this time and this time only, thinking backward holds the answers. It doesn't solve the problem, and the solution does not really come from the backward thinking, but it grounds you firmly enough that you can find the inner strength to deal with the problem.

Ultimately, what helps you solve a problem without losing your mind is deconstructing the problem, figuring out the expected outcomes, and accepting that they are inescapable. After that, you factor the problem into the future plan and go ahead accomplishing what you set off to accomplish.

This NLP technique of inversion, embracing problems, and making them part of the storyline is best embodied by Elon Musk. Elon is an entrepreneur who has encountered numerous problems in his career, from getting fired from his own company to losing millions of dollars' worth of NASA supplies. Despite the challenges, he powers forward and never wavers from his chosen path.

Entropy

Entropy is a philosophical principle that postulates that chaos is inevitable. However, much we try to prevent problems, they will always persist because no system can ever be maintained in a chaos-free state. This is an important principle for managers to understand, especially when they are dealing with problems at the workplace. Not every tiny problem will require your personal interference.

More importantly, you must not worry about small problems. Most people feel indicted by problems that arise in their department. This could never be further from the truth, as indicated by the entropy principle. The sooner you realize this, the sooner you can stop worrying and beating yourself up when things don't go according to plan.

To the extent that they don't disrupt much or disrupt you from pursuing your vision (micro problems) embrace the chaos and let it motivate you. As for any other sort of disruption, you must dedicate yourself to beating back disruptions from every area of your life. The way to do this is to be disciplined, conscientious, and methodical planners.

NLP Exercise to overcome entropy

1. Embrace the mental model of entropy; life is designed to resort to a disorderly fashion. You cannot control the future or anything that happens in the present.

2. Clean up your room; just because the world resorts to disorder does not mean you let disorder take over.

3. Adopt orderliness.

4. Determine what you can do for the community and do it.

5. Practice consciousness in everything you do.

First and second-order change

Every action we do has consequences beyond the immediate result. When you manage to stop a valuable employee from quitting by offering him or her a generous pay raise, you will have to deal with other employees who may feel that they deserve a raise as well. You will also give the impression that people can get their way with you by holding you hostage to ransom. These are the second-order consequences that every leader must consider when solving a problem.

When using NLP techniques like the swish pattern to change negative thoughts or habits, we use the conscious, not unconscious, parts of the mind. This means that unconsciously, parts of the mind that were associated with the old habits are left untouched. If you don't account for the second-order changes that the unconscious will demand, the habits changed will simply be replaced with new ones. For example, knuckle crackers who use a swish pattern to change their behavior to flexing their fingers would soon realize that they can crack other parts of their bodies to derive the same satisfaction they got from cracking their knuckles.

As a business leader, it falls on you to keep in mind the second-order consequences of your actions, especially when solving problems. The best way to do this is to find the root causes of a problem and endeavor to change that instead of treating the symptoms. In our example above, instead of rewarding a salary raise, you should figure out exactly what the employee needs. Sometimes appreciation is more important than money and making your best employees feel appreciated goes a long way. By simply thinking about the consequences of the actions you do to solve a problem, you will prevent a lot more problems from following in the wake and conserve a lot of your resources.

Reframing

NLP principles teach that the most constructive thing to do when faced with a problem is to use reframing to get a positive spin on the problem. This reduces the distress to our brains and dims the fight-or-flight response that is responsible for that mind-numbing freeze-reflex when faced with a problem. Instead of thinking what an inconvenience a problem creates for you, try and think about the mental and character strength you will reap from solving it.

Reframing can entail changing the perspective on the angle from which you look at a problem or the seriousness of a problem. To deal with the latter, you simply break the challenge down into smaller pieces. These will be easier to deal with. And while you are at it, coming up with a solution to the smaller problems (which is easier) will embolden you to deal with the bigger challenge, however big it seems.

By combining NLP with willpower exercises, you will embolden yourself to move away from the problem and focus on the solution. The recommended time allocation is 20% on the problem, getting all the facts right and considering the implications, and 80% on the solution.

Anticipation

When making plans, you are required to use NLP's future pacing to visualize the outcome to motivate yourself to pursue it tirelessly. When you are a leader, the visualization must take into account possible issues that may arise during the implementation of action plans. This is called anticipation. It helps you prepare in advance for challenges and have an idea of how the problems could be mitigated. Essentially, anticipation entails answering the question, "What could possibly go wrong?"

Anticipation does not just help you solve the problem; it also helps you anticipate them and put in place measures to ensure that the problems never arise in the first place. To do this, you must start with a thorough breakdown of all the tasks and activities you associated with the project. Answer the following questions:

- Are there any weaknesses and if there are, what are they?
- Is the plan foolproof?
- What specific areas present a possible risk?
- What is the cost of risk occurrence?
- What can be done to stop the problems before they arise?

Not only does anticipation help you avoid risks, but it also helps you to limit any possible damage they might cause.

The "what" model

When you ask the question "why" about a problem, you get to its cause. When searching for the solution, however, the starting point should be "what," not "why." This way, you stop looking for a reason why something happened and simply find a solution. It is an important strategy, especially when you don't have as much time to spend finding the root cause of a problem. However, asking what you can do about a problem rather than why things are going wrong has other advantages. It opens your mind up to finding solutions instead of challenging your whole system for causing a problem.

Next time you are faced with a real problem at work, ask the following five questions about the solution you formulate:

- What would (insert role model) do to solve a problem like this?

- What explanation can I give for choosing this particular solution and not any other?

- What am I trying to achieve with this solution?

- What will I think about the solution I came up with within 10 years?

- What information am I relying on to justify the solution?

These questions give you perspective and take you out of your comfort zone, allowing you to examine a serious problem with a fresh outlook.

NLP problem-solving exercise

- Review the history of the problem you are trying to solve. Write down a detailed description.
- Using the NLP technique of well-formed outcome, imagine that you have already solved the problem.
- Think of everything you can do to solve the problem. Brainstorm as many solutions as possible.
- Settle on the most suitable solution and focus keenly on it.
- Let the realization that you can solve the problem wash through you, relaxing you. There is no reason to worry, you got this!
- Close your eyes and visualize the problem being solved.
- Your inner mind will continue to work on the problem in the most fulfilling way. This could go on for up to half an hour.
- You will start feeling the urge to move when your mind has resolved the problem. Most of the time, you will come out of the exercise with a strong urge to do something about your problem.

- Create an action plan for the duration it will take you to solve the problem, detailing the steps you will need to take.
- Follow the action plan strictly to ensure that you get the outcome you desired.

Decision making

Decision making uses all the concepts discussed in thinking and problem solving to formulate the most appropriate course of action for your department to achieve its goals. While problem-solving can be about a range of issues and concerns, decision making is more specifically concerned with the long-term end result.

When making any decision, you must keep the vision in mind. In fact, the vision is the single most influential consideration in decision making. Only those decisions that will further the strategic cause of the organization are worth making. In this section, we will look at the approaches to decision making that a good leader must follow.

Confirmation bias

Let's discuss first things first and start with the biggest hindrance to decision making. Confirmation bias is a sort of fallacy that blinds us to all information but that which supports our views. In decision making, people are very likely to notice and acknowledge information supporting a decision they already made. In the same vein, any information that is contrary to a decision will be dismissed. So, if you decide to venture into a new area and diversify, you will be more likely to find evidence supporting the concepts of diversification. Even though the risks are still there, your confirmation bias will lead to you glossing over them.

Obviously, this is a very dangerous trap to be caught in. If you cannot identify or acknowledge evidence pointing to mistakes you have made in a decision, this could have disastrous consequences not just for you but also for the whole company.

Even more worrisome is the fact that human beings tend to form an opinion about things really fast. Confirmation bias does not just affect the decisions you have already made. It influences the ones you make. So, if you are more inclined to an idea or a solution, you will gravitate towards evidence that points towards its suitability. If you don't check this inclination, you risk making decisions based on personal rather than business considerations. These decisions will obviously be flawed and will be more likely to bring about even more problems.

NLP decision-making process

Luckily, you can make good and unbiased decisions using the concepts of neuro-linguistic programming. NLP strategies present the master key to effective outcomes for every decision that you make.

Begin with the end in mind: The main reason why confirmation bias distorts your decision making is that you have a personal opinion about the decision. The problem arises when your problem is not backed by the facts.

However, if you can start by considering existing information, both quantitative and qualitative, you increase the chances of your decision is based on good information and factual reasoning. Henceforth, your personally preferred decision will be based on objective information and cannot thus be fallacious. In fact, by beginning with the end in mind and using factual information to verify it, you pave the way for your instinct to kick in and guide you towards the ideal decision.

But as much as your decisions affect the whole group you lead, it is also a personal victory for you when you make a winning decision. So, visualize the outcome of the decision you are about to make and see, hear, and feel it. If it is a good feeling, go for it. But if a big part of the outcome doesn't look or feel good, abandon the idea at once.

1. Elicit values/vision: in the event that you have already created the vision and mission statement for your division, making decisions is simply a matter of

consulting the vision statement and considering the impact of your decision on the attainment of the same. Why is it important that you get the outcome your current decision will bring? Can you do without it? How essential is it that you make the decision? How urgent?

2. Activate the desire to achieve: making a decision is not just a matter of choosing to do something. It is also a commitment you make to pursue a particular aim to the end. In this step of the decision-making process using NLP, you must increase your determination to get to the desired outcome. Part of this entails visualizing the outcome as a picture and enhancing your vision of it to all the senses. Smell it, taste it, see it in your mind, and feel the thrill of victory. This is your outcome picture and you should be able to recall it anytime you need to motivate yourself to pursue the desired outcome.

3. Keep the timeline in mind: every good outcome must be timed. So, when you make the decision to pursue a particular end, make the decision as specific about the timeline as possible. For example, if you decide to diversify into new markets, a more effective way to make the decision is to say, "Diversify into new markets within the next two years." When you hold yourself to a

specific timeline, you become more accountable and thus more driven to achieve.

Decision making and self-awareness

Perfect decision-making capabilities are almost exclusively a preserve of highly driven people. Studies have found that personality plays a major role in the decision-making process. One of the most important aspects of personality that affects decision making is self-awareness. When you are self-aware, you know exactly what you want to achieve in a week, a month, a year, and ten years from now. You also know your limitations and capabilities.

The former allows you to make decisions faster because you simply ask yourself "How does this decision get me closer to my ultimate goal?" People who go through life without any set pursuit or goals don't just make bad decisions. Sometimes they avoid making them altogether by avoiding situations that might require them to choose. If you habitually struggle to make decisions, your sense of self is the first place you should go to look for a solution.

Having no awareness of our capabilities also brings about doubts. When you doubt yourself, you open the door for insecurities to ram you down and erode your decision-making capabilities. So, if your decision-making capabilities have been hampered since you earned that promotion, it is high time you analyze the real emotions you harbor about it. Sometimes you could be avoiding making decisions because you don't feel qualified to make such big choices. For improved decision-making capabilities, increase your self-worth.

Modeling

When working to improve our decision-making capabilities, we use two similar NLP techniques: metamodeling and modeling. Metamodeling is the practice of observing and understanding our own mental models and ways of doing things. It also doubles up as the easiest way to identify personal limitations that could be hindering the attainment of our utmost desires. We use it to find out ways through which we have been hampering our own success. And by employing the concepts of modeling discussed in chapter 1, we are able to replace the constraints that stop us from making good decisions with concepts borrowed from the best business leaders.

In metamodeling, observe your reaction to decision making. What goes through your mind when an opportunity to make a big decision comes by? Are you invigorated or frightened? If your reaction is negative, what could be causing this? You must reach a position of being comfortable making huge decisions.

While observing your thought patterns, it is important to pay attention to the negative patterns of generalization, distortion, cause-effect statements, and cherry-picking. With generalization, you form a universal statement based on an observation of a few events. Distortions happen when you read people or situations wrong and make erroneous interpretations. Sometimes setting a high goal and not meeting it might lead to a rebuke from your boss. Hardly will you ever get fired for going out of your way and failing unless you were targeted for the sack anyway. But a common impediment to decision making, especially of the strategic kind, is the cause-effect idea that you might get fired if you fail. Finally, cherry-picking is the mental model that powers all the thought patterns listed above. It allows you to ignore all evidence contrary to your distortion, generalization, or wrong cause-effect association and blow up the supporting evidence.

After identifying your shortcomings in decision making, you must then find an outstanding business leader with excellent decision-making ability and copy their practices. These include business leaders like Lee Iacocca, Bill Gates, Anthony Robbins, and Steve Jobs among others. Below, we discuss the common decision-making habits the outstanding leaders listed above exhibit that you can model.

NLP exercises for decision making

When you use NLP in your decision-making process, you must incorporate the visual, auditory, and kinesthetic senses. But more specifically, some of the most effective NLP practices for decision making include:

Recognize the reality

You must understand perfectly the options available for you to choose from. Some minor issues might be misconstrued as problems until you actually evaluate them.

Understand your options

A dilemma may turn out to be anything but, as soon as you articulate the options. This is why some people use a pros-and-cons list to make decisions. It allows you to actually think about the different reasons why you might want to make a particular option. While evaluating the options, be sure to keep your eyes on the big picture. As the saying goes, "Don't step over a dollar to pick a dime."

Trust your gut

Decisions can either be supported by rigorously analyzed data or it can be sensed by the heart. While it is not 100 percent reliable, instinct is a very powerful asset for decision-makers.

It relies on unconscious information to come up with a decision that you can feel but not necessarily explain.

Have an alternate plan

While some people believe that having a plan B is rooting for plan A to fail, successful leaders call this common sense. Because failure is unavoidable, the only way to insure yourself from massive losses is to have an alternative in the event that your first idea does not initially work out. Even if, in the way of Elon Musk, your plan is to start all over again, you must be willing to carry on when things do not initially work out as you planned.

Chapter 4: Productivity and time management

As a leader, you want to make the most efficient use of your time and boost productivity. This is the measure that employers and observers everywhere use to determine your ability to lead. To attain the highest levels of productivity possible, you must be skilled at time management. These two skills go hand in hand. Time management influences productivity and high productivity inspires better time management. In this chapter, we will evaluate both using NLP techniques.

Personal productivity

Ultimately, your success as a leader will be judged by the level of productivity you will achieve. This judgment will be made based on the performance of your whole team, but it will be driven more by your ability to attain high rewards using the least possible resources. On a personal level, productivity can be achieved by adhering to NLP processes like the four-step process known as PDCA (plan, do, check, adjust), removing distractions, overcoming procrastination, and understanding how the brain works.

PDCA

The PDCA cycle of productivity is an interactive strategy for continuous self-improvement and the resolution of challenges to productivity. It was created in 1950 by Dr. William Edward Deming to help business managers refine their project delivery processes and has been adopted into NLP to help people increase their personal productivity.

Plan

The awareness of what you are working for is very crucial for productivity. If you don't have a good idea of what goals you want to reach, chances are you will spend your time flitting from one task to another without ever getting anything done. At best, you will achieve moderate success. But if you really want to be a roaring success, you must have a coherent plan of how to get where you intend to get to. The best way to devise a plan is to make it SMART for reasons discussed further below.

Do

The only way to ever be productive is to actually do something. You must be willing to do the things you need to do to reach your goal. Breaking down an objective into smaller tasks is one way to simplify the accomplishment of goals.

Check

Unless you monitor your progress, you can never be sure if you are actually getting anything done. In making smart goals, the M stands for measurable. Your productivity must be measurable. How many new clients per month is good enough? What is the ideal amount of time to spend bringing them in? What percentage of growth in sales or profit is acceptable? All these are quantifiable measurements that you can track.

To ensure that you are on course to reach your goal, check up on your own progress every once in a while. The closer you get to your goal, the more motivated you will feel about doing the work you do.

Adjust

If you have been working hard but not getting anywhere on your goals, it might be time to change your behavior. You are supposed to act on the observations you make about your own work. If you have been doing well, give yourself a reward. If you are not getting closer to your goal, consider adopting a different approach.

Eliminate distractions

Even though our brains can only process about nine bits of information at a time, our brains process up to two billion bits in the conscious and unconscious mind. The distractions that hamper our productivity could be as small as annoying noises, the unsuitable temperature in our place of work, or an uncomfortable chair or desk. Distractions grow in size up to social media and unresolved personal issues, including psychological ones like lack of self-belief, among others.

You should eliminate as many of the distractions you know as possible to give your mind the chance to focus on the most important tasks. Environmental distractions like the hot or cold room can be eliminated simply enough, but dealing with psychological distractions is a little more complicated.

NLP exercises for personal productivity

But by using NLP, it is possible to create an environment where you can still get some good work done despite the mental distractions. This can be done using visualization exercises or anchors.

Anchoring exercise:

- Take note of your environment every time you are in a very productive state.

- Come up with a phrase that captures this moment or a gesture (or both).

- Perform the gesture or say the phrase every time you are in the zone of high productivity.

- Use the phrase or gesture to get yourself into a state of high productivity when you are feeling lethargic.

Visualization exercise:

This is something to do every morning as soon as you get to your office. It sets you up for high productivity through the day.

- Close your eyes.
- Visualize a time when you were at your most productive.
- Let the image consume your senses and give yourself up to this feeling of success.
- See yourself being this productive throughout the day.
- Be productive throughout the day.

Take breaks

The brain is capable of working for a maximum of 90 minutes at a time when you keep distractions to a minimum. Limiting your work sessions to 90 minutes at a time can be a way to attain massive productivity because it gives your brain time to refresh. The breaks present you with the perfect opportunity to network and observe the work environment. If you have spent the first 90 minutes of the day in a meeting, try to spend the next session doing something else. This rotation of tasks ensures that your mind never tires and will always be productive as ever in every new session.

Avoid procrastination

Above anything else we might discuss here, the ability to put off short-term gain for long-term benefits determines your level of productivity and ultimately your success. The only problem with this is that people derive greater pleasure from short-term indulgences. We are biologically engineered to gravitate towards them. However, you can still get the satisfaction of short-term indulgences from doing long-term stuff. This NLP practice utilizes positive reinforcement and reward systems to motivate the highest levels of productivity and satisfaction from work that is ordinarily tedious and monotonous. If keeping on top of your inbox is something you struggle with, give yourself a reward after replying to every email and reading every important message. You will start to associate the task with the satisfaction you get from the reward and be more inclined to do it.

Workplace productivity

When you are the leader, the productivity of the team you are in charge of determines your own success. And while it might be challenging to motivate everyone in your team to pursue success or selflessly commit to the group effort, you can use NLP to turn around any negative attitudes that derail work, inspire employees to change bad habits, and improve the general productivity of everybody in your team.

Set objectives

A common objective in the workplace improves productivity by pooling resources together. A common objective directs the team towards a single purpose, with employees working harder to deliver. See, most of the time people don't fail to achieve success because they are incapable. It is simply a matter of not understanding what is expected of them.

When you set an objective for the whole team to pursue, you should make sure that you assign tasks to each and every employee. This way, they will recognize their role in the whole process and work harder knowing that their success is the success of the whole group, which is their success. Follow that? If an employee succeeds, the whole group succeeds; if the whole group succeeds, the employee succeeds. The failure of a single employee in a team effort leads to double failure and their success to double success.

Boost morale

The only way employees will recognize and appreciate their role in the success of the whole team is when they are motivated to excel. To succeed in leadership, you must consider the morale of your employees. Why should you bother? Well, because unmotivated employees will frustrate your best efforts at productivity. That's why.

You can use team-building exercises to foster a spirit of togetherness, but more importantly, you must consider your employees' personal dreams and objectives. Failure to account for the goals of employees will result in feelings of alienation, poor motivation, and possibly sabotage.

Communication

Communication is the foundation of every strong relationship. To get the best out of your team, you should improve the way you talk with them and how you communicate your goals and objectives. This you must do with all players involved in your workplace, from subordinates to bosses and outsourcing partners. If communication between you and any partner breaks down, the consequences will be felt across the board.

Improved delegation

Delegation is one of the most important tools in your managerial toolbox for improving productivity. This strategy might appear like something that improves your own productivity more than that of the team. But in a real sense, delegating does more to boost the productivity of your employees. It gives them the sense that they are part of the team and can be counted on to play an important part. Of course, you must know the difference between delegating and shoving off your work on the most eager employee. It only builds resentment in the long run and does nothing whatsoever to improve your productivity or that of your team.

Learning and development

To improve the productivity of your team, you must perfect the art of bringing out the abilities of your employees. By using NLP, you can unlock the wealth of potential and knowledge in every one of your employees and make the most of them to boost the productivity of the whole team. By teaching employees the NLP techniques for unlocking their potential, you empower them to take charge of their careers and to be more proactive. Proactive employees do more to bring success to the whole team and serve as an example to others.

Change bad attitudes

If your team has a bad attitude to work, chances are you are not responsible for that since you are new. Bad attitudes at the workplace develop when managers neglect the psychological needs of employees. Overworking is one chief cause of bad attitudes. Mismanagement, poor communication, favoritism, and lack of direction are other causes of bad attitudes. To reverse the harm done by poor leadership, teach employees to recognize their own role in their work-life balance and satisfaction, then work with them to create a nurturing environment.

Finding the state of flow

The peak of productivity is reached when you get in the state of flow. Here, the demands of the activity at hand consume all our attention, skills, and awareness. When you get in the state of flow, you can achieve astounding levels of efficiency and the ability to accomplish tasks that are otherwise challenging. To achieve the state of flow, our highest, purpose-driven goals have to be aligned with the smaller task-driven goals. For example, you can say that you are in flow when you manage to reach the target number of new clients in a week while working towards the higher aim of doubling sales or profit for the year.

Other than boosting productivity, being in the state of flow allows us to grow as individuals as well as with the team. While it is not entirely impossible to get in a state of flow alone, it is always so much better when the results you get are earned by a team effort. And even though happiness is not the foremost emotion you will be feeling while in the zone, you will experience massive growth afterwards. You will also find the whole experience fulfilling and extremely addictive. And if you can manage to get your whole team addicted to extreme productivity, then your quest for success as a leader is already half won!

NLP exercises to get into a flow

The state of flow sure does sound like the ideal workplace atmosphere to have, doesn't it? A state where productivity is boosted to the highest levels, not just for you but your whole team, is the ideal situation for any manager to find him or herself in. So, how exactly can you whip up your team into a state of flow and consistently hit your targets and achieve your goals? Well, NLP has got you covered!

The most important NLP exercises to get into the state of flow are anchoring, visualization, and reframing. The anchor conditions your mind to go back to previous moments of high productivity and visualization excites you to work towards the desired outcome.

1. First off, you must create a vision for your team and ensure that every member is fully committed to it.

2. Before starting the day, gather your team around and guide them through a visualization exercise envisioning a future when you will have achieved the vision.

3. Create a catchphrase to start every meeting with to create a deeper connection to the team for every member.

4. Whenever you achieve a goal, bring the team together for a reward like champagne, cake, or whatever every member likes. A reward, especially one that is enjoyed

together, fosters teamwork and creates an anchor for success.

5. Be sure to make a toast to your team's success, invoking the catchphrase you have created for it. This further strengthens the anchor your team has towards collective success.

6. Respond to concerns, both personal and professional, of all your team members. This is very important to avoid disharmony when some members fall out of touch with the rest of the team.

Reframing comes in handy when you turn out to be unsuccessful. And the chances are high that you will face failure at one time or another, regardless of you and your team's commitment to the goals. You must lead your team in reframing any undesirable events, whether you will pivot in another direction and develop strategies or change strategies and carry on as before. When dealing with failure:

1. Recognize the failure in all its scope. Be as specific as possible and put things in perspective. For example, the failure to meet a target of 50% growth in sales is not as big if you got to 30% growth.

2. Find out why you failed in your quest. Was it too high? Did the team break down? List all the factors that led to the failure.

3. Rationalize. If you failed to reach the target because it was too high, you might want to scale it down a bit. If you do this, remember to celebrate the small victory to keep morale high. Sometimes teams fall apart not because they failed, but because they did not meet a high goal. Even though technically they succeeded, failing to celebrate the success, even underwhelming as it was, led to demoralization and worse, failure.

4. Celebrate the small wins. A small win celebrated is more motivational than a big win that is not.

Time management

You only have so many hours to do what you need to do every day. If you don't plan your time properly, you will end up spending all your time on the unimportant things and having no time for what really matters. Of all the resources we have, time is the most valuable. You can get more money, learn new skills or hire people with them, you can learn new things and become knowledgeable, but you can never get more of a valuable resource called time. When a day goes by, it is gone forever and can never be recovered. If you made proper use of it, it will leave you enriched. Fail to maximize the opportunities that come to you throughout the day and they are gone, possibly forever. The value of every minute, every hour, and every day comes from the things you accomplish and the demands that are made of you.

And as a leader, you will be required to do more every hour of the day. Not only must you get the most out of YOU, it falls on you to ensure that your whole team performs at optimal levels. In this section, we will look at time management at the personal and team levels.

NLP Time management strategies

On a personal level, the proper use of time will be determined by several factors including your sense of direction, creating focus areas, milestone checking, and developing skills.

The proper understanding of long-term goals is very important for time management. It determines the amount of time we allocate to the most important activities. These important activities become our focus area, places where we dedicate most of our energies and time. Focus areas are supposed to be the activities that play the biggest part in getting us to the long-term goals.

These activities are demarcated using milestones, which allow you to verify your progress along the way. Only by tracking progress can you know when or if you need to up your game.

And whether or not you need to up your game to achieve your goals, skills development comes naturally with the pursuit of personal goals. Your ability to accomplish a particular task increases in direct proportion to the amount of time you spend doing it. Ultimately, you find that you need less time to do the same amount of work overtime.

To ensure that you manage your time in the best way possible for maximum yields, the following seven strategies will come in handy.

Set your priorities right

The best strategy to set your activity of main concern is to leaf through your vision statement and determine which three activities will bring you closest to the target. You should then figure out how much time your focus should remain on the activities before moving on to the next step. When your priority activities are clear, your time allocation becomes clear also, mostly because you are able to give precedent to the most important tasks even when the demands on your time are overwhelming.

Build your energy

Energy is another resource that we have in limited quantities. You start with a full tank of energy in the morning and use it up until you are running on empty by nighttime. The only difference between time and energy resources is that you can increase the amount of energy you have at the beginning of the day by resting properly, exercising, and proper dieting. Emotional energy can also be boosted by visualization exercises and meditating, ultimately building your focus, energy, and effectiveness. More energy means that you get more out of your day every day which is the ultimate goal of time management.

Establish a routine

It takes quite a lot of energy and time to start a new routine, but maintaining a routine is the least time-consuming activity ever. The most important routines for good time management are the morning and evening (sleeping) routines. They are especially important because they boost not just your ability to manage your time but also the capacity to get the most out of it.

Make the diary your best friend

A diary is an ultimate tool for the budgeting of time use. But every other manager can schedule their activities in their diary and manage their time just fine. When you use NLP time-management strategies, you pay special attention to hotspots in your diary and plan to do certain activities at the times most suitable to do them.

You see, all hours of your day are not equal. Some are suited for difficult tasks and some are best suited for relaxation. To note these different times of the day, you must practice full awareness during the day. Notice how you feel in the morning, midmorning, early afternoon, and the evening. When do you feel most alert? At what times is your brain sleepy and lethargic? Schedule intellectually demanding tasks when your mind is at its sharpest and engage in more physical activities when your mind is less sharp—activities that involve movement, for example.

Ask yourself a question… or two

Time management does not just happen by accident. It is something we do consciously by ensuring that we make the most out of every hour throughout the day. Questioning the time used for tasks and activities increases the value we place on time and fosters better time management. Questioning your time allocation for tasks allows you to keep improving on both the time allocation and task accomplishment.

Ready, set, go!

The most important time to mark when doing something is the start and finish times. You must start every activity you intend to finish and you must finish everything you start. Observe this rule and you will increase the utility of your time every single day. In between the starting and the finishing line, you must pace yourself. A steady pace with occasional sprints is the best strategy, especially for tasks that require a lot of time to get done.

Create a structure

We form habits because we do something over and over again and derive a measure of pleasure from it. However, there is another strategy to form habits: creating a structure of actions. A structured workday ensures that you have specific times for doing the most important things like eating, sleeping, exercising, and working. Every activity should be scheduled with strict timelines to reinforce the need for you to do them at the right time.

The 4 Ds

In a more simplified manner, you can manage your time by adhering to the 4 Ds of time management. The 4 Ds of time management is a way to help you put your time to the best use by determining how you handle tasks. It classifies tasks into four groups, namely: the ones you delete, the ones you delegate, the ones you do, and the ones you defer.

Tasks to delete

As a leader, you should only give your attention to the tasks that are absolutely necessary. If an activity does not really help you get closer to your ultimate goal, then you must strike it off your list of to-dos. To determine the activities that are not worthwhile and that are best deleted, use the Pareto 80/20 rule. See, in most cases, 80% of what we do only brings 20% of the benefits. Activities that fall in this bulk category can be deleted with little to no negative impact on our productivity but with massive amounts of time freed for more productive work.

Tasks to delegate

As the team leader, you will be responsible for the management of time at the workplace, especially for projects. In the course of your day, you will be put in a position where you must decide whether or not an activity is important enough to tackle right away or tackle it at all. You will also have to prioritize between activities happening simultaneously, like a meeting with an old client and an interview with a prospective one. When this happens, you must pick one activity to place your focus on and hand over the less important task to your subordinates. However, don't completely abdicate by handing out any difficult task and washing your hands of it. Only hand over the tasks you must and follow up to ensure that whoever does it meets the quality standards.

Tasks to do right away

Any important task is a task worth doing straight away. With "do it," I mean that you must follow up on the task to completion. The biggest mistake people make is to start a task then leave it halfway through and start doing something else. By the end of the day, you will have started to do, but not completed, so many tasks it will be difficult to gauge your level of success. Ultimately, the numerous task folders open in your mind will leave you feeling stressed and anxious. Don't get trapped in the paper-shuffling trap. Finish every task you start as soon as possible then move on to the next thing.

Tasks to defer

Obviously, as you go through your to-do list, you must prioritize some tasks over others. This means that you will have to put aside some other tasks for some other time. These are the tasks that are important but not as urgent, so they can be delayed without affecting the ultimate goal.

The best way to classify tasks into the 4 Ds is by going through your to-do list each morning and using the Eisenhower Matrix to group your tasks. You must do the urgent and important tasks, delegate the urgent but not important ones, defer the important but not urgent ones, and delete tasks that are neither urgent nor important.

Chapter 5: Communication, negotiation, and presentation

Communication and interpersonal relationships are critical components of neuro-linguistic programming. They also play a big part in the professional work of a manager, because a lot of what you will be doing will be coordinating the efforts of various stakeholders to achieve a specific goal. In this chapter, we will look at the role that communication, negotiation, and presentation play in the makings of a great business leader.

Communication

One skill that you must develop to a high standard as a leader is the ability to communicate clearly, convincingly, and consistently. The vision you develop for your team (which we have said several times is a very stabilizing force to your leadership) can only be realized if you convey it in an effective manner. This is the conventional view of communication and its relevance to leadership. However, with NLP, we know that communication goes beyond the words you say to your employees or clients to the way you absorb and process ideas and information from the world. In this section, we will look at all the ways that leaders communicate and how you can enhance your communication for success in your management career.

Communication filters

All forms of communication take place in five channels, namely: visual, auditory, kinesthetic (feelings, touch, pressure), olfactory (smell), and gustatory (taste). These input channels make up the communication model used in NLP to help us absorb, process, and react to information from the environment including what other people say, do, and how they look, as well as the environment where the communication takes place. However, the ultimate information that reaches us is determined not by the other person or the environment but our own filters. These filters delete, distort, and generalize information from the outer world and could impact in a big way how we deal with the rest of the world.

In deleting, our input channels omit some parts of the messages absorbed from the world and leave only the important or useful bits or whatever we perceive to be the most important bits. One instance where deletion occurs is when we use a phone and drive at the same time. The visual channels are overpowered by the information that needs to be absorbed, resulting in poor performance in both.

Distortion occurs when we misrepresent the information we absorb to create different meanings than what they actually give. On one hand, distortion can be a powerful motivational tool that can help us create a rosy future for ourselves in our minds. When we do this with enough conviction, we can create powerful visualizations.

On the other hand, distorting information can lead to serious misunderstandings. If you don't know what someone means when they do or say something, it is best to wait till you have gathered enough information before interpreting their actions or words. This saves you from potential misunderstandings which can be catastrophic when you are a manager charged with offering leadership and guidance.

Generalization is a breakdown in interpretation that happens when you draw universal conclusions based on a single experience. This leads to stereotypical thinking that could be very dangerous and interfere with your ability to lead. Information should be interpreted as independent of past experiences.

Intrapersonal communication

One of the many definitions of communication is simply "the means of transmitting or receiving ideas or feelings." Most people believe that communication only occurs when there is a direct exchange of information between two people, but in truth, communication takes place even when we receive and decode information from our environment. On the one hand, you must understand that your brain is always collecting information from all around you. Our thinking and decision making are influenced by both the information we perceive consciously and that which reaches our minds at the unconscious level. Being aware of the power of these unconscious communication pathways can boost your effectiveness as a manager.

The things you say to yourself also count as a form of communication because they entail the exchange of information between the conscious and the unconscious parts of our minds. These forms of information exchange are known as intrapersonal communication and they entail planning, calculating, internal monologue, and daydreaming. Using NLP, you can enhance the use of internal monologue and daydreaming to impact your mind with greater productivity.

Internal monologue includes the things you say to yourself about yourself, the things you do, and things that happen around you. Listening to your internal monologue is one way of examining your own psyche to determine the state of your mind. And because it is a window into your unconscious mind, you can also exploit internal monologue to impart yourself with positive and inspirational messages.

Chanting is one positive way of imparting positive messages into your mind. Consistently saying something about and to yourself eventually tricks your brain into believing it. As a new manager, you might need to utilize the gift of chanting to lift your confidence in your ability to take on the duties of your job with confidence and do so to great success.

Simply mattering things like "you got this" under your breath can calm you in a tense situation. When you do it over time, your mind takes in the message and starts to act it out. This means that you will find yourself actually being in control of situations, however stressful, without losing your mind. All because you said it to yourself and you believed it.

Daydreaming is an unconscious means of communication that you can use to enhance your skills as a manager. Any time you are daydreaming is a time when you transport yourself into an ideal future situation. This communicates your deepest desires, which is why you mostly find yourself daydreaming when you are excited about something. The only problem with most people is that they daydream without purpose. It is something they do when bored and needing an escape. By doing it with intent and committing your mind to the process, you can convert daydreaming to future pacing and use it not just to visualize a future with a prospective mate but also to visualize your successful future and goals.

Leadership communication

All the forms of communication that take place between managers and their subordinates, peers, and their seniors are called leadership communication. It is underlined by the need to convey the capacity to lead at all times. When communicating as a leader, you will see greater results if you make it grounded in your own vision as a leader and the organizational values. The culture and climate of the organization must shine through your communication.

Leadership communication models include significance, cadence, values, and consistency. Regardless of the perceptions of your employees, peers, or bosses have about you, these aspects will factor into their interpretation of whatever you say. This is especially true for official communication. Anything you say will be treated as significant, including a random compliment to an employee about the quality of their work. It is very important that you keep this in mind to avoid sending the wrong signals. And especially when communicating with your bosses, the values of the organization must shine through when you communicate. Your vision and mission statement plays an especially big part of your communication strategies as a leader.

In fact, affirming the vision you have created for your team and how it falls within the vision of the whole company is one of the most important purposes of leadership communication. With proper leadership and communication, junior leaders can even create a vision that shapes the whole organization. When General George C. Marshall was the Chief of Staff of the

US Army during World War II, he created a plan for the entry of America into what most considered a European conflict. He then appeared in Congress several times to convey his opinion about the need for the country to mobilize and take an active part in the war. For his ability to communicate his vision for the military and convince his superiors (the president of the United States and Congress), he was rewarded with a five-star rank in the military, an appointment to the position of Secretary of State under President Harry S. Truman, and a Nobel Peace Prize award in 1953.

This is the power of good communication driving transformational initiatives. Without General Marshall, the United States Military would not have been able to mobilize the massive resources he secured to advance its defense and assault weapons systems and practically win World War II for the Allied forces.

Leadership communication also allows you to galvanize your employees, peers, and seniors to rally behind an initiative. This is important because it is impossible to achieve any worthwhile thing in business without the help of others. Even if you have the best proposal with great potential for profit to the company, you will probably see little support until you convince all the stakeholders to get behind you on it.

Another purpose of leadership communication is to coach your junior employees. Since they look up to you for leadership, any instructions coming from you will make them feel valued and seen. Sometimes that is all an employee needs. As for you, the coaching you do will pay you back with greater productivity and efficiency from employees who actually understand what is expected of them and who knows how to deliver. Even if you offer coaching through contracted professionals, it still speaks to your desire to see the people who work for you build their skills.

Finally, when you are a leader, communication is as much about talking as it is about listening. When you listen, you communicate volumes nonverbally, like the fact that you care about employee, peer, or senior input in your work. Communicating without expecting, asking for, or listening to feedback is destructive and is likely to result in an eventual breakdown.

The Milton model of communication

The Milton Model is an approach to communication that borrows from the language patterns of hypnotic communication. It was developed from the concepts of noted hypnotist Milton Erickson and is considered to be a method of accessing the covert elements of our personality through language-induced trances. From the Milton model, we have three other communication models: rapport, indirect communication, and unconscious interpersonal communication.

Rapport

We use the concepts of hypnosis to create a better model of exchanging ideas and responses to information. This is an important asset to have as a business leader because much of the communication you will be doing will be aimed at convincing people to do something they might not necessarily be willing to do. When you can make a person empathize with you, you will realize that more of what you say meet a positive response.

Using NLP principles, you should mirror the body language of your audience to tune into their world. This includes matching their body language, breathing, posture, and tone of voice. After mirroring their nonverbal cues, you occupy the same state of being with the person, with him or her being the object and you the reflection that copies their actions. However, you can take over and start leading by changing your behavior and gestures in a covert and dominant manner. Rapport is very effective when you are trying to sell an idea to a higher authority. Once you have established a rapport, they will be more likely to agree with your ideas. Not only that, the person will probably be eager to do so.

Indirect communication

This entails using the NLP technique of metaphors to gain access to the unconscious mind of a person. This way, you can implant ideas into a person's mind by giving them a metaphor with a correlation to what you want them to do. This is called an indirect suggestion. It is accomplished with the use of purposefully vague metaphors. See, it is harder to get someone, let's say your boss, to agree with you if you go to him or her and say, "We need to invest in this new technology. It will boost our bottom line."

But you could approach him or her and vaguely suggest that the bottom line is not as strong as it used to be, but this new technology is really paying off for the people who have invested in it. If you launch into a different topic, he or she might not even notice the metaphor. But the power of a metaphor is in the way it latches onto the unconscious. Don't be surprised if the next time you talk, he or she asks you to tell them more about the technology you mentioned. You may even ask for the opportunity to explain it with a PowerPoint presentation because, after all, he came to you! Indirect communication using metaphors can be a very useful resource when used the right way.

Unconscious interpersonal communication

This Miltonian NLP strategy uses ambiguous language and nonverbal communication to achieve almost the same results as indirect communication. The only difference is that this strategy uses blurred boundaries of meaning to distract the conscious mind rather than metaphors. The aim of unconscious communication is to give the unconscious mind the opportunity to shine through, allowing recall and the invocation of relationships. This communication model allows you to say something without actually saying it. It can be indispensable when you are trying to communicate covertly.

Negotiation

Contrary to popular belief, most negotiations, even for a business leader, happen outside the boardroom. Any time you try to make someone with a different view come across to thinking like you and doing what you want is a time you are negotiating. With that being said, you will do a lot more negotiating in your new position as a manager. The stakes will also be higher, so it is something you might want to perfect.

Building your negotiation skills

NLP teaches about outcome setting using fundamental approaches. With an outcome setting, you learn how to win in a negotiation by recognizing a few important facts about negotiation. These include:

Information is key to negotiation

Negotiation is a form of decision making. In fact, the decisions you make during and at the end of negotiation are the most important ones you will ever make. When you are more informed, you negotiate better and make healthier decisions. To do this, you might have to get the professional services of an investment consultant, a headhunter, a lawyer, or an accountant. These professionals clarify some of the more complicated things for you and also give advice. With sufficient information, you will be better placed to understand the whole scope of the situation and also to reach a winning deal.

Moreover, information flows faster in a negotiation than any other time. The situation you leave in a morning negotiation could be very different from the one you find in the afternoon. If you buy a software package shortly before a more superior one enters the market, it will leave your company at a huge disadvantage when all your rivals adopt better technology and start to outperform you. A slight change creates a massive shift, and anyone who doesn't know or appreciate the changes risks getting screwed over in the negotiation. Keep your finger on the pulse, as the saying goes, to avoid possible ramifications down the line.

Anything is only as valuable as the buyer makes it

People set the value of objects based on the value they perceive it has, not necessarily its real value. For example, hardly anyone ever complains about the cost of healthcare because people value their health more. The same rule applies to negotiations. Whatever is under contention will be valued based on the perception of the marginal buyer, i.e., the person who is interested in it. You can sell something for more than its market share if you can capitalize on the interest another person shows in it.

You are not immune from influence

Sometimes, we make the decision to do something based on impulse rather than good reason. Skilled negotiators use psychological principles like reciprocation, social proof, and scarcity to influence their rivals into giving ground beyond the make-sense point. Let's touch briefly on these principles.

Reciprocation exploits the evolutionary urge every human being has to reward every good deed with another. So, rather than start with exactly what you came to the negotiation table for, a wily negotiator will give their rival a "free" gift, often out of the blue. Even though we may not be aware of it or we fight hard against it when we are aware, studies have shown that we are more likely to concede ground when we feel that we are reciprocating.

Social proof is a tool whose use many salespeople have perfected to an art form. You go to buy something, say conferencing equipment for your office, with a pretty concrete idea of the qualities you want in mind. It is cheap, reliable, and recommended. But the salesperson you meet, working for a different company selling a different product, convinces you to buy something more expensive simply because they tell you that it is the equipment that Mark Cuban or Zuckerberg uses. Your desire to fit in leaves you susceptible to manipulation.

Finally, we have the oldest but still most effective trick in the book—scarcity. People value scarce things higher and will be willing to pay more for something simply because the opportunity is closing or there is a short supply. The worst mistakes made on the negotiation table are those that followed one party (often the most unlikely) pulling out or expressing the desire to pull out.

How to make it a win-win

The outcome of a negotiation defines the relationship you will have with your negotiating rival afterward. If you crush someone in a negotiation, he or she will probably be left feeling cheated and taken advantage of. This tends to happen when you go to the negotiation with a must-win mentality—the notion that the other person must lose for you to be satisfied. Any concession you give to your rival will make you feel cheated, which results in mutual dissatisfaction on both sides. So, the disaster of approaching a negotiation with a must-win mentality is not just that you destroy any chance at a relationship afterward but that it also turns out to be a lose-lose outcome.

A much better approach, especially in the long run, is to find a way for both of you to walk out of the negotiation with what you wanted. If that is not possible (and that is the case most of the time), then at least you should both come out feeling satisfied with the outcome. This is where it gets a little complicated and where NLP comes in handy.

By using the NLP strategy of total-win, you foster cooperation, rather than competition, with your negotiation rival by using strategies such as:

Establish your positions

Three out of five times when people reach a stalemate in a negotiation, it is because they are too fixated on getting their own way or they misunderstand what the other party wants. Nevertheless, people will go out of their way to try and make sure that their adversary doesn't get the thing they think he or she wants. Keeping an open mind is important when you are going into a negotiation. Make no assumptions about your rival's interests. In fact, you should be as clear as possible as to what they hope to gain from the negotiation.

When Steve Jobs was buying the parts to build his first computer, he negotiated two deals with two different merchants, one to get the parts he needed to build the computer and the other to market the computer—on credit. Without this genius piece of negotiation, the Macintosh may never have been born.

What are the interests?

Whatever your position in a negotiation, your interest in the outcome will always be infinitely bigger. You try to negotiate with the best salesman in your field because you want to bring him to your team—that is your position. But what you really want is to become the best-performing junior manager in your company—that is your interest. See, it is very easy to negotiate for our own interests because they are the very thing that drives us.

Understanding the other person's interests, however, can be a little bit more complicated. It requires a level of empathy and consideration that many of us don't have. But if you can discover your rival's interests, you will have gained the key to winning the negotiation for both of you. Interests can be driven by everything from tangible gains to beliefs, cultural values, and status. And because people rarely ever do anything that is against their values, it is something you need to appreciate during a negotiation.

Focus on achieving mutual gain

Good leaders know exactly what to do to get their way. Great leaders try to make sure that everyone gets a good deal out of their dealings with them. This calls for the ability to brainstorm as many inventive ideas to reach an agreement as will be needed to find the one solution that enriches both teams. Even when you crush an opponent in a negotiation, you can reframe the outcome so that they don't feel like they lost too much.

The conditional close is one way that mutual gain can be implied even when it is not, in the strictest terms, achieved. The conditional close is used to overcome objections with the promise of a sentimental reward that your partner did not expect but may value more. This requires that you understand their interests so that you can twist arguments around to appeal to them. The conditional close could be anything from promising to give a reluctant target hireling an indoor mini-golf course if they sign a five-year deal to promising to buy all your supplies from one seller if they give you a really big discount. The conditional close momentarily removes the negotiation from the key issues and boosts your chances of winning. It can be especially effective when your interest in the outcome of a negotiation is outsized and your chances of winning are low.

Compromise

In every negotiation, an agreement can only be achieved by the willingness of both parties to settle. This is called compromising, whereby each one of you gives something up to get closer to the other person's position. The best compromise is one that is created from the objective analysis of your own position. Before starting the negotiation process, sit down and ask yourself what you are willing to give up. Be objective about it but keep it under wraps until you get down to ironing out a settlement. Ideally, you should convince your rival to take your position without giving anything up. But when it comes down to it, it is much better when you know exactly what you can and cannot give up.

The BATNA, or Best Alternative to a Negotiated Agreement, is a kind of alternative outcome every party in a negotiation has. If you negotiate with the best salesman in the city to join your team but realize that he or she is too costly an acquisition, your BATNA might be to get the second-best or incentivize your own team. A good BATNA helps you go through negotiation without falling for a terrible deal simply because you think there is no option.

Influencing others

As much as you will try to make a negotiation ends with a win-win situation, you must cultivate the ability to influence others. Look at it this way; it is better to hold all the cards and be generous than count on the generosity of other people to get what you want. As a leader, you want to leave nothing to chance. You want to have the power to influence the outcome of negotiation as much as possible. Well, with NLP techniques like rapport, mirroring, and pattern interruption, you can get just that.

Building Rapport

The ability to reach a satisfactory win-win settlement in a negotiation relies in part on your ability to establish a connection with your negotiation partner. In the last chapter, we touched on rapport as part of the Milton model of communication. Well, turns out making eye contact, synchronizing body language, and matching vocal patterns also help you in negotiation. This helps you reduce the chances of cognitive dissonance and puts your partner more at ease. All round, rapport building creates a connection that makes it easier to come to a favorable conclusion.

Pattern interruption

Pattern interruption is a very powerful, subtle mind-control tool. When you make someone do a series of actions a few times, their unconscious mind takes over and starts to expect the next action in the series. This establishes a pattern. Breaking the pattern entails simply removing one of the actions in the series and redirecting the person into doing something they normally wouldn't have done. Some mentalists use pattern interruption to achieve results as impressive as talking strangers into giving them their wallets. You can employ pattern interruption along with other NLP techniques like anchoring and metaphors to establish a quid pro quo of actions that results in you getting what you want.

NLP negotiation exercise

One of the most effective NLP negotiation exercises is the agreement frame. It follows a simple procedure of pacing and leading to influence the pace, direction, and outcome of a negotiation. The steps are:

1. You open the negotiation by telling the other party your expectations and the solution you want.

2. Ask your partner to state their best offer for what you want

3. Use pacing and directing to agree AND offer a counterproposal. Avoid words like but, however, and other such contradictory terms.

4. Work towards a greater agreement by discussing your positions and the interests behind them. It is always best when you get the other party talking about their interests in making the deal because it gives you clues as to what conditions you can give for a mutually beneficial close.

5. Talk to the other party into agreeing with your condition by highlighting the benefits and downplaying any perceived weaknesses.

6. Check that there are no objections and close the negotiation as swiftly as possible.

Presentation

Public speaking is an important skill for a business leader to have. Good presentation skills allow you to talk to a large group of people and pass on the information you need to. Presentations serve the purpose of informing, demonstrating, persuading, and inspiring. They make up a big part of leadership communication.

Over the course of your career, you will be requested to make presentations to present detailed information to your employees, seniors, and or peers. Demonstrational presentations are useful for showing how a product works. It can be for a new technology you are hoping to adopt or the prototype of a new product for your company to produce. Persuasive presentations are more important because they are supposed to appeal to the audience and generate a specific reaction (agreement) from them that they might not be very willing to give. Finally, the ability to make inspirational presentations can come in handy when you need to motivate and stir up the interest of your employees and peers towards a specific course of action. For example, the presentation you make while selling your vision for the department is inspirational.

You can make the same kind of convincing and inspirational speeches that Steve Jobs used to sell his iPhone. But to do this you need to use NLP techniques. They entail:

Two-minute anecdotes

An anecdote gives you the perfect start to the speech. It can be a story about something that happened to you, an interesting article you recently read, or a statistic. If you make it humorous, an anecdote will also break the ice and leave you feeling more confident about talking to your audience. Steve Jobs opened up his presentations with a thought-provoking story that got the audience hooked on his every word. He also used one-word notes for his presentations that made it easier for the audience to recall what he said.

Use sensory language

Words can be used to invoke all five sensory experiences of sound, sight, feel, taste, and smell. The use of these words pulls the audience into the plane of thought you have created and allows you to appeal directly to their senses. Steve Jobs was able to peg his audience to his every word by using carefully worded statements that turned ordinarily boring and technical presentations into engaging and awe-inspiring ones.

Anchoring

A good presenter uses the stage in a very particular way. Instead of just moving around, designate specific areas of the stage for specific types of information to unconsciously engage the audience in the presentation. For example, if you choose to be tough in the center-forward position, firm on the left, and playful on the right, your audience will unconsciously expect to feel these reactions whenever you get to those positions.

Anchoring can also be accomplished using gestures. If you watch Steve Jobs's presentation, you will notice that he does it quite a lot. Animated gestures (in moderation) engage the visual sensors and draw attention to your nonverbal cues while on stage. The nonverbal cues, in turn, allow the audience to absorb all of the information that comes from your mouth.

Focus on the aim, not the content

The outcome of a speech is more important than the content of the speech itself. Focusing on the ways your speech will affect the audience rather than the things you will say helps you develop your presentation skills in a number of ways.

1. You are more intentional in the words you use.
2. It imparts the need for you to work harder to connect to the audience.
3. Taking the focus from what you will say reduces the anxiety of making a presentation.

For Jobs, it was usually to drum up support for a new product, and people would line up outside Apple stores to buy his product. He would sell the benefits with simple yet effective visuals. Because he understood that the aim of communicating is to elicit a specific feeling, Steve Jobs perfected the art of presentation in his years at Apple. Today, he is one of the most admired and studied business leaders in history. The biggest attraction point, especially for managers, is his presentations.

Chapter 6: Anxiety and stress management

Anxiety and stress are quite common in the demanding life of a leader. They are two commonly related issues but are caused by quite different mental and physical states. You will feel stressed when the demands of your workplace or new changes put a strain on your mental and physical faculties. Anxiety, on the other hand, comes about when you dread or are worried about a future situation. The main difference between anxiety and stress is that the former mostly occurs before a demanding event while the latter commonly follows afterward. In this chapter, we will look at the two states and how they can affect your ability to perform as a newly promoted manager.

Anxiety

Anxiety occurs when we feel threatened by external factors or, surprisingly, when we are anxious. It adds "freeze" to "fight or flight" and makes it harder for you to do things that other people find easy. Unlike stress, anxiety is a mental condition that can impair social and professional functioning in the long term. And even when anxiety occurs for a short span, the impact can be just as serious to your social and professional life.

Causes of anxiety

Some of the reasons why you might be feeling anxious include:

Self-doubt

Normally, people use to fight or fight to tackle big problems, either fighting it out or fleeing to avoid dealing with them. But when you are about to embark on a huge inevitable task but you don't feel capable, you are trapped in what your mind perceives to be an impossible situation. You cannot run and you feel incapable of fighting, so your mind settles for option three and freezes up. This form of anxiety is very common when you are faced with a huge task.

Limiting thoughts contribute to self-doubt by making you feel incapable of doing something. Whether from previous experiences or lack of previous experiences, your brain can make you feel fearful (of going back to a place where you have failed before) or worried (about the prospect of doing something you have never done before) and cause you lots of anxiety.

Choices

For people who are prone to anxiety, the choice can be very incapacitating. It paves the way for self-doubts about your ability to make the right one. Big choices with serious consequences are especially notorious for inducing stress. Making a choice under pressure, where the chances of making a mistake are even higher, is even more anxiety-inducing. People who are prone to anxiety tend to find the process of making a decision daunting, spending hours worrying about the chance of making a mistake. The choice mostly causes anxiety among those with anxiety disorders rather than common bouts of anxiety. The anxiety caused by choice points to a lack of confidence in making decisions.

For leaders, choosing between two bad options with bad results means that people might lose their livelihood, careers might be destroyed, or other bad consequences might follow. Even with great decision-making capabilities, the choice could still cause anxiety.

Lack of options

On the other hand, the lack of choice is just as anxiety-inducing. The choice is a reason why freedom is one of the most important things for humans and why democracy is celebrated as the best form of government worldwide. On a personal level, nothing makes people as anxious as the perception that they are trapped in a bad situation. When you have to choose between two choices that will both lead to adversity, the very idea of having to deal with any of the consequences could freeze you right up. A sensation of entrapment often results and anxious feelings crop up.

Preventing anxiety

To ensure that anxiety does not interfere with your work, you must use NLP to avoid it. If you can manage to overcome anxiety before it happens, you will live a happy, fulfilled life. Your ability to lead will also improve dramatically. Some of the strategies you can use to get there include:

Rename it

The things that scare us are often daunting in name only. When you actually think about them, they are actually quite harmless. The idea of renaming the things that cause you to be anxious borrows from the NLP technique of reframing. Simply put a positive spin on things: challenges are growth opportunities, the opposition is a chance to win big, and failure is just a minor setback. By reframing, you also put things in perspective so that you don't have to beat yourself up or be apprehensive about future events that are not even in your control.

Limit your choices

If the idea of making a choice makes you anxious, then you must find a way to make choices in advance. A clearly stated vision is the first place to start. It narrows down your options to only those things that help you move closer to the ultimate goal. Making your choices through visionary thinking further enhances your decision-making capabilities and reduces the level of your anxiety overall.

In the rare event that you have no option but to decide between two or more options, a pros-and-cons list can be a simple yet elegantly effective tool. It narrows your choices and gives you a way to make choices in an objective manner.

Create an exit strategy

The reason why most people feel trapped in the notion that they have no option whatsoever. To avoid the possibility of that ever happening, an exit strategy or plan B comes in handy. Even as you dedicate all your energies to achieve plan A, the knowledge that you have a backup plan in case anything goes wrong is both reassuring and settling. An exit strategy is especially important if you are prone to anxiety attacks.

NLP treatment

In the event that anxiety gets past your defense systems (and this is highly likely), you can use still use the following NLP strategies to remedy it.

Change your thinking about anxiety

Anxiety hinders so many people from achieving their goals because it comes as a double threat. The real instance of anxiety happens when the dread of doing something causes you to freeze and be unable to do it. But sometimes the anxiety happens much earlier, when you start fearing the freeze before it actually happens—anxiety about anxiety. This is because most people who have experienced negative impacts of anxiety—missed deadlines, failed tasks, and poor performance—start to associate their failures with the anxiety attacks. It becomes a big threat to their wellbeing and easily gets blown out of proportion.

NLP anxiety training helps you overcome it by helping you recognize that anxiety is actually nothing. It is simply a creation out of your own mind, a monster of your own making that nevertheless terrorizes you. Anxiety is not even an emotion; it is a thought process that happens when you face a threatening situation. When you change the way you think about anxiety, you will start to normalize it and, at the very least, tackle any anxiety you might have about anxiety, which only makes it worse.

Turn it around

You can use the NLP presupposition of the capacity to turn your thinking about anxiety around. The NLP presupposition of capacity states that we are only incapacitated by our own minds. Realize that what is in the future cannot hurt you now unless you represent it to yourself as something that can hurt you. When you worry endlessly about something, you only increase the creation of double jeopardy whereby you will suffer for an event that might not even happen and because it has already happened in your mind, the chances of it happening in the real world also increase.

So, if you are anxious because you think a huge deal you have been negotiating for your company might fall apart and get you fired, you will be unable to focus on getting it done, fail, and get fired anyway. But if you turn an anxiety-causing event around and make it less of a big deal, your own fears about it will diminish as well.

Be in the moment

What anxiety does that is so devastating is that it deceives our minds into believing that our worst fears are real and happening at the moment. So, not only does it rob us of the opportunity to live every moment of our life, it transports us into the worst-case scenario future. But you can overcome it by remaining rooted in the present moment, doing what you can do to make the future as beautiful as possible. You can use self-hypnosis to remove the negative images of the future from your mind, swatting them away any time they try to resurface. Experience every moment of your day and only consider the future in an objective manner.

Know what you can and cannot do

We are most anxious about the things we think we are supposed to be able to do even when they are completely impossible. You will never be anxious about crashing a spacecraft into Mars because you know that would never happen. Only the things that you are capable of doing will make you anxious. The limit of your anxiety, therefore, is the limit of your potential.

Do it anyway

Nelson Mandela said, "It always seems impossible until it is done." This is true for every task that makes you anxious. As difficult as it seems, at one point you will look at it and remember a time when you thought you couldn't do it. Splitting up a huge job into smaller tasks can make you feel more confident about your ability to do it. Once you have started to do it, you will start to feel less scared of doing it and effectively banish your anxiety. The trick is to not be afraid to feel the fear because fear is part of the achievement.

Harnessing anxiety to excel

Studies have shown that brain anxiety can unlock certain parts of the brain and enable you to do so much. People with high levels of anxiety can use their panic and worry to function at a more productive level. This can be done by following the following process:

Allowing anxiety

The first and most important process in harnessing anxiety is to accept that you are anxious. But instead of thinking of your anxiety as being destructive, think of it as a force of nature that sharpens your reflexes, heightens your awareness, and gives you greater strength. This takes the fear away from the equation and allows you to go to the next step in the process.

Befriend your anxiety

Think of your anxiety as a wild stallion. You cannot tame it if you don't calm it down enough to ride it. Understand the causes of your anxiety so that you can get into the right position to solve them. Instead of thinking of it as the enemy, think of it as the sentry alerting you to a problem. The sensations you feel are simply your body trying to get you ready for some action. Let the anxiety fill you at your terms. Feel it increasing sensation to your arms, legs, and mind. Feel the adrenaline pumping through your system, giving you strength, focus, stamina, and speed. There's nothing to worry about here!

Channel it

As the energy, stamina, focus, and speed course through your body bring your mind about to the thing you've got to do. Focus the anxiety towards the activity at hand and visualize yourself getting into the state of flow. Anxiety will be your fuel until you emerge, having accomplished the task you set out to do. If you can create a productive relationship with your anxiety, there is no reason why you shouldn't be able to achieve new levels of success and productivity in your new career.

Stress

Stress occurs in less subtle ways than anxiety, and prolonged stress is actually believed to be the leading cause of a majority of lifestyle diseases because it affects the functioning of organs, worsens the effects of cancer, and hampers circulation. The thing about stress is that unlike anxiety, it is very real and very often completely warranted.

Causes of stress

In your management career, stress can come from many areas. A bad working relationship with a senior manager can be a stressful thing because he or she can make your work so much harder. Constant failure in your pursuit of a vision or a goal can also be very stressful.

Lack of work-life balance

As you settle down into your new job, you will almost certainly have to apply yourself even harder to the job. Sometimes, this means that your home life suffers. A bad work-life balance can be extremely stressful because it means that you will have no conduit to drain the stress of your job at the end of the day.

Poor health

Your new job comes with added responsibilities that with most likely turn your life upside down. Your old healthy habits fall off and your eating habits deteriorate. This all leads to decreased energy levels, energy drinks and coffee, poor sleeping habits, and increased levels of stress.

Poor planning

"Failing to plan is planning to fail" so the saying goes. Well, turns out that poor planning is also a recipe for stress. Poor planning means that you never foresee challenges and put in place the measures to mitigate them. You will face numerous problems that make it harder to achieve your intended outcome, increase the pressure of your job, and blow up your stress levels.

Stress management

Slow down

Sometimes all the body needs are the opportunity to recharge. When you don't give yourself some downtime to replenish your energies, you only increase your stress levels. Even when you are engaged in a big project, taking a break can be very crucial in alleviating your stress levels. Go out for a drink, watch a movie, sit and read a book, just take your mind off whatever is giving you stress.

If you simply cannot find the time to slow down, you can use NLP's future pacing to achieve the same effect for a fraction of the time.

1. Simply recall a time when you were calm, relaxed, and at peace.
2. Close your eyes and focus on that one thought
3. Expand the details and immerse yourself fully into the picture. Activate all the sensory organs for a more realistic experience.

When your mind relaxes, so does your body. All the stressors will be dispelled, and you will be left feeling refreshed and more alert.

Create awareness

As much as people maintain that their stress is caused by a bad boss, difficult project, or whatever they attribute their stress to, nothing ever stresses you out without you giving it the permission to do so. The way you react to a situation is the real culprit. If you deliberately choose to not get stressed, then that will be your new reality. Whenever you feel a negative reaction to a distressing event building up, practice the following NLP exercise:

1. Take 10 deep breaths

2. Bring your mind to the present and be wide aware of everything about you. Activate every sense to perceive the current situation as clearly as possible

3. Visualize a present moment when everything is perfect, and you have no reason whatsoever to worry

4. Realize that you really don't have to be worried about a thing

Be positive

The best weapon to deal with stress is to be positive on purpose. When you let your brain process thoughts at its usual rate, 70% of what goes through your mind will always be negative. It is only when you are mindfully positive that you can be positive indeed and overcome stress. Whenever a negative thought comes to mind, accept it as one among many and replace it with the direct opposite (positive thought). Think about your goals, past happy times, and anything that makes you feel excited and you will achieve a state of true optimism and positivity and stop the stress even before it happens.

Make time for family and to hang out with friends

Work-life balance is critical to stress avoidance. Keeping in touch with your support group offers a great source for stress relief and positivity.

Have a laugh

If you have to watch cat videos or watch stand-up comedy to laugh, do it. A good laugh is one of the best tonics for stress. The more you do it, the less stress you will have to deal with.

NLP stress management

Any one of the following NLP exercises can be very effective for stress management;

1. Simply floating your awareness out of the body can help you to disconnect from a stressful situation into an imagined world of peace and tranquility.

2. Imagine that there is a glass wall in front of you and all the things that are stressing you are on the other side. They cannot get to you because you are protected by the glass shield

3. Turn down the volume of the stressful thoughts going through your mind until they are quiet. This includes any negative self-talk associated with a stressful event

4. Send the images away, away, away. Stress sometimes manifests as ugly images going through our minds. To remove the stress, imagine the images leaving your mind and propel them as far away from you as possible.

Chapter 7: Motivation

We pursue goals and visions because we are motivated to do so. As a leader, you will need to stay driven and focused on the vision for your department. The job of keeping your employees hungry for more achievements will also fall on you. Your ability to keep everyone motivated will affect your productivity and, ultimately, your success. In this chapter, we will look at how you can use NLP to keep both yourself and your employees motivated even in the face of failure.

NLP techniques to motivate yourself

The following strategies have been used by the majority of the world's most successful business leaders to get where they are today. I hope that using them will make you stay motivated and driven to excel more today than you did yesterday.

Focus on one thing

The first tip for motivation is focusing on one thing at a time. This might be harder when you are a manager and your to-do list is overflowing with tasks, but trying to do more than one thing at one time will only lead to overloading yourself, probable failure, and disenchantment.

Motivation comes, in most part, from the confidence you gain over time because you can do something really well. In fact, it is very hard to remain motivated after failure. This is why businessmen like Elon Musk, who has continued with the same passion even after failure, are so inspirational.

Discover your big WHY

The reason why Elon Musk, Steve Jobs, Tony Robbins, Bill Gates, and any other successful leader have all continued pursuing excellence to the top of their fields was that they were doing something that gave their lives purpose. Each one of us has that one thing, but most are not even aware of what it is. But if you want to stay motivated, if you want to surprise yourself with superhuman feats of drive and ambition, find the one thing that will give your life meaning. What you are doing matters little if the reason why you are doing it does not align with your life purpose. And when you do something because it aligns with your big WHY, you can withstand any challenges and remain strong enough to pursue it regardless of your failures.

You should apply the big why on a project-by-project basis. Any good manager has a clear-cut vision that drives their every action. Whenever you do something, answer the question of why the desired outcome will contribute to the fulfillment of your dream. You will realize that your motivation in doing something will be as compelling as the reason why you are doing it.

Visualize your goal

Visualization is a powerful motivational tool. It connects your body, your mind, and your emotions and works as the fuel that powers your motivation to work. To help your mind along, create a specific representation of your goal as possible. Use all the senses to visualize the moment of success, and if possible, a visual representation. When you visualize a specific, rather than vague outcome, your emotions and your body take over and start to help you to get there.

Picture the worst

As we discussed in chapter 6 above, our brain has the capacity to expand and accomplish exceptional feats. Untrained, this expansion of the mind pours over as anxiety. But when we tame this beast, we can harness the power of the anxious mind for motivation. You see, our brains respond exceptionally well to a negative stimulus versus positive. So, while visualization is a valid tool for the attainment of goals, picturing not achieving an outcome is even more terrifying and easier for the brain to do.

If you can see the outcome of not achieving your goal on the second, third, and nth try, chances are that your brain will already be terrified by the third level of consequences. This serves as the perfect deterrent to your mind, which will then lead to you doing anything you can to make sure that it does not happen. This serves as the "away from" motivation, what you are trying to avoid by working hard.

Picture the benefits

More than just picturing yourself achieving your goal, there are numerous benefits to be reaped from imagining the perfect world of achievement after reaching your goal. It works as an additional "toward" image to your visualization, albeit in a wider and less intense way. Picturing simply entails daydreams of the consequences of achieving a goal.

Your employee lifting your shoulder higher, popping champagne, an article about your genius in *The Wall Street Journal*. It is all very invigorating to think about it. And the best thing is that even though you will be motivated by the visions, it is highly unlikely that you will be disappointed when they don't happen because you will already be pretty damn thrilled to have reached the goal!

Don't overreach

It is all right to dream and have a big vision, but you must make sure that your dream/vision is within the make-sense zone. Things that are beyond your control only serve as a recipe for disaster because you will hardly ever achieve them. The only outcome worth pursuing is one that is within your control to get. When the goal is unrealistic, our brains often respond by shutting up, creating even more anxiety and making it harder to find the motivation to work.

Know the price

For everything you commit to pursuing, you will be foregoing putting your focus on something else of equal or more value. Family, relationships, and other interests are some of the things that you might have to give up (or have less of) to achieve your biggest goal. You should only commit to doing something after figuring out the price you will have to pay for it and determining that you are okay with it.

Measure your progress

When you set a vision to work towards, make it measurable. The work involved in subdividing it into smaller tasks and budgeting for time and other resources will also help you determine whether or not it is achievable. You can then measure your progress along the way to verify that you are on track as well as for motivation. See, what you will find out is that even the smallest evidence of progress can be very motivational. When you are feeling overwhelmed, looking at the progress you have made over time can push you to work even harder to get to your destination.

Make a total commitment

One of the leading causes of procrastination is future options: the notion that something will happen in the future to make your life that much better. The reason why this causes people to procrastinate is that it kills the motivation to work right now. Few people would work now if they were assured of being all set in the future. The mind is no different. It shuts up and ceases functioning (at least in part) when there is an opening for that.

Failing to commit 100% to a decision only makes room for doubts, lethargy, and laziness. As soon as you make up your mind to pursue a certain outcome, you should banish every other option from your mind. Even a plan B, while essential, can be an excuse for your mind to half-ass its way through plan A.

Create the right environment

Your environment plays a big role in the pursuit of any outcome you set out to achieve. Environmental obstacles can either be physical or mental. Both can be detrimental to motivation. Environmental obstacles can be avoided by changing locations or refurnishing your office if your furniture is blocking your motivation. You must be willing to do what you need to do to get your mind in the right state for productivity. Mental obstacles are somewhat more serious killers of motivation because they are a bit harder to banish. If you want to achieve a particular goal, you must get your mind in the right state; otherwise, you won't find the incentive to do much.

Get the right people

The only way to grow your motivation is to insert yourself in a nurturing environment. This means that you must surround yourself with positive, growth-minded people who will add to your energies rather than draining them. The good thing is that as the manager, you have almost free reign to hire the right people. A good team will not just tolerate you; they will support your dream for the department heartily and with good cheer.

We will discuss motivating your team below, but this is also a contributing factor to your own motivation and must be mentioned here. Your ability to follow the guidelines discussed below to create a motivated team will have a cyclic impact on your own motivation.

Start working in advance

Chance favors the prepared, so the saying goes. Well, so does motivation. The best way to keep yourself motivated all day long is to have a clear idea of what you will be doing in the day. So, obviously, the best time to plan for your day's activity is yesterday.

And before going to sleep, it is good to take a few minutes to look through the to-do list for the next day. Look over the items on that list and visualize, very briefly, yourself doing them. Don't go into the details. Just make sure that it is the last thing that you think of before falling asleep. Your mind will be working on the items subconsciously through the night so that you will wake up feeling energized and eager to start working. This also helps you say no to distractions.

Use the Pareto principle

The Pareto equation states that 80% of your outcomes will be generated by 20% of your efforts. The most effective people are skilled at determining the 20% and focusing their energies on it. They are able to achieve more with less effort and retain much of their energy, being always motivated and ready to rock it out. When you are a leader, your job should be to figure out ways of achieving the best results with limited resources. The Pareto principle can be a great way to ensure that your resource allocation produces the most outcomes. It is also very gratifying on a personal level when you see such massive results as 80% from doing 20% of something. It grows your motivation exponentially.

Focus

You have probably heard about the exceptional power of NO. As a manager, you should learn to say no to shallow work like logistical support that does not require any special skills. Instead, focus on the deep work, taking the lead on the accomplishment of mentally demanding jobs that will allow you to get into that state of flow where motivation and skills meet to produce exceptional levels of productivity.

In the current content-filled world, take pride in being delightfully ignorant of memes, comfortably absent from "hot" social media trends, and hard to reach. Unless you are a social media manager, these distractions do nothing to make you better at your work.

Fake it till you make it

Now I know that this is a contentious concept, but it is also one of the most effective tools for personal motivation. Regardless of what people say, the people who act as if they are already achievers in whatever field their desires lie are infinitely more motivated than the rest of us. They have achieved something that few others can ever boast of having—a state of perpetual visualization. Furthermore, isn't modeling a critical concept of NLP? If you decide to start acting as you have already reached the levels you want to get to, your brain reacts by thinking like the image you have made for yourself. Acting as if you have already reached your outcome motivates you to work the hardest to make it a reality.

NLP techniques to motivate others

Motivating others is a skill that every manager needs because it falls on him or her to motivate his entire staff. The best leaders are able to motivate their teams to achieve above and beyond everyone's expectations. You can motivate your team by using the strategies of coaching, relationships, dialogue, and credibility.

Coaching

Motivation in the workplace comes from the confidence of being able to do one's work competently. This is especially critical for the employees who perform the technical jobs in the company. And since motivation goes hand in hand with the ability to do their job well, increasing their competence is guaranteed to boost your employees' impetus to work.

As a manager, you will be responsible for molding your junior employees in accordance with your vision for your division. The mentoring you do encourages them to pursue excellence, increases their skill set, and motivates them, all at the same time. You can even go a step further and hire professionals to teach curricular and extracurricular skills. The more the skills your employees have, the greater the dedication they will show to their job.

Relationships

The environment you create for your employees will play a big role in their dedication to working. It is important that you foster a relationship with every member of the team. Find out their interests and talents and figure out the best way to match them with the company objectives. That way, every member of your team will have a role to play in the pursuit of your vision and you can all draw motivation from each other.

The relationships you create with your employees form a two-way support system which will come in handy when you are dealing with stress. A support system of coworkers is more effective in the management of stress because you all have a firsthand understanding of the stressful conditions you face. A nurturing environment boosts morale and motivates every member of your team to work even harder.

Team building

Team-building exercises do a lot to foster relationships. Whether you will take your whole team to full-day or weekend getaways or you will keep the bonding at the workplace, conducting NLP exercises like visualization can create a very strong bond between employees and contribute towards a nurturing environment where every employee is motivated to achieve the best.

Rapport is a very important thing to foster a team spirit. So, ensure that you use the smallest excuse for teamwork to make your team do the same thing, even aerobic exercises. It connects everyone together and, when you are at the forefront of the rapport-building activity, cements your position as the leader. And because of the rapport you have established with them, your team will be more likely to keep an open mind when considering and implementing your ideas.

Dialogues

With every word to speak, you have the opportunity to motivate someone or crush their spirit. This is especially true when you are in a position of influence because your opinion is highly regarded. So, whenever you speak to your employees, you must watch your words to avoid killing their motivation. Even criticism should be offered in a constructive manner or not offered at all. But constructive criticism is not the only way to motivate others through communication. You can also use vision setting and presentations for this.

Vision

The vision acts like a stimulus that channels the relationships and allows a large team to cooperate in the attainment of a common goal. Using an NLP principle called the logical levels of change, you take the company blueprint and apply it to the six levels of thinking. At the workplace, you start with the environment and surround your whole team with the concepts of your vision and mission. This serves as their own personal vision and mission whenever they are at work and motivates the highest levels of productivity.

Speeches and presentations

Another way to motivate others is to make speeches or presentations. This is a strategy that has been used by some of the world's greatest leaders. In the early days of Microsoft, Bill Gates used to make his entrance to the company's annual general meeting in dramatic fashion, including an incident when he rode in with a gang of Harley Davidson bikers. He and his cofounder would then rouse their employees with song, dance, and drink to celebrate every financial year of great results. The motivation and productivity of his employees remained at all-time high levels all through the 70s and 80s and enabled him to get closer to his vision of putting Microsoft software on every computer in the world.

Other leaders who use charismatic motivational tools to energize and motivate employees are the duo of Warren Buffett and Charlie Munger. To this day, these two celebrated leaders hold an annual general meeting where presentations usually include humorous videos of the two men. The Berkshire Hathaway AGM is one of the most popular events in the city of Omaha where it is held.

Credibility

As much as the vision is supposed to have the input of everyone in your team, it is essentially your prerogative to think about the future of the department by considering the overall vision of the company and how your department can contribute towards it. People follow leaders they can trust, and teams that have no clear leader always fall apart because there is no direction. So, to make sure that the team pursues your vision with gusto, ensure that you exhibit the qualities of integrity, intent, capability, and results.

Integrity means that you don't apply double standards when dealing with your employees. Don't treat anyone better or act in an entitled manner. The hardest working person should always be you.

People trust men and women who show good intentions for everything they do. Even if someone does not agree with something you did, they will judge you less harshly if your motivations were not ill meant.

It matters a lot whether you got to your current position by merit. People respect capable leaders, and your capability and skill set should be impeccable to earn the respect of your team. Incidentally, people with high capabilities value capability in a leader even higher. Therefore, this is a quality you will want to cultivate if you want to get to the levels of productivity you desire.

In the end, little else matters apart from the results. If you constantly achieve beyond their wildest imagination, people will hold you in high regard and be more willing to do what you ask of them.

Conclusion

Neuro-linguistic programming (NLP) is the art and science of using mental models and language to alter harmful behaviors we exhibit into constructive ones. There are numerous techniques of NLP, but some are, naturally, more applicable than others. Future pacing is one of the most powerful and easily applicable NLP techniques. It allows us to visualize desired outcomes to get motivated to work and also helps us shift our perceptions of the present to overcome anxiety and stress. The swish pattern is another indispensable NLP technique that helps us to modify behavior by replacing negative thoughts with positive ones. It is very important to behavior change. In hypnosis and persuasion, metaphors come in very handy. By simply implanting an idea into the mind of a target, you can recruit their subconscious mind to work in your favor to convince someone to do whatever you want. Reframing allows us to adopt a new perspective to a situation, focusing on the positive rather than negative for perpetual positivity. Finally, anchoring helps us create associations between events and our minds by employing gestures and words as memory anchors. This makes it easier to recall a memory and comes in handy for stress reduction and improved self-confidence.

You must have noticed that vision was mentioned is almost every chapter of the book as a factor affecting everything from problem-solving, decision making, time management, stress management, and pretty much everything you do as a leader. Your vision powers everything you do as a leader. You will only be as successful as you let yourself be and you will do this with a vision too big, too small, or SMART. This condition applies to personal and team success. If you can manage to sell your vision for the division you lead and get the team to buy into the idea enough to fully commit, you will most probably achieve massive success. And most of the NLP techniques discussed throughout this book have something to do with vision setting or achievement. They include anchoring, future pacing, well-formed outcome, and state management. Even reframing, swish, and covert hypnosis that help modify behavior contribute to our pursuit of the vision by putting us in the right frame of mind.

Thinking is a big part of what you will be doing as a manager, so it is very important that you do it right. We discussed the ways you can apply NLP techniques to your thinking, problem-solving, and decision making. This will be immensely critical to your career. Because the one thing that sets apart the world's best leaders like Elon Musk, Warren Buffett, and Steve Jobs, among others, is their unique thinking. They applied their unique thinking styles to innovate and to solve problems as they arose. They were defined by the big decisions they made, and so will you. We also offered some NLP exercises to help you to start thinking like a leader and win like the best business leaders who ever lived. Only when you have mastered these techniques will you be in a position to step into your destiny and achieve the vision you have crafted not just for you, but for your whole team.

Results make leaders. We also touched on the importance of productivity for your career, including the NLP techniques and exercises that you can use to attain the highest levels of productivity. The most important tip for efficiency—understanding the way the brain works and tailoring your work around the high peaks of productivity. And to find the state of flow with your whole team, we described a series of NLP exercises that include anchoring your wins and visualizing the goal of every task you embark on.

With its close relation to linguistics, communication turned out to be an important message in the book. It plays a big part in sharing your goal, negotiating successfully, and motivating your employees. With NLP, you can unlock unconscious messaging, an element of communication that most people overlook. With unconscious communication, your negotiation and presentations (both critical to good leadership) will be boosted. You can then use negotiations to foster good relations with partners by ensuring that everyone wins, even when it would have served your immediate needs better to crush your opponent.

For motivation, the main thing is to discover your big why. This is the one thing that has propelled leaders in business, politics, sports, and academics to the pinnacle of their respective fields. Anyone who wants to become a good leader must first search within themselves for their purpose and only do things that help them get there. And at the workplace, everything you do ought to be in service to the vision that you set. In fact, you should make the big picture a reference point when making your to-do list for greater motivation.

We also touched on stress and anxiety management among leaders. Stress management is an area most managers struggle at, but with simple NLP techniques, we discussed how you can ensure that your mind and body are always relaxed and primed for action. With anxiety, it is better to try to make use of it rather than straight out avoiding (or trying to). The anxious mind has been found to be highly effective by studies as recent as 2017, and our "Allow, Befriend, and Channel" (ABC) strategy ought to help you harness anxiety to bring flow to your work and increase productivity.

If you are to take one thing from this book, let it be vision setting and pursuing. A good vision is key to solving every problem that a junior manager like you faces. As a bonus, let the second lesson be using NLP to pursue the excellence you desire.

And there you go, the complete guide to leadership using NLP as promised. A solution for every communication, decision making, vision setting, stress coping, and adopting concern you will ever have as you settle into your new office. I hope you have as enjoyable and transformation a journey reading this book as I had written it. All the best!

Part 3: Thought Models for Leadership

Use the mental techniques of the world's greatest and richest to make better decisions, improve your career trajectory and gain more respect at work

Introduction

Lately, my colleagues and I were talking about the things that we usually see on social media like on Facebook, Twitter, Instagram, and even in Google News! We have a wide variety of topics that are very prominent on Facebook starting from current events, weather forecasts, historical flashbacks, down to funny trivial ones that didn't concern us at all. Aside from those topics, we were discussing our own lives and realizations as we age. Getting older each day gave us a panic attack that we talked about things that we don't usually get into the discussion. I am with my friends and colleagues for some years now and that made us bonded and comfortable with each other's presence. Recently, we had been asking each one, where we are right now? What we already achieved? Are we satisfied with what we have? Where are we heading?

Now, it seems unbelievable that the officemates and friends that I used to be drunk with and who didn't have time for serious group discussions because they were a bit awkward are already having a gradual change in their perspectives in life. That literally left me amazed and flabbergasted, just like what is totally happening to me. Nowadays, we are very much interested in talking about the security of our future, how to invest smartly, how we spend quality time with our families, how we can maintain a good healthy lifestyle. how to deal with toxic people, and other things that can cause us stress and anxiety. We can say that we are taking our maturity to a higher level.

To attain the mentality that we currently have today and to achieve the change or security that we want to happen in our lives means that we are learning not to repeat the mistakes that we had committed when we were younger. We must learn from our mistakes and rise from the ashes of our failures to have positive patterns that are affecting our growth. We learned from the repeated mistakes brought by an impulse that are constantly pestering our peers and other people around us. We have learned to observe recurring events and to perceive new concepts that are becoming **mental models** that we are looking at. Yes, we have **mental models** that are repeating ideas that gave us mental images of scenarios, which become a *model* that we can utilize in similar circumstances. These models are very powerful tools that are not universally acquired at any academic level. You can possess mental models through practical life experiences, reading other individuals' practices, and your own observation in life.

You might be using mental models without being fully aware that you are actually applying one. So, this book is good for you so you can learn more about mental models that can help you become a more effective decision-maker. Even I, earlier in my life, I was not aware that I was already using mental models. By listening to other people's suggestions on how to fix my problems, I was able to use the mental models that were proven effective for them. That is one example of a mental model, when you listen to other people's experiences and how they managed to solve problems effectively. For us, social validation is essential so we can save time, energy, and effort in solving problems. Furthermore, it is a normal reaction to be disappointed if the outcome doesn't go the way we wanted it to be. That's when we rely on our own or, we will try another way until we solve the problem. In this process of trial and error, we are collecting mental models and we discriminate if one model or combination of it would be effective in solving one situation.

Also, in this book, you will learn different mental models that you can apply in situations personally and at work. Every day, we are making decisions that can be right or wrong; decisions that will surely affect the future and the variables in our surroundings. You will meet toxic people and unexpected circumstances that will surely challenge your patience. In my experience, I have been supervising the newly hired employees in the company I am working at. Being a mentor at the beginning was like a blessing and a curse at the same time. To nurture the minds and develop the skills of the trainees that I was handling gave me fulfillment. I said that I found the purpose of staying in a career that I was starting to dislike. Then, my struggles started when some of my haters started to question my capabilities as the newly appointed trainer. I was appointed after I celebrated my first-year anniversary. The pressure became heavier when my trainees violated some of the basic company rules. Since I wasn't trained as a trainer, it allowed me to create my own techniques and I started to follow my instinct. I prepared my own training materials, formulated my own topic syllabus, reinvented myself during discussions and formed my own way of instilling disciplines among my trainees. Every time that I was discussing at the training room, I felt like I was the master of my own universe. I got addicted to the adoration of my trainees. And the saddest part of all, I took advantage of the little authority that I had once. Until one day, everyone in the office seemed to hate me and even my closest allies were abandoning me.

I can say that I decided to teach to help a company and it is also my decision to be eaten by work and superiority. The most important lesson I learned is always to be down-to-earth and do not forget the people who helped you when you are still a nobody. I deserved all the wraths of the people around me. That was when I decided to change, and I reached out with the people who were always there when I need them the most. When I was abusing my authority, I was always depressed and there was no happiness in my heart. I was very impulsive with the stupidity of others. I tried to be a better version of myself and begun my holistic rehabilitation. I had to keep myself low and extended the boundaries of my understanding. My collection of mental models helped me to be a better version of myself and I won the support of my friends and colleagues again. I have proven that mental models helped me always to look back and to remember the person that I was once.

I know that you are dealing with problems and you want to have the best decision to apply in all of your difficulties. I do understand your needs personally and professionally. I want to expose you more about how mental models will help you achieve the success that you want in your life. Mental models can also help you gain the income that you are dreaming of. Further in this book, you will get to know successful individuals who relied heavily on mental models and how they became billionaires, speakers, authors, and inspirations to people around the globe who always wanted to achieve what successful people have accomplished. I had cited Charles Munger, a self-made billionaire, who has deep wisdom about mental models because of his expertise in many disciplines and you will learn about his techniques as you dive into the pages of this book. I learned a lot from that guy, and I am sure that you will also idolize the partner of the famous investor, Warren Buffett.

Life has many chances and mysteries to offer you. All you have to do, in order to have a peaceful and successful life is to build your own personal concepts by learning by the experiences of those people who knew a deeper secret regarding their existence. With this book, I can give you a glimpse of how people become successful and attain a meaningful lifestyle by utilizing mental models and applied them to be effective decision-makers.

I believe that after you read this book, you will be capable of collecting your own toolbox loaded with powerful mental models that you can apply to various challenging situations. I am looking forward to helping you produce successful decisions that will benefit not just you, but all the people around you and your environment as well. Upon learning the fundamentals of mental models, you can also teach their concepts to your family, friends, or anybody else. You can bring positive change to yourself while sharing the gospel of mental models.

Now, I want you to find a comfortable place… where you can absorb everything that is written in this book. Gather yourself together, muster your energy, and go deep into concentration as you dive inside the wonders of this book. I will join you in a new realm where mental models and their proponents give reality to the success you've been seeking.

Chapter 1: Why We Use Models?

Television and social media are highly regarded as the fastest and effective way to advertise products and disseminate information. The most common effect that they can build to everyone is how people perceive things with multiple facets or definitions. Like for example, when we talk about models most people would agree that the term is used to describe people whose faces are printed in magazines. Those people who are walking on runways, or it can be device prototypes. These definitions are correct. But what we are going to discuss in this book is a way deeper and helpful to professionals and other working individuals.

Models are very important when you actually want to attain a specific goal. For example, education starts at home and parents are the first teachers who guided us to gain good manners and right conduct. I can still remember when I was young, and my mother was lecturing me about giving to the poor and sharing what little I have to other children who were in need. She used to tell stories about the generosity and selflessness of Mother Theresa who was elevated to sainthood in 2016. Until today, the heroic deeds of Mother Theresa still linger in my memory and I even shared her stories to children whenever I have the chance to act as a volunteer teacher in one of the organizations that I am actively participating in. My mother recounted Saint Theresa and used her as a factual model to effectively instill to my brain the importance of sharing. Surely, your parents had used superheroes, biblical characters, or other prominent figures in history that have impacted the persons that we are today. Different kinds of models have also been utilized in different fields for the advancement of humanity. Theoretical models are used in business industries to maximize profits and to sustain the global economy. There are also different infrastructures in the field of information technology (IT) that continuously evolve like the emergence of artificial intelligence. Even regular people are following models that govern their day-to-day existence. There are essential models that are innately part of humanity and we call them **mental models**.

If you haven't heard about a mental model, it simply explains how a thing works and it is a recurring concept. It is also a label for any kind of perception or concept that we carry in our minds. Mental models are very vital because they help us understand the essence of life and make the way we live much easier. Game theory is among the popular mental models because its fundamental purpose is understanding the importance of trust and relationships. Mental models are vital gears for knowledge compilation, and they create a wide base of information. Our knowledge starts with grain and it keeps expanding as we get older and earn more experiences. When we find missing pieces or gaps between parts in our information base, we tend to find and add new pieces to form a connection that would fill out those gaps. With mental models, you can have a better approach when dealing with problems. By identifying where you are effective and good at, you can start right there and think of strategies that would solve the problem partially or the whole of it.

Decision-making is a tough job that every one of us is undertaking and there are situations where we need to choose and weigh in carefully our options to select the best solution. Mental models are relevant in decision making because they mostly led to success when properly executed. But it doesn't mean that having a mental model will always end up successfully. There are moments that following a specific mental model brings a person to fail. When a person is weak at making decisions, failure means that another mental model should be used or even change that person's setting to save his face. I want you to instill in your mind that even failures can pave the way to a much better opportunity. I think it is important for me to tackle the factors that make a decision.

Smashing Magazine published an article in February 2019 on how people usually make decisions.[1] Emotions play an important factor in decision-making and most decisions are not logically planned because emotions interfere. Most decisions are also made unconsciously. There are researchers who observed brain activity and they could successfully predict what decision people would do within 7-10 seconds before they even realize what they made as a decision.[2] It means, even when we think that we are making a logical and conscious decision, there are still chances that we are not really aware that we already made a decision unconsciously and its implication to others and to the environment. When we are in fear and doubtful, we always choose decisions that are safe enough to avoid conflicts. It is a major problem in decision-making if you can't feel emotions and if you can't also empathize with other people. Our instinct depends on what we feel. Let us go a bit scientific. There is this specific part of the brain that regulates fear and that is the *ventromedial prefrontal cortex* (vmPFC). Other parts of the brain, like the amygdala in particular where conditioned fear reactions are created, tell us when to be afraid and what to be afraid of while vmPFC is opposing the conditioned fear and stops a person from being afraid in certain scenarios. When vmPFC is active, a person can ignore conditioned fears that enable decision making. To make an effective decision, you need to admit that emotions are necessary and play an important factor in planning. Instead of focusing on logical arguments for validation, you are more likely to produce wise and effective decisions by understanding situations and be more empathic if there are other people involved. According to studies, there is a specific kind of neuron that travels into the brain that allows people to act when the brain is confident enough of a decision. It is more likely based on instinct that made this matter subjective once a decision is not based on the data collected but a product of mere confidence.[2]

In fact, the outcomes of a certain decision are unpredictable. No matter how logically accurate your data are, there might be unexpected or unpredicted factors that affect our decisions, causing them to fail big time. I know that just like me, you had experienced making a decision which turned out opposite to what you were expecting. It was a very common reaction to explain why it failed and to regret it afterward.

Let us take the case of the war between Spain and England in the 16th century. Spain and England dominated the European political arena during the second half of the sixteenth century. Spain was ruled by the prudent Catholic king, Philip II; while England was ruled by the Protestant and virgin queen, Elizabeth I. King Philip and Queen Elizabeth were siblings-in-law because Queen Mary was Philip's wife and half-sister of Elizabeth. Upon the death of Queen Mary who was the ruler of England for five short years, Elizabeth ascended to power. Papal authority was a prominent force during this era and since Elizabeth was a Protestant, with one wrong move, she could earn an excommunication. Protestantism was still young at the time and Elizabeth was the ultimate champion of the newly established religion and she supported Protestant allies, an act that was distasteful for the Roman Catholic Church. Elizabeth was poised to be excommunicated but Philip protected Elizabeth at all costs from the Papal wrath.

Philip was helping Elizabeth because he wanted to marry her for political alliance and to put England back to Catholicism. Until Elizabeth begun to support the Dutch against Spain, military intervention in the Netherlands, the beheading of the Catholic Queen Mary of Scots, and the ambush of English pirates against Spanish ships tolerated by Elizabeth were the major factors for the launching of the Spanish Armada in 1588.[3] This so-called invincible Armada was consisted of 130 ships that carried 2,500 guns, 8,000 seamen, and 20,000 soldiers. Such a figure worried Elizabeth and her subjects that they relied heavily on divine intervention.[4] The heavens seemed to smile at England because many ships of the approaching Armada were ruined by the storm. The exhausted Armada was confronted by the waiting English naval fleet to protect the boundaries of the English coast. Obviously, the Armada outnumbered the English forces but because of the raging storm, the Armada's ships decreased and left the other ships damaged. Elizabeth had brilliant naval officers that led the English to win the war. The Armada lost at sea and it was among the most humiliating defeat in Spanish naval history while England entered a golden age and became the Empress of the Seas governed by the pure Queen Elizabeth.

With Spain's wealth and military might, it can crash England easily. Sending too many soldiers carried by gigantic ships brought fear to Elizabeth. But there were unexpected circumstances that made it possible for England to win the war like the storms that injured the Spanish Armada and the experienced English officials who made effective tactics that destroyed their enemies. Yes, King Philip regretted his decision because being defeated by Queen Elizabeth weaken his popularity and increased the latter's capacity to rule. Well, nobody wants to experience a war and to see one country beaten by another one. King Philip by that time thought that launching his Armada in 1588 was the best time to oppose Elizabeth and to completely restore Catholicism in England.

Success is sweet and is always attributed to good decision making while failure is constantly explained by bad decisions and a series of bad luck. In my experience, good decisions can also lead to failure as well and vice versa. Decision-making is like your gambling because data and other factors might be helpful, but you are not sure where it will lead you. That's why it is a normal reaction while making a decision to ask yourself the possible outcomes of your options. For Darius Foroux, that is an incomprehensive method not to question the decision-making process because you are more likely looking at the possible outcome.[5] That is why mental models are important because it is your thinking mechanism about how you perceive things. There are times that we tend to skip the process and decided right away, and several factors might include a lack of resources, familiarity, or time. To bypass a decision-making process makes a person a bad decision-maker. You have to focus on how comprehensive your process is rather than focusing on the success rate of your choices. In fact, you don't need to know all about mental models. All you just have to do is to internalize the fundamental core and find models that are effective for you and for situations that you need to apply mental models. Do not be like other professionals who speak about mental models but lack the system of application to achieve meaningful goals. Always remember that knowledge without even applying it is useless at all. We cannot see the future accurately because we are not psychics, nor even understand all the mental models. By studying and applying a comprehensive thinking process, it can give us satisfaction no matter what the outcome is. And in that way, we can avoid any forms of regret that might hurt as deeply. Inaction is a kind of regret that can literally make you unhappy. Always keep in mind that mistakes are lessons that make us better individuals.

There are countless possibilities in our world and uncertainty is just around the corner. With mental models, they help us to reduce some doubts about our decisions. Now, we will dissect how mental models enable you to become smarter and effective decision-maker.

Simplify Things to Make a Better Impact

There are too many things in our lives that we take for granted. There are times that we are very inconsiderate about the fact that what happens to us is created by countless possibilities brought by different phenomena that are pulled together to yield a certain product. What we see initially is just something on the surface and not the outcome beneath it. If you have the power to manipulate or to play the things that directly affect the outcome, then you might bring it on your side to produce the result you want. The question is, how would you identify the variables to play along with?

It is like suicide if you will try to influence everything and be disappointed with the result. That's when you use mental models to give you the full potential to filter unnecessary elements and improve your decisions. To give you an example, we have this famous topic in statistics known as Pareto's Principle which is known as the power law. This principle states that a very little portion of essential variables has more of an impact on the outcome than all of the rest combined. The billionaires Charlie Munger and his partner, Warren Buffett, used this principle when they are making investment decisions. They don't buy stock without undergoing their system that evaluates if a certain company is undervalued or not relevant to any industry. They are thoroughly looking for potentials from small stuff that will produce massive profits.

When you study their corporate records, most of their earnings came from a very little section. By being highly aware of the model you are using, you can utilize it in other situations where your sole judgment is put to the test. It provides you a strainer to filter the most important variables to work and focus on and which ones to disregard. Other models have different outlines that can be used to determine correct and important details. Mental models do difficult tasks on our behalf and they help us to simplify intricacy.

Omit Hidden Dimensions for the Betterment of Your Problem Solving

The human mind is very fast to discriminate and to establish cause and effect which can be considered as the brain's strengths and weaknesses. We are more likely to be blinded by the initial result rather than looking at a deeper level. Yet, this factor is actually a mental model because it allows us to sort things to make sense out of everything and it gives us an easier way of understanding our environment. Somehow, it also permits us to take shortcuts in learning new things. And that is also when it becomes bad because what we are connecting with is often wrong.

Charles Munger loves and an advocate of the idea that it is better to minimize shortcomings by evading errors than it is to be perfect. According to Munger, if you are doing things that are exposing you to destruction, your luck will be exhausted no matter how brilliant you are. As humans, we have innate blind spots that expose us to harm. Behavioral economics states that we don't comprehend our surroundings rationally because we have different kinds of biases which are more potent than the way we think. By using mental models, we are making ourselves aware of those biases and think a way better. Also, because of these biases, once it becomes evident in a situation, we can think twice or more before making a decision. By formulating a checklist that will help you find the right mental models when making big choices, you are significantly reducing the possibility of losing and committing mistakes.

Be Realistic by Using Multidisciplinary Approaches

Charles Munger became a wealthy and very successful person because of his habit of collecting diverse mental models. It seems that he believes in the idea that the whole is greater than the sum of its parts, or that two are always better than one. Munger famously quoted that it is best to have multiple models since the human psychology is so powerful that you have the ***capacity to torture reality so that it fits your model***. He is exerting that you must not give up trying until you get the very fruit of your labor. These models have to originate from multiple disciplines because of the very fact that all the wisdom that exists in this world is not found in just one academic faculty.

What You Do is Who You Are

What we practice in our career tells us who we are or what we specialized in. A businessperson is inclined to evaluate decisions using disciplines that have planted in his mind at work while a scientist and a researcher are relying on experiments and hypotheses. If you see, they have limited frameworks that they can use to discriminate before coming up with a final decision. The world offers so many dimensions other than what we learned through our existence. For your mental models to be effective, they must be proven and compete with others by attacking different situations. Always assume that individual models are somewhat wrong, but a good collection combined can mitigate and filter these errors and pave the way to a winning decision.

You don't have to be an expert in every discipline. Because mastering them requires energy and a great amount of intelligence. Attempting to master every discipline might leave you insane. You just have to understand the fundamentals of many disciplines and use them to make decisions in your everyday life.

This is What You Need

There are many of us who are trying to use status to dictate the factors of existence. The higher the income, the more entitled others are projecting themselves. That is a very limited way of living, and it is also damaging to one's image, reputation, and pursuit of life. Let us take another look at Charlie Munger who is typically shy under the media's presence. But when he opens his mouth to deliver his speech, his audience listens because what he shares is valuable. His deep knowledge and practical application of mental models offer a remarkable tool in decision-making and problem-solving. There are countless ways to get and to utilize mental models to improve our lives. You can always use notes, reminders, checklist, and raise consciousness about mental models.

Mental Models at Work: The billionaire who made it!

Mental models are really powerful tools that can lead you to success and can give you access to a much more meaningful life. There are many moguls in different parts of the world who dominated their corresponding fields of expertise because they use mental models effectively. So effective and helpful that they suggested their mental models whenever they were invited for an interview or during their public speeches. The best examples who used mental models are the billionaires Charlie Munger and his partner, Warren Buffet. Let us take a ride and explore the mental models Charlie Munger, a self-made billionaire, who used effectively to be a successful man that he is today.

Charlie Munger, also famously known by his nickname Charlie, is considered to be one of the great minds of the 20th century. He is currently the vice-chairman of Berkshire Hathaway Corp., owned by a famous investor named Warren Buffett. Munger is also the chairman of the Daily Journal in Los Angeles. He is the director of Costco Wholesale Corp. He is a longtime resident of Pasadena in California and he was born in Omaha, Nebraska in 1924. During his teenage years, he worked at Buffett & Son, a grocery store owned by the grandfather of his future business partner, Warren Buffett.[7] He studied Mathematics in the University of Michigan but eventually dropped out a few days after his 19th birthday to enter in the United States Army Air Corps where he served as a second lieutenant. He then continued college studying meteorology at Caltech in California. His curiosity and thirst for knowledge led him to take advanced courses in several universities including Harvard University where he completed law school. He graduated as *magna cum laude* with a J.D. in Harvard Law School in 1948 and he was a part of the Harvard Legal Aid Bureau.

Munger founded and served as a real state attorney at Munger, Tolles & Olson in 1962 which is currently a prominent law firm. He concentrated on investments, he gave up practicing law and partnered with Otis Booth in real estate development. Munger is highly associated with his business partner, Warren Buffett, whom he met in 1959 and formed an investment relationship. As per Buffet's essay entitled *The Superinvestors of Graham-and-Doddsville* published in 1984, from 1962 to 1975, Munger operated his own investment partnership that generated compound annual returns of 19.8%.

Munger's success in the field of law and financial investment made him a self-made billionaire and inspired millions of people across the globe. His groundbreaking methods in achieving a winning life prompted different universities, organizations, and organizers to invite him as a speaker in their seminars and other functions. His speeches, as well as his best-selling book Poor Charlie's Almanack, introduced the model of **elementary, worldly wisdom** which also relates to the field of business and finance. Munger believed that high ethical standards are vital to his principles of success.

Through the years, Munger developed a comprehensive system of **multiple mental models** and thanks for his love of academics that he was able to attain his dreams. His reinvention through his commitment to studying different fields aside from law and business include psychology, economics, physics, biology, and history. His mental models made him capable of having an accurate solution to complex problems. His viewpoint about career and life is very rare, accurate, and standout with surprising reliability. This method is called by many as the **Munger approach** which is difficult. But once you undertake and understand its fundamental code of belief, it will help you to wipe out the uncertainties in your mind easily. Munger once shared the secret to his success and it is simply because he is a rational being who applies rational and attainable solutions.

Munger is typically shy and doesn't want to be pestered by the media until he gave his very famous speech in 1994 at USC Business School and ushered the world to the general framework about making wise decisions. He and Buffett are learning machines, a fact that made them successful and produced billions of dollars in profit. They are collecting mental models on how the world works and utilize what they learned to solve every problem in different ways before having the best final solution. As the famous proverb says, *two heads are better than one*. One mental model alone is not entirely perfect and effective, but with a good collection permit us to see everything around us from a better angle.

Charles Munger is really an inspiration and an idol to look up to. His mental models allow him to have an optimistic vista of the world and its components. He made the best decisions especially in the field of business that made him a sought-after investor and team player. His assets provided for him and even his philanthropic works which are helping many people and organizations in great needs.

Chapter 2: You Want to be Right

The advent of technology has brought significant development in the field of biology. Nowadays, people who wanted to modify their body parts can consult plastic surgeons and undergo expensive procedures to be desirable and for the sake of aesthetics. Imagine that you have been riding on the elevator, going down to the lobby, you have seen a person with radiant skin, a pair of healthy breasts, long attractive legs, long straight hair, and wearing a revealing red cocktail dress. Of course, what you have witnessed is a perfect example of a lady, a naturally born to the female species. You were mesmerized by what you saw. You stepped out from the elevator and went out to grab a taxi. Back in the elevator, the lady that you have encountered went back to her room to get an identification card that will be used on some errands. The name that was written on the card is SMITH, MARK W. Mark Smith who just completed his gender reassignment operation. Mark is still currently in the process of healing and is on the way to meet his lawyer to take legal actions on changing his name and gender and be identified as a transsexual woman. A situation like this is a good example of *"What we see is what we get"*. It is, of course, easy to believe in the evidence and with your intuition, jump into the conclusion that you have seen a natural woman. You believe in what you saw without further validation and you are convinced that his persona as a natural woman is true. That is very dangerous if we believe instantly to something that we have just seen. This is an example of ***confirmation bias***.

Confirmation Bias

According to Psychology Today, confirmation bias happens to start from the direct influence of desire on what we believe.[1] It can also be defined as the tendency to collect and interpret new data in a biased way to validate preexisting principles. Another example is when people still stick to obsolete theories in the presence of apparently obvious evidence. When we want a certain concept or thought to exist, we end up believing that it is true. Therefore, we are being inspired by wishful thinking, or else, false hope. This mistake leads some of us to stop collecting data when the variables gathered, in the long run, validate the views or prejudgments that we desire to be real. The moment that we have created an image, we are gladly embracing the information confirming that what we believed is authentic and correct. Doing this process allows you to reject or to ignore evidence which contradicts your own established facts. Confirmation bias also suggests that we don't see situations objectively. We gather bits of information that make us happy due to the fact that it confirms our belief. Sad to say but in reality, it makes us prisoners of our own assumptions.

The Reality About Maps

A map is a very useful tool in humankind. According to Merriam-Webster, a map is a representation that is usually on a flat surface of the whole or just a part of an area.[2] A map also emphasizes relationships between variables of various space-like objects, places, or themes. They are very helpful for navigators and other professionals who work with maps. Just like everything that exists in this world, maps are imperfect. They are flawed and yet very vital. They are replicas of reality, and as replicas, they are reductions of their reference. Maps don't have the exact qualities or attributes of what they are portraying. Maps are no longer useful to humanity if they were to represent things with perfect symmetry or they are no less than a reduction of the real object.

The Map and the Territory

Alfred Korzybski was born on July 3, 1879, in Warsaw, Poland in an aristocratic family known to produce several scientists and mathematicians for generations.[2] He studied engineering at Warsaw University of Technology. Later, he entered the Second Russian Army during World War I as a volunteer and served as an intelligence officer. His service brought him serious internal injuries and badly wounded his legs. After the war, he decided to stay in the United States where he continued his academic endeavors. The first-ever world war is an ugly part of history which brought a deep impact to Korzybski and he questioned why people involved in such catastrophic and senseless actions. This prompted him to compare human behavior to animal behavior to find the differences. Such a venture allowed him to publish his first book in 1921 entitled *Manhood of Humanity: The Science of Human Engineering*. It was a success and he ventured in the field of psychiatry. Korzybski is famously known for giving birth to the field of general semantics that is a philosophical approach to language. Its formulation seeks to navigate the connection between the totality of language, its function, and efforts to stimulate an individual's capability to express thoughts.

Korzybski presented a paper on mathematical semantics in 1931 in New Orleans, Louisiana. For a layperson and a non-technical reader, the mathematician's arguments on the connection of mathematics to human language, and to reality are difficult to comprehend and unnecessary. But Korzybski's string of ideas on the formation of language promoted his concept that **the map is not the territory.** Meaning to say, the usual description of an object is not the object itself. That the model is not authentic and not even the reality. That is abstracted is not abstracted. According to Korzybski:

A map may contain a formation that is the same or not to the formation of the place.

1. Two identical structures have identical *logical* features. Therefore, if you apply it in a correct map, Dresden is provided between Paris and Warsaw and an identical connection is available in the actual place.
2. A map is not a definite territory.
3. A perfect map must contain the map of the map and its map, and so on. This characteristic can be called ***self-reflexiveness***.

Maps are very important, but they are imperfect. In this context, maps are a representation of the concept of what is real that includes explanations, philosophies, prototypes, and the like. To fully understand the map, we need to have an abstraction or a definite concept that will guide us to solve our problems. We always have to admit reality. In order to solve any problem, our minds produce maps of reality to better understand and interpret the situation due to the fact that the effective way we can identify the difficulty of reality is by abstraction. Most of the time, we don't understand our own maps and what their limits are. In reality, we are so clingy on the abstraction that we are accustomed to utilizing inappropriate models and patterns because we often believe in the idea that it is better to use *any* preference than *none at all*. An example of such a dilemma can be found in the workplace. I have a colleague who had confessed the craziest step he did so far in completing a project on time. He used to submit things on time or earlier than due. Then, there was this project that would have been completed ahead of time if updates were applied and saved correctly. My colleague was very busy and there came an incident that made him cram until the next day. His computer went dead for several minutes because the person sitting in front of his station triggered an unknown peripheral that turned off his computer. He was problematic because he didn't save the edits he applied so, he started to repeat the process. Adrenaline rush came in and since it was the project's due, he decided to send an incomplete file. Feedback is usually given a day or two. So in case the client notices that the project is not yet done, my colleague would tell me that he sent the wrong file and the updated version will be sent right away. Or, since he was confident that he would finish the project the next day, he will tell the client that he sent the wrong file and then will upload the completed version of the file. What happened was the latter, he emailed the client and the client responded nicely. What my colleague did was a bit risky because the client could have reacted differently. He can tell the truth, but he decided to compromise his image, with the name of the company stipulated on him. He was really lucky at that time because the client was very polite.

Even the most prominent and accurate maps have limitations. According to Korzybski, some of their limitations are: they could be wrong without us noticing it; maps are a reduction of the actual model that loses vital information and they need a scientific interpretation that usually causes major errors. With the groundbreaking discoveries in modern psychology, another issue has been raised about the human brain: it takes vast leaps and detours to interpret and understand the environment. Charlie Munger once stated that a decent idea and the human mind work like the sperm and egg – that when the first good idea comes in, the passage seals. This possibility may cause major problems for the sake of simplifying reality. Once we try a certain model and it works, we tend to overuse it even to situations where it is not potent at all. We have the difficulty of categorizing it and its uses that often cause mistakes. Let us discuss another corporate sample.

Ron Johnson was a force to be reckoned with in his success to change the marketing strategy of Target from an elite department store to a quality-yet-affordable retail shop for all types of consumers by the late 1990s to early 2000s. His successful maneuver of the Target Corporation was not left unnoticed came into the knowledge of the late Steve Jobs, the famous CEO and co-founder of Apple, Inc. Johnson's success in building the Apple Stores into prominence was gradual and yet undeniable. According to the report released by Fortune Media in 2011, Apple Stores were the most productive worldwide on a per-square-foot basis and became a supreme force in the retail world.[3] Apple's sales put the famous jewelry store Tiffany's on the second spot. After taking charge of Apple's formidable position in the business world, Johnson was hired by other legends of the financial world including

Steven Roth and Bill Ackman. His next task was to modernize the image of the old-fashioned department store chain JC Penney. The store was in a very dire situation and a transformation must be done. The retail market share consumed by department stores had declined from 57% to 31% between 1992 and 2001. Compared to other struggling retailers at that time, JC Penney was still making some considerable profit because it had a valuable real estate and mall positioning. Plus, the rent was cheaper compared to other retailers which were a major advantage. Therefore, JC Penney had enough money to fund its transformation.

Johnson applied the technique he did for Apple that included the best customer service, static pricing with no markups and markdowns, attractive displays and quality products. Johnson envisioned to convert the stores into tiny malls-within-malls. This approach would make JC Penney trendy and reestablished as a prime and competitive retailer. During corporate meetings, Johnson discussed his idea persuasively that led to the store's soaring stock price from $26 in the summer of 2011 to $42 in early 2012. But it didn't last long because of the failure of Johnson's new model which eliminated discounting. Consumers who relied heavily on discount coupons rebelled and most of the products on display were seen too chic. The transformation of JC Penney which is originally known for its affordable sweaters was not a hit for its loyal consumers as well as the general public. As a consequence, Johnson was later fired for the expensive transformation of JC Penney which caused millions of dollars of operating losses.

Here is the question. What went wrong to Johnson's approach to JC Penney? We cannot question Johnson's effectivity and competency as a strategist. Even if we forget his success in Target and Apple, he still managed to propel JC Penney's undervalued stocks for a short period of time. The problem is, the success was not sustained longer than expected and losses soon came after. Its regular customers were not pleased by the sudden transformation of JC Penney from a mid-range to a high-end, trendy store. Obviously, Johnson used the old map he used in his previous campaigns, was proven ineffective and it even ruined his reputation. He utilized a map that he no longer needed because JC Penney's situation was demanding for a new map to be explored. Johnson had a wonderful vision and promoted a strategic proposal about retailing that was compatible in some situations, but not applicable in anymore in other cases. The landscape had changed, but the sad part is there is no innovation because he was hooked and stuck in the same old idea.

Warren Buffet is a successful investor who is fond of taking risks. At the same time, he advocated the use of multiple mental models. As the founder and owner of Berkshire Hathaway, he ran it smoothly without relying on computer models because it consumes a lot of resources like space, cash, and manpower. For him, it is better to admit that he has no power to see the future and depend greatly on his practical experiences.

Selective Perception

The emergence of mobile phones in the late '90s is unstoppable, and it led to the product's continuous innovation up to this era.[4] From the simple capacity of sending messages and making calls, today, mobile phones are powerful enough to control appliances at home or to manage financial transactions. Thanks to the available technology and resources that made such visions possible. And speaking of phones, we always have our favorite brands and personal preferences when acquiring one. Some of my friends have iPhones, some are loyal to Huawei, and I put my trust in Samsung. When my friends asked me why I love Samsung, I explained the pros and cons. They reacted without interest and talked about their phone's capabilities and suggested me to change my brand. Of course, I won't change my brand because it works for me. In vice versa, when I asked my friends to change their brands, I got their smiles and they ignored my pitch no matter how hard I tried to convince them.

When our favorites are being subjected to scrutiny, we are defensive and protective. We reject any forms of criticism and ignore what others are saying. This perceptual process is what you call *selective perception*.

Selective perception

A method in which an individual only accepts his desires and sets aside other's methods or beliefs.[5] There are factors that could influence selective perception. Like us, our past experiences have a direct bearing on selective perception mechanisms. Seymour Smith is an advertising researcher who said that individuals embrace advertisement that conforms on their beliefs, attitudes, conditioning, preferences, and a lot more. Selective perception can also be affected by biological factors such as age, race, and gender. The most powerful factor that may affect selective perception is the person's emotional extent, needs and wants.

Perceptual vigilance and **perceptual defense** are the two types of selective perception. Perceptual vigilance is the lower degree of selective perception and it connects to the method wherein the person notices and realizes the stimuli that may be vital for him at some level. **Stimuli** are actions, conditions, or persons that provoke a response.[6] Perceptual defense, on the other hand, is a high degree. It happens when a person is trying to make a shield against the stimuli to be protected against acquiring knowledge of it. Commonly, these stimuli are known to be intimidating or disagreeable, like vulgar words and abominable actions. This level of selective perception often ignores the negative facts of the subject. Research shows that people with a high degree of perceptual defense tend to have a powerful perceptual wall that acts as a filter, allowing them not to perceive unpleasant stimuli.

Based on early research, when selective perception is done consciously, it may lead the person to have a sight of things he wants and ignore its opposite. The best example of this case is the classic research that included subjects from famous universities of Princeton and Dartmouth. Respondents from these universities were instructed to watch a recorded football game between the two. According to the result, respondents from Dartmouth noticed that Princeton accumulated too many violations compared to its opponent. While subjects from Princeton, on the contrary, noticed the Dartmouth had the most violations during the game. This case shows a selective perception of opposing teams.

Selective perception can be tested and many professionals during the early 21st century conducted experiments and research to amass information and understand more the concept of selective perception. The most well-known selective perception test was conducted in 1999 by two psychologists Daniel Simons and Christopher Chabris.[7] The test was called the ***Invisible Gorilla Test***. This test was filmed and to give you a glimpse of the said video, allow me to describe it to you.

There were six people and the three of them are wearing white shirts while the other half is wearing black. You will be instructed to focus and do a silent count of the number of passes the players in white shirts can make. In the middle, a gorilla appears in the focus of the camera as it thumps its chest and then goes away. You definitely saw the gorilla. But when the proponents of the experiment conducted the live test at Harvard University, half of the participants who were instructed to count the number of passes didn't notice the gorilla. They simply focused on the instruction and ignored the animal. Therefore, the experiment reveals two important things. One is that we are missing many things around us. The second is, we are not aware that we are already missing too much.[7] People can concentrate on a single stimulus or event and tend to be **blinded** to what is coming ahead unexpectedly. This effect is known as ***intentional blindness***.

Ideology

There are things that we stand up for and we are trying our best to live the life that we are comfortable with. Ideology is the word globally utilized to define the fundamental values, ideas, beliefs and rules that mold the behavioral method to economic, cultural, political, and social norms of a person or a group. In a larger scope, there are worldwide ideologies like fascism, conservatism, socialism, Christianity, Buddhism, and the like. A common ideology, shared by people with the same goals and advocacy, frequently work together as one to achieve a significant and ideal social impact for a valuable outcome.

Ideology roots during childhood that we start learning from people around us. At first, we are participants guided by older individuals like our parents, siblings, grandparents, etc. These people made us players in an event or activity wherein we were taught to copy or observe the responses and attitudes of the people around us. This is what we call **socialization**. Also, during this childhood development of ideological schema, it is vital to recognize the ideological factors that will serve as our guide in the future. We tend to imitate our elders until we find our own imperatives that shaped the ideals that we are fighting for and to believe in something.

Our ideology allows us to filter every information that is coming to us and accept the best ones that fit our ideals and ignore the rest of those that are unnecessary.

Google is an Eden for IT professionals and business executives because of its in-demand and trendy services. Google knows how to value its clients as well as its employees. It offers a competitive salary, countless benefits, free food, flexible working hours, and a lot more. The best perk I've seen personally is your pet can tag along with you once you become an employee. Google's management believes that pets and other recreational activities, except substance abuse and gambling, during working hours help their employees to be more productive, creative, and responsible. I hope that every company around the globe has the same ideology as Google but of course, some work environments are too hostile and having pets and doing recreational activities during working hours can compromise productivity.

Framing

Our minds respond to the situation in which a thing is attached and not just to the object itself. Framing is a very vital function of our brain. It is one way to look for patterns in disorder. It is another way to form sense out of insignificance. Every day, we are subjected to the framing battle which is one of the basic difficulties we can encounter as we continue to exist. The events, things, experiences, methods, and facts we learned are the components that give meaning to reality. Reality is dynamic, contextual, and actively constructed. The building process includes choices that we want to apply in our experience. What we want to have in every experience is of great importance. The framing options that you select identify the value, essence, limitations, and design of your experience. The rules of framing can be actively controlled by different social players like organizations and people around you to impose their personal agenda. The best example can be observed in the political landscape where different factions are framing and fighting over issues that greatly interest the public. If the majority of people believed that marijuana affects the brain negatively, marijuana use would be seen as illegal.

Framing can disturb you in different ways. If back at work you feel unhappy and undervalued, what could be your problem? You can make your own version of reality by framing that you have hostile and narcissistic bosses and find a better one. Framing has been greatly studied in behavioral economics wherein Israeli-American psychologists Amos Tversky and Daniel Kahneman found how framing influences many dimensions of decision-making. When they observed how individuals work with the unknown, it was revealed that there were constant biases in the responses. These biases could be products of **heuristics** or **mental shortcuts**. Some of these shortcuts were very obvious and people are more likely to make inferences from their personal experiences. For instance, if you felt like you were not giving your best at work and you were not doing things right, you have the tendency to overestimate and see yourself unemployed anytime soon. Tversky and Kahneman conducted another experiment by asking their subjects to estimate the number of African nations that were members of the United Nations. They had a wheel of fortune that generated random numbers. A big number was selected, and estimates went up. They discovered that with the wheel, they could influence their subjects' responses.[9] Other samples can be, a condom with signage of *95% effective* is more marketable than the one with a label of *5% chance of failure*. Or it sounds more frightening when there is a *70% chance of an earthquake* rather than *30% of* *not having one* — the bigger the figure, the more likely that it affects our perspective.

Framing can affect the way we see things and how we handle them. The famous golf player Tiger Woods once said that if you don't feel nervous, that means you don't care. Patients that undergo psychotherapy are often instructed to frame a situation that can be a challenge or an opportunity. The research found that patients who do such simulations are stronger in the face of stress. Words are good examples of frames because they create various mental schemas. Like euphemisms which are effective frames because their purpose is to distract and to lessen the weight of something offensive or unpleasant. An example is a good veterinarian, instead of saying that he "killed" your pet because of the complications of cancer, he would likely to say, "I put your pet to sleep."

Aside from the words, the overall tone of the language is a powerful frame in association with the different origins that built the term. For instance, the general and scientific Post Traumatic Stress Disorder that was used during the Vietnam War originated from Shell Shock and Battle Fatigue during World Wars I and II respectively. Framing is an inevitable process because we always have a point of view in everything that we know, and it forms biases the way we see things around us. Of course, once biases are structured, we omit or devalue other situations or ideas. Always keep in mind that we have the power to win against the unexpected pitfalls of framing. That is why you have to be careful because if you don't keep an eye on the framing battle, you will become the biggest loser. First thing first, you have to be aware that the framing saga is always around and present all the time. Awareness of what is happening in your environment makes you prepared and gives the control back to you. It is also possible that you make it a habit to study and to collect different frames that you can use to understand a situation and your future decisions.

For Your Application...

I interviewed a friend of mine and her name is Lalaine. She is currently working as vice-president of a pre-press company located in Maryland, USA. She gladly recounted to me the lesson she learned from being an impulsive leader.

Lalaine is a Vice-President for more than a decade now. A single mother of two, she has a maternal instinct for her subordinates, but she is also strict during working hours. In her earlier years as a VP, she checked her employees and their production by roaming around the company premises and silently observing the employees. It is a normal scenario for her to see employees, who are not aware of her presence, eating in their workstation and that is a violation of company rule; employees who are talking about things that are not work-related; and the worst, those who are sleeping and those who are having *extracurricular activities* during production time. So, she used to raise these issues to her supervisors and they gladly complied. Then, after a week or less, the employees were coming back on their unprofessional habits. After a few years, *CCTV cameras* became a trendy monitoring system and Lalaine was happy to see the company attached CCTV cameras in every corner of the company. Since the installation of the cameras, Lalaine decided not to roam discreetly within the company premises and stay longer at her station to work. Lalaine was very vigilant and she took advantage of the CCTVs. She watched her employees from her computer monitor and she often called the attention of those people who are violating company rules and remind them to focus back to work.

There was this one department that was causing a lot of headaches to Lalaine. On her computer monitor, she noticed that a lot from this department was not focusing on their assigned projects and it seemed that they were constantly moving from one station to another. She got a suspicion that they were just talking things that were not work-related. Since production time was recorded to an online system, she asked their IT personnel to generate a productivity report of the employees involved to see how productive they were. According to the data, some of them were productive, some had suspicious records. Before the report came into her hands, she already had a confirmation bias and the things she witnessed in the video recordings allowed her to frame that some of her employees were not working seriously. No matter how good their productivity time, they can do much better if they will just focus on their tasks. She also got reports about noise issues from other departments. She raised this issue to the supervisor in-charge to investigate and take necessary measures in case the employees were not focusing and if the reports were true.

The supervisor held a meeting with the employees involved and informed them about Lalaine's observations and the concerns of other departments. According to them, they needed to switch places in some instances because the applications that they were running were compatible with other computers that were vital for their tasks. They also cleared the issue that was noisy and rebutted that they have to discuss work-related matters as a group and they didn't think that whispering out was enough just to please other departments. They also became honest that they were having a friendly chat to kill boredom, to refresh their brains, and to avoid themselves from sleeping because the atmosphere sometimes was inviting them to take a nap. Moreover, they didn't have any backlogs so far and they finished their projects on or ahead of time.

The supervisor discussed this to Lalaine during a meeting with the HR supervisor. After Lalaine heard the side of the employees involved, she understood now the situation. She decided that in order to avoid moving stations, a seating plan must be applied for the convenience of her employees and to maximize their production. Regarding the noise issue, the HR supervisor defended the employees because she overheard once the extent of the discussion that they were having, and it was work-related. She also realized that having a little friendly talk is okay as long as the production is not compromised, and due dates are assured to meet on time. Anyway, that was the productivity report suggested so far. Lalaine soon became more open-minded and instead of constantly relying on the CCTV footage, she went back to silently roam to conduct a surprise inspection, a routine she hadn't done for so many years.

Instead of being clouded with assumptions and false judgments, it is best in a corporate setting to see things in actual and to rely on a practical basis. Before jumping on into conclusions, it is best to investigate if there are suspicious actions to prevent hurting the feelings of the people around you who are doing their best. Providing a friendly work environment to employees will set a good production rate and quality output as long as company rules are enforced correctly.

Chapter 3: Answering All These Questions

To lead yourself to the ladder of progression is not easy and you need to face painstaking battles along your path to gain approval or promotion from most of the people you are working with. In the corporate world or any work environment, there is a famous saying that I know you are already familiar with which is essential for aspiring leaders. There was once a wise man who said, "**A good leader is a good follower.**" In my experience, listening to instructions and taking down reminders are vital in successfully completing a specific task. To be a good leader as well, you must be strong no matter what failure comes in and it is important to learn from mistakes. Leadership means that you are responsible for anything that is related to you. If it is hard to lead yourself, it is much harder to lead people or to lead a territory and to secure them.

Doing things for the very first time reciprocates more room for errors and knowledge to accommodate. Let me give you a list of the common mistakes of beginning leaders that you might be doing, or you will probably encounter once you have a promotion. So, grab your highlighter and mark those that interest you.[1]

1. ***Always make yourself presentable.*** It is a common mistake for beginning leaders to be intimidated by their officemates because of the new position that has been given to them. No matter how good your outfit is, if you are not wearing self-confidence, you put yourself in deeper scrutiny making you uncomfortable as a result. So, communicate with eye contact, make an appropriate facial expression, and speak with confidence. How you present yourself and deal with others speak a lot about you.

2. ***Maximize your time learning from your mentors.*** Most of the time, we get intimidated by the leaders who train us. Training is important, especially when you are about to handle more complicated and demanding tasks. Typically, during promotion, you need to fill in someone's position which is either promoted or resigned. Instead of being a keen listener and observer, be inquisitive and always ask questions if there is something that is not clear enough or you do not understand completely. Review your manual and modules ahead of time so that, you can validate things that are not thoroughly discussed. It is best as well if you will ask for advice and techniques for you to become more effective.

3. ***Don't let your failures put you down.*** Failure is important for you to learn more and grow as a person,

always keep that in mind. Nobody is perfect and even the biggest CEOs' and leaders around the globe are imperfect who committed perfect mistakes. Your mistakes also allow you to be more compassionate with your subordinates who are aspiring to be leaders as well.

4. **Do not be complacent.** Once you officially take over a position and you learned the things that you must learn, it is time for you to put yourself to the test. If you are handling a safe or prosperous team or territory, do not be contented with what your predecessors achieved and established. You must think of other ways that will make you unforgettable in a positive manner. Do not be stagnant like most of the leaders around you. You must act and make a difference!

5. **Take time to pause and to think.** Overall management is part of leadership and that makes it tedious, demanding, and somewhat exhausting. Whenever you feel drain and tired because of how busy you are, find some time to breathe out. Relaxation helps you to think correctly and that equates in making wise and correct decisions. Resetting your whole system will make you fully prepared again for tackling any challenges.

6. **Do not be so judgmental and impulsive, be transparent.** Remember Lalaine in my previous example? When you hear reports about your

subordinate(s), conduct your own investigation and ask the persons or parties involved. Do not be judgmental and make assumptions, especially when your favorite one spilled the beans. Assumptions often lead to more and complicated conflicts. So, be transparent and be an ambassador of peace.

7. **Don't let your position get into your head.** If you are a fan of *Game of Thrones*, you are familiar with the *mother of dragons,* Daenerys Targaryen. Her lady-in-waiting and confidant used to enumerate her titles to tell how important and entitled she was. As the series goes, her emotional breakdown and too much entitlement led to her demise. As a leader, you become humble at first. Stay that way no matter how long you are in that position. Always remember that respect is earned and not imposed.

8. **Be careful in accepting advice.** As everybody does, we get advice from people who are really close to us. In the corporate environment, listening to people who don't know the extent of an issue leads to managerial downfall. To get wise advice, you must ask yourself if the person is connected, competent, and candid.

9. **Believe in yourself.** Be bold and take the risk to your sure ideas. Instead of being discovered, you must act and discover your own success.

10. ***Explore.*** Do not just be stagnant and explore other areas of your field or the areas of other fields. Life is a learning process, and so is leadership. The more you learned, the more you will become effective. Staying in the same territory brings boredom and dissatisfaction.

Some of the problems I enumerated above are inevitable and vital for your growth. Just make sure that it won't happen again unless you are trapped in a very difficult situation. The question is, what are you going to do to prevent yourself from repeating the same mistakes? Well, it's time for me to give you the mental models that have been effective and still used by successful people in different industries.

Mental Model #1: The First Principles

One of the best ways of thinking that have been effectively used by Charlie Munger and Elon Musk is the ***first principles***. This mental model was used as early as the ancient times and was famously used by the famous philosophers in history like Aristotle. Its function is to reverse-engineer complex situations and establishes creative opportunities. Also known as *reasoning from first principles*, it dissects complex problems into basic parts and assembles them back once the root of the element has been revealed. This method allows you to think for your own, unleash your creativity, and provides non-linear outcomes.

A first principle is a root assumption or information that can also stand alone. It cannot also be deduced from another assumption. Perception by first principles omits the unnecessary elements of propositions. Through this, what is surely left is of importance. It is one of the most effective mental models that you can utilize to improve your perception and the way you see things in a deeper manner. First-principles can be explained further using **the coach and the player scenario**.

A game coach creates the game itself because it is the one who thinks what to do best in order to win against the opposing team. A coach assesses the physical possibilities, the strength, and weaknesses of the opponent, and create a strategy that is formulated to give a team an advantage. Creating strategies is a risk and each of them must be tested in order to find what works for a certain situation. Every coach has its basis from the first principles. Every game has its rules and these rules are the first principles. Rules dictate what you can and cannot do in a game. You can do everything as long as it is legal and conforms with the rules. Players are to execute the tactic presented by the coach. The coach and the player are separate entities and they generate different results. The coach can analyze why a game is successful or not and is capable of adjusting his tactics while the player doesn't generally have an idea about what is going on and what is working or not since he completely relies on the coach. We are in the segment between coach and player who reason by first principles, by analogy, or a combination of both. The first principle of reasoning breaks through tradition and brings light to the darkness. While reasoning from analogy is so traditional and it might lead you further from the answer that you are seeking for. Utilizing it will help you see the world from a deeper perspective and be more open-minded to possibilities. We are rational beings and some of us hesitate to take advice from the people around us. It is because their experiences are different from our own and we see things differently.

There are various techniques to establish first principles effectively. On top is **Socratic questioning** using stringent analysis. A disciplined questioning process, it is used to establish truths, reveal hidden assumptions, and divide knowledge from unfamiliarity. Socratic questioning pursues to detect first principles is an organized manner. You can also use the **Five Whys** which is very common to children whose inquisition is unstoppable unless satisfied.

Since we always want social validation, the bits of advice and thoughts of others suppress us if we don't know how to be independent and think for our own. Reasoning using first principles enables you to get out of the past and traditional wisdom. You could have the tendency to see what is possible when you understand the underlying principles and utilize your own methods or mental models. Reasoning by first principles is best when you are trying something as your very first; facing difficulties, and trying to understand things that you are not used to. You can eradicate those problems if you stop making guesses and prevent others from getting into your head. With the first principles, it unleashes the creative part of you and sets you free from analogies which is a good start for you to understand more deeply. You are also more likely to come up with better answers, adapt to changes, accept reality, and bolder to grab opportunities.

Elon Musk and His First Principles2

Elon Reeve Musk was born on June 28, 1971, in South Africa. He is currently residing in Los Angeles, California and a father of six. He is known to be one of the boldest entrepreneurs this world has ever witnessed. Being a founder and heading some of the most successful companies like SpaceX, he seems unstoppable. Musk was recognized by Forbes as one of the most powerful and richest people in the world. With a jaw-dropping net worth of $19 billion, everybody wants to know his secret.

He believes that in order to understand reality, you should start with what is true. He begins with what he wants to achieve and traces the first principles of the problem. A true visionary, Musk wanted to send people to Mars, and he found rockets absurdly expensive. He wanted to make cheaper ones. So, he studied what rockets are made of and only to find out that they two percent higher of the original price. There was no stopping Musk to create cheaper rockets. He is a studious person and has a degree in economics and physics, and he taught himself rocket science. That led him to establish SpaceX to see if he could build cheaper rockets.

Musk utilized the first principles in SpaceX to have gradual changes at low costs. According to his blueprint, battery packs are expensive, and they will always be because that's the way it has been which is pretty dumb. Because when you applied it to new things like a car, you cannot just say that horses are great, and it is a way better than cars because we're used to it. That's very traditional reasoning. So, in order for him to save more and to fulfill his visions, he gave an interesting example with battery packs. Traditionally, they are worth $600 per kilowatt-hour. To understand its price, he used first principles by breaking down the problem's components and their actual price in the market. So, the batteries got cobalt, aluminum, polymers, nickel, carbon, and steel can. These materials are available at the London Metal Exchange for an affordable price of $80 per kilowatt-hour. He said that you just need to be clever to acquire those materials and combine them to create a battery cell. There you have cheaper batteries.

In an interview with Larry Page, he was amazed at Musk because he is unusual and he also knowledgeable in business, organization, governmental, and leadership issues.

Mental Model #2: The Thought Experiment

Thought experiments, just like our first mental model which is the first principle, can be traced back as early as the dominance of ancient Greeks and Romans.[3] This mental model helped them to enrich some of humanity's greatest innovation and advances from philosophy to physics. A thought experiment is actually a way of exploring an idea, concept, or hypothesis by deep thought. When looking for practical evidence seems unattainable, the best way is to utilize thought experiments to understand complex ideas. Its purpose is to promote rational thinking, assumptions, and to alter models. Once used, it might also help you to come out of your comfort zone because it will allow you to realize that you must confront reality and to find answers to your questions that you have difficulty to answer. This mental model reveals to us that there are limitations on what we know and there are things that we cannot identify.

There are different types of thought experiments.

(1) *prefactual* which involves potential outcomes;

(2) *counterfactual* which is contradicting facts;

(3) *semi-factual* that contemplates if a different past can still lead to the present;

(4) *prediction* that theorizing future products based on available data;

(5) *hindcasting* that runs a reverse prediction to find out if it predicted a situation that had already happened;

(6) *retrodiction* that moves backward from a situation to find out the root cause; and lastly,

(7) *backcasting* that considers an outcome and works on the present to assume its causes.

Thought experiments are highly important in philosophy and integral to its evolution since ancient times. They provide answers to subjective philosophical hypotheses that empirical evidence cannot. Philosophers utilize this mental model to convey philosophies easy to understand. The goal of thought experiments is to illustrate a particular concept, like free will, and dive into abstracted situations. The goal is to create new ideas and not to dismantle what is proven to be correct. Plato provided an early example of a philosophical thought experiment known as the *Allegory of the Cave*. The narrative goes with a group of people who were born and live within the confines of a dark cave. Living in that cave for most of their existence, they saw nothing but shadows. They don't have any idea what's outside and they don't want to leave the cave either. A time comes that they were led outside, only to realize that the world is more than mere shadows and that the world is far more intriguing and so has much to offer. If these cavemen returned to the cave, their lives would be very different and unsatisfactory. They will start to regret that they went out. Plato used this allegory to convey his great appreciation of educating ourselves. That our first move to get out of the dark cave is dismantling ourselves to be educated and start to seek things that would help us understand the world.

Thought experiments have been helpful as well in the field of science. Empirical pieces of evidence are vital for this body of knowledge while experiments are used to create hypotheses. There are hypotheses that cannot be tested like the string theory. This mental model is often used by theoretical scientists to provide a provisional answer. Andrew D. Irvine is a Canadian academic who wrote a paper entitled *Thought Experiments in Scientific Reasoning*. He explained that this mental model is a key part of science which is in the same territory as physical experiments. It wants all assumptions to be reinforced by empirical evidence. The idea must be feasible and must give answers to intricate questions. A thought experiment must have the capacity to be wrong. An example of a thought experiment is *Schrodinger's Cat* that was developed in 1935 by Edwin Schrodinger. This experiment wants to show the counterintuitive part of quantum mechanics in a more accessible manner. The experiment goes with a cat, which can be alive or dead, inserted within a box. In the box, you will see a small amount of decaying radioactive material and a Geiger counter. Over time, the radioactive material may decay or not. If it decays, a tube of acid will crash and poison the animal. Without even opening the box, it is impossible to find out if the cat is dead or alive. The only indication that we have is the angry cat will start meowing if it is alive. Like the majority of experiments, details are subjective. Schrodinger's wanted to imply that quantum mechanics are unclassified. According to the astrophysicist John Gribbin, nothing is real unless it is scrutinized and that there is no underlying reality in the word. Schrodinger himself also stated that we do not fit into this material world that science created for all of us because we are outside of it. We are just its audience who can be amazed, shocked, or scared to its revelations. We believed that we are all part of it because we see ourselves in the picture.

Albert Einstein and His Application of Thought Experiments

Albert Einstein was a theoretical physicist and is considered as one, if not the most, famous physicist of all time. He is forever associated with the scientific world because he provided the modern foundation of physics: the theory of relativity.

Einstein was born on March 14, 1879, in Germany. Since childhood, Einstein was an exceptional student who greatly had an interest in math and physics. He then took math and physics in college at Federal Polytechnic School and a Ph.D. at the University of Zurich. The year 1905 was the turning point of Einstein's career as a physicist. He published the Annus Mirabilis papers which contained four articles that contributed greatly to the foundation of modern physics. These articles are Photoelectric Effect, Mass-Energy Equivalence, Brownian Motion and the Special Theory of Relativity. It also included the famous equation, $E=mc^2$.

The thought experiments mental model helped Einstein to his important discoveries. The most famous where he applied the thought experiments were on a beam of light that was later made into a brilliant kids' book. He asked himself, "What would happen if you catch a beam of light as it moved?" As he was looking for the answer, it led him to a different course that changed his life forever and benefited the field of physics as well. And the special theory of relativity was born. His services for the advancement of physics made him a Nobel laureate.

Mental Model #3: The Second-Order Thinking

As humans, it is our common trait to be judgmental and we often believe in what we initially see. As the saying goes with *what you see is what you get*. But we must keep in mind that there is something more beneath the surface and that things aren't always as they seem. There were times that we tried to solve a problem and we end up accidentally making room for another one that is even worse. The best method to check the long-term effects of our options is to utilize **second-order thinking**.

It is easier to recognize when you didn't consider right away the second and consequent order influences. For example, in business, there is a narcissistic boss who always wanted attention, but he doesn't want to work that much and be more active in his other activities. To secure that his presence is still active in the company, he created a right-hand that will manage and oversee on his behalf. Being the right-hand means that you are powerful enough to do your boss's function. The right hand is always present in the company and always attends to the needs of the employees that he gained the respect and loyalty of them. One day, the boss stayed at the office and observed how warmth the employees' greetings to his right hand compared to him. He realized that the affection of the people that he always wanted went to his right hand. It was not a good move after all for someone who is always craving attention.

The capacity to analyze things in the midst of challenges to the second, third, fifth, until infinity and beyond, is a powerful device that charges and expand your thinking. If there is second thinking, it is a good thing if you are asking yourself about the first one. First-level thinking is very simple and shallow; every one of us can apply it. First-level thinkers are already satisfied with the opinions of the people around them.

Second-order thinking demands a lot of action because it is difficult to think in terms of time, principles, and connections. Applying this mental model means that you are intelligent to divide yourself from the rest. It helps you to improve your ability to think by constantly asking yourself and by thinking through time.

Ray Dalio and His Application of the Second-Order Thinking

Raymond Dalio was born on August 8, 1949, in New York City. A son of a musician, he started investing as early as the age of 12 when he decided to buy some shares of Northeast Airlines for $300. This investment went tripled when the airlines tied with another company. He later received his bachelor's degree in finance from Long Island University and his MBA from Business School. Today, Dalio is a billionaire investor who founded the world's largest hedge-fund firm, Bridgewater Associates.

The second-order thinking philosophy helped Dalio to reach the peak of his success by choosing what he wanted in life and avoid temptations no matter how hard to ignore them. Like, if you want to be healthy and more attractive, you must avoid eating too much and conduct a proper diet as well as regular exercise so you can achieve the appearance that you want. This is how Dalio became a mogul in the business world. He always thinks first the implications of his decisions before he put them into action.

Mental Model #4: The Probabilistic Thinking

We are living in a world where countless unexpected events are being ruled by a dynamic set of influences. We need a mental model that would help us predict what would happen the most likely, and ***probabilistic thinking*** is a perfect fit for the job. If you are mathematically and philosophically inclined, I could say that this is the best mental model for you. Probabilistic thinking is vitally attempting to estimate, with the help of math and logic, the incoming situation. It is one of the mental models that improve the accuracy and success of our decisions.

We are short of perfect information about the world and this fact makes way to all the existing probability theory. We don't have the power to see the future as accurately as psychics do. The best possible way that we can do is to estimate what lies ahead with the help of practical and realistic probabilities.[6]

Thomas Bayes and Bayesian Thinking

Thomas Bayes was born in 1702 in London, United Kingdom. His alma mater is the University of Edinburgh. He was a notable English minister in the early half of the 18th century and he was famous for publishing An Essay Toward Solving a Problem in the Doctrine of Chances. In 1973, two years after his death, a friend named Richard Price, a British philosopher, was very impressed and brought the paper to the attention of the Royal Society. The essay paved the way to the Bayes Theorem which is concerned with how we will adjust probabilities when we come across new data.

The very core of Bayesian thinking lies with the thought that, by default, we have limited but convenient information about the world, and we are continuously meeting new ideas. We keep on believing that before the new idea pops out, we are already knowledgeable. This mental model enables us to utilize what is essential material in making decisions.

Mental Model #5: The Inversion Principle

The ***Inversion Principle*** is based on a proverb "*invert, always invert*" by the German mathematician Carl Gustav Jacobi. This mental model has been highly promoted by Charlie Munger. According to him, in solving a problem, it is important to approach the issue from the opposite side. By this tactic, it will ensure that you have thought everything that would greatly hinder you from achieving your goal. What we conventionally do is to confront problems starting from where it begins. It is highly suggested that we could make a different approach and start backward. By inversion, you have to think of the worst possible problems in order to provide probable effective solutions.

There are three easy steps for you to apply the inversion principle to develop better output. You should **define the problem** first. Then **invert it** thinking the worst possible problem you could encounter. Lastly, **consider the solutions** that you can apply during the second step.

The Evolution of the Inversion Principle

It was in 63-65 AD when Stoic philosophers practiced the *premeditation Malorum* or premeditation of evils to oversee the worst factors that could affect every event. Then here comes the fast forward, it was in 1820 when the German mathematician Carl Jacobi stated that complex problems could be verified by inverting them. The famous Charlie Munger has made Jacobi's maxim widely known over the past twenty years. In 1989, Deborah Mitchell, Jay Russo, and Nancy Pennington discovered that event imagination boosts the capacity to recognize reasons for possible results. While Gary Klein, a psychologist, and best-selling author, in 2004 proposed a pre-mortem guide to prospective hindsight. Tim Ferris in 2017 provided premeditation malorum an easier name and guide in his TED talk. He believes in the sequence identify fears, benefits of risks, and loss of inaction.

Mental Model #6: The Loss Aversion/Fairness/Endowment Effect

We all hate to lose things, especially those that are very important to us. Repeated sequence of losing is even more painful while gaining gives us pleasure. When you acquire something, it becomes a member of your system and ***loss aversion/fairness/endowment effect*** is responsible for that process. As these materials become part of you, you value it more than the way if they were not yours. You become angry seeing them taken away from you more than you would appreciate them being given to you. Individuals have a powerful inherent sense of fairness which is connected to their right they believe they have control over. Whenever you break this sense of fairness, it can lead to the development of *deprival super-reaction syndrome.* This syndrome is always associated with the loss of fairness and you tend to shout the words, *"It's unfair!"*

This mental model allows you to be more helpful to others while helping yourself at the same time. You know the feeling of being in pain of losing and you become more empathic with others. By understanding loss aversion, you find ways to help people overcome their agony or you can think of solutions to help them without giving up anything. With this, successful negotiation outcomes may come on the way.

In the corporate industry, you may apply it to win some deals by preparing proposals that lead to a win-win situation.

Understanding About Deprival Super-reaction Syndrome

Charles Schulz, creator of the comic strip "Peanuts", created a panel where his famous Peanut character, Lucy, was deprived of her birthday party and she said, "it's not fair!" then she had tantrums instead of understanding her mother, a very typical reaction of a child who didn't get what she badly wants. This is a classic example of deprival super-reaction syndrome which is always partnered by exclamations of unfairness which paves the way for us to believe that individuals have a sense of fairness.

According to Richard Thaler, an American economist, economists believed that fairness was a senseless concept mostly utilized by children who don't get what they wanted. Going back to Lucy, for her, it is not fair that her mother didn't keep her promise that Lucy will be having a birthday party. There is really an essential angle on expectations with our sample. It is crystal clear that Lucy held on to her mother's promise and that she had a right to have a birthday party. That is actually a part of her endowment –– or her rights and possessions.

When you have something and you have the natural or legal rights to own it and suddenly taken away from you, it is normal for you to feel unfairness. Going back to the Peanuts comic strip, when can see the fact that Lucy will celebrate her birthday once a year like everyone does, therefore, she didn't always have to do it that it became a good reason for her to expect. The mere fact that the comic strip specified that the party was promised, it became a part of her endowment since it was promised. So, hypothetically, what Lucy might have felt and done are quite rebellious to show that the promise was violated. She was definitely not happy, didn't even talk to her mom, felt betrayed and left behind, shamed on herself because her friends were expecting the party, didn't do her daily chores back at home, and a lot more than you can imagine. It is clear that the anguish and agony experienced by Lucy upon the cancellation of her birthday party greatly exceeded the pleasure she once felt when the party was announced and promised by her mom.

Mental Model #7: The Sunk Costs/Commitment + Consistency Bias

The concept of this mental model can be easily explained. Time and money are vital to our existence and you cannot take them back once you spend them or they're **sunk costs.** Since you cannot take them back, you have to focus and spend your energy on other things like building for your future. Sunk costs, if not fully understood and utilized correctly, can lead you down to horrible situations like despair, and death as the worst implication. The best example that history can offer us is the wars that destroyed many lives, including our natural resources. War is very expensive and destructive. Teaching yourselves to have a practical intuition of sunk costs aids you to think of better decisions. Sunk costs as a mental model is a kind of trait that you can utilize in certain situations like other models.

Consistency bias which is also called as *thesis drift* goes with the concept that you are doing an action for a better cause, but this reason changes eventually, and you are still doing the same thing. It usually garbles your decision-making. In a different course, you can utilize that situation to advertise unity, but you should be aware that the implications of small actions can make way to sunk costs that you have to justify.

Richard Feynman and His Sunk Costs

Richard Phillips Feynman was born on May 11, 1918, in New York. He was a theoretical physicist and his contributions in the field of physics led him to earn the Nobel Prize for Physics in 1965.

Feynman assisted the US in developing the atomic bomb known as the *Manhattan Project*. He experienced sunk costs in this project. He joined the project because he saw the Germans as dangers in society. He felt immoral because along with the success of the project and the defeat of Germany, he forgot the reason why he supported the project. Since the successful launched of the atomic bomb in Hiroshima and Nagasaki, they partied and got drunk while so many innocent people were dying in Japan.

Mental Model #8: Product vs. Packaging/Action Bias

If you are a shopaholic and you bought something, you used to ignore and throw away the packaging without reading it to enjoy the product within it. Practically, others scrutinize the packaging that tells the totality of the product. This mental model gives you another way of getting ideas which is adaptive. But you must also be aware that in some instances, it can lead you to odd and irrational behavior. For example, being industrious without being productive or counterproductive. If probabilistic thinking suggests that we must begin making analysis by focusing on the packaging, the ***product vs. packaging*** mental model recommends that we need to take our analysis to a different level to ensure that the product is what the packaging says.

Product vs. packaging enables you to have some time thinking about situations intellectually and emotionally. For example in a corporate setting, overproduction is not good because it leads to major problems with throughput, inventory, and other various aspects. Sometimes the more you act, the more your situation becomes complicated. That doing more is worse than doing nothing at all. This mental model is highly related to one of the paradigms formulated by Stephen Covey and that is, *to begin with the end in mind*. You must know your destination, where your decisions will lead you. Always be observant because you might be working very hard to reach the far end of the ladder to progression, only to find out that it is leading you in the wrong direction.

So, whether you are a leader or a member of a team, your focus should always be on **how to be more effective** and **not on how to be busy**. Culturally, we tend to connect busyness to being more productive, even though in reality that it is stressful and generally bad. Bad because being busy doesn't always lead you in the right direction. Sometimes, giving heavy labor to your workload, you tend to forget the most important things that you must accomplish or even the essence of why you are working.

Stephen Covey and His Stand on Busyness vs. Productivity

Stephen Covey is a motivational author who became famous for his best-selling book entitled The 7 Habits of Highly Effective People. This book has relations with different mental models including a deeper understanding of product vs. packaging in the specific area of busyness vs. productivity. Almost an entire chapter was dedicated to it.

Covey provided a four-quadrant model in his book and we will focus on three of the specific elements.

- **Butt in chair** – proposes that some deeds are more valuable than others. This element agrees that most of our best accomplishments are a product of creativity and novelty. Doing too much work and we have no time to think creatively and acquire a far greater perspective about our surroundings.
- **Visible Markers** – It is a cliché that in order to prove that we are making progress, we have to do and acquire a lot of things. This element conforms with that idea, as long as we see our progress in

visible markers. This element is observed when we accomplish things that give us satisfaction and motivation to do more because of a sense of purpose.

- **Type of day** – This element greatly depends on the discussion of chronotypes — a term that actually used in zoology that refers to the time when animals are active or inactive.10 In the corporate world, it determines if you are an early bird or a night owl. This element discusses when we are more productive and creative. Our body clock is our label for the productivity that we can offer in an organization.

Mental Model #9: The Base Rates

A ***Base Rate*** mental model is a form of probability that defines the possibility of an event when new or more accurate information is lacking. This mental model covers the highly likely chance that something might or might not happen, which doesn't conform with the recent information that might change the possibility that essential for an expected event. Therefore, base rates tell what commonly happens if nothing is available to influence the outcome. Part of this mental model is ***the base rate fallacy*** which refers to our capacity to ignore information that allows us to predict what could happen because we tend to concentrate on the latest, previous, and fascinating data instead. ***Bayes Theorem*** also comes helpful in this mental model since it is a mathematical equation wherein you can include the Base Rate for a situation with the possibilities associated with the latest data to extract the actual total possibility for a predicted event.[10] One example that we can have is the probability of the gross income of an established company.

Utilizing this mental model will help you to become more ready and equipped with solutions that you might encounter in case that your Base Rates predicted a not-so-good outcome for your future endeavors. Being highly prepared will give you prestige among your workmates because of your strategic analysis of things that are still on the way.

For Your Application...

Now that you have learned about other mental models that have been utilized by different business tycoons and other prominent luminaries in different fields, you can enhance your ability to lead and to have a more positive perspective in any situation that you will be involved as you live each day.

The First Principles mental model allows you to trace the very roots of a situation for better understanding and for you to find a more creative decision. And to be creative, you have learned under the **Product vs. Packaging** a deeper knowledge about **Busyness vs. Productivity** that you must have time to relax to be more creative and not to be eaten by working too hard without even knowing the very purpose of your labor. In a corporate setting, your problems are not answerable by just one answer or a single mental model. To find a solution that would fit your problem, the **Thought Experiment** teaches you to explore ideas, concepts, and hypotheses, then apply them to various situations, and identify what really works on which. Upon the identification of effective mental models, the **Second-Order Thinking** leads you not to be contented with what you see on the surface, but to dig more and see the lifelong impact of your decisions. The **Probabilistic Thinking** and **Base Rates** show you the imminent use of previous data to form new information by forensic prediction of future outcomes. Solving issues from the start can sometimes lead you to a more difficult situation. You can utilize the **Inversion Principle** and change your perspective by dealing backward to form a decision. The **Loss Aversion/Fairness/Endowment Effect** and **Sunk Costs/Commitment + Consistency Bias** mental models make you a good leader by putting yourself first in the position of others that allows you to be empathic. Through this, you gain more information about the situation enabling you to create win-win decisions and proposals. And those are the powers you have to unlock and learn more from these mental models.

Chapter 4: Optimizing and Systemizing Productivity

Leaders are given the hardest tasks that demand the most complex decisions. That is why they tend to do everything on their own and without relying absolutely on their subordinates. This is a common habit of beginning leaders. They want to do every bit of the job and make it perfect all at once to prove that they deserve their promotion. They want to win the respect of all and secure the good projection of their image before they rest and create other leaders. Because of such impulse, they are also prone to errors and put themselves in difficult situations. Most of the time, they exude too much confidence and self-glorification that they make decisions directly, without thinking a million times and without asking for help from their superiors. They work too much, and they think a lot that they even bring their jobs at home and constantly think about work. They cannot sleep properly at all and they sometimes lock themselves away from their social circle. Committing such suicide leads to possible burnouts.

I don't want you to mess up your life while assuming your professional duties. That's why I prepared more mental models and healthy suggestions that will allow you to enjoy your corporate and personal lives. First, let's begin with **stress**.

Dealing with Stress

You may always associate stress with your career, your boss, the deadlines that you have to meet, and other personal factors that are demanding your full attention. These factors are constantly giving you so many headaches and confusion to the point that you want to divide your body to accommodate them all. The stress that you identify, brought by trying your best to meet important matters, shouldn't be considered stress at all. What you are feeling is **pressure**. Pressure, as defined by Merriam-Webster, *is the burden of physical or mental distress*.[1] There is no inherent stress even if the demand could be intense. You can avoid stress or let go of it easily if you know how to react to pressure and the sudden changes in life. You always have options to choose from. Always remember that you have to be resilient or flexible and the key to it is to avoid converting pressure into stress. The number one cause of stress is **rumination**.

Rumination

Mental process of repeated thinking about something negatively. The basic symptom of rumination includes waking up in the middle night and having difficulty going back to sleep because of the things you haven't and should have done. I know that you have experienced this because I myself had been in the same situation many times! Rumination can also bring back the past that contains negativity and worries that don't do any good. Individuals who don't ruminate could be suffering from a lot of difficulties by they are not stressed by it. For you to prevent rumination and to live a better life and lead effectively, I prepared a list of mental habits to reduce your stress and intensify your resilience.[2]

1. **Live in the present.** You have to wake up and live in the present, live in reality. Do not let your past hinder your present that will affect your future. Admit it or not, we have dull moments that we daydream. We look back at things and regret some of our decisions in the past and we conjure that *what if? question*. It gives us stress most of the time because we feel bad for things that help us grow somehow. Gather yourself and focus back on your present and be positive about your future. Living in the present will help you to see the real mechanism of the world.

2. **Be always in control.** Once you gather yourself and come back in the present, do not be distracted to things that won't contribute to your growth, to your production, and that will take too much of your time that cause you no good. It is correct that we are not in control of what will happen to us, but you have the power to control your attention. So, practice attentively on putting your attention to the most important things and strategize for your long-term happiness and success. Being in control will also help

you to predict and manipulate the odds when you make decisions.

3. **Believe in the power of distance.** If you the irrational and distressed about someone or something, then you have to save yourself and create a space and distance yourself from things that keep you away from the peace you deserve. Detachment gives you the ability to preserve yourself and to maintain your perspective. Sometimes, we are not aware that we are investing a great deal of our time and energy into things and people that are temporary. They the things are keeping us from growing because that's the way we like it. If these things are causing you stress and you feel tired and toxic because of their out-of-place demands, it is time for you to detach. As long as you keep things that are unhealthy for you physically, mentally, emotionally, and spiritually, you are prone to commit errors that will also affect your relationship to others and your performance at work. Do not allow your emotions and your past to hinder your journey towards growth. So, detach and gain yourself once more to reflect and strategize than to ruminate.

4. **Breakaway.** There are mental models that we are using in order to solve our problems professionally or mentally. If you find some methods that are ineffective and causing you more trouble like being pessimistic,

learn to break away and let go of things that give you more suffering. Aside from what your brain is projecting, let go as well from uncertainties, negative emotions, and bad habits that do not contribute to your growth and might also affect your capability to decide efficiently.

5. ***Be occupied with positivity.*** Another thing that you must practice is to be occupied. Being occupied in a way that won't burn you out but will help you propagate success. So, in case you are facing a problem, then play along with time and think of strategies that will help you out from that situation. Conduct a SWOT (Strengths, Weaknesses, Opportunities, and Threats) analysis for you to identify every angle of your decision. If you are in a very harmonious situation, then think of things that will sustain the happiness that you are enjoying. Positivity reflects not only for you and with everyone around you.

6. ***Always be adrift.*** Remember that problems are always just around the corner and they can offer you growth and lessons that you will value for the rest of your life. If you are being flooded by overthinking or rumination, do not get drowned no matter how strong the current is. Open your mind, have high hopes, and be optimistic –– these things will help you get above

them all. Self-preservation and your goals in life allow you to find the best strategies to attain what you want in life.

- **Reflect.** The mind is a very powerful organ and whatever we feed to it, dictates the outcome. If we think negatively, we feel doubt and uncertainties that lead us to problems and regrets. When we think positively, we become much stronger and empowered resulting in success and good decisions. Ruminating does you no good and it will constantly give you setbacks and uncertainties. Reflection serves you with a purpose by getting ahead and a plan for a brighter future, and acknowledge that your shortcomings are your springboard in achieving your goals. Reflection is also a healthy way to activate your senses and make them in harmony with your mind. It causes relaxation and you can find better solutions to problems that you find exhausting.

Be Highly Concerned About Mental Health

Thinking too much about work, aside from your personal matters, brings many possible mental issues. Overdoing tasks, working beyond your capacity, bullying, and paranoia are some of the possible factors that can affect your mental health. Leaders are models and should set as an example for everyone in the workplace. They are also responsible for promoting emotional and mental welfare. So, voicing these issues out in the workplace must be tolerated for the awareness of everyone and to help those who are in need. This is necessary to spread hope and empowerment. Aside from that, being a paragon of the importance of mental health awareness brings challenges for the promotion of such endeavors. You have to be highly prepared and informed about the facts concerning mental health so you can spot people who cannot directly announce that they are suffering from certain mental issues.

Below is the list that will help you to raise awareness and promote the importance of a healthy mental state.[3]

1. **Show that you genuinely care.** As a leader, you need to spend an ample amount of time with your subordinates and bond with them. You can set a group dinner or team building to have quality time with them. You can ask and talk anything under the sun as long as you maintain everything professionally. Of course, you must be extra emotional and sentimental so they could feel your sincerity and show them that you actually care. I personally do a one-on-one talk to my trainees and often ask them about their professional insights and a bit about their personal lives. I found it very effective in establishing a strong rapport and letting them feel that as a leader, I am accessible and can

respond to their professional needs. Providing your subordinates and coworkers with genuine care brings a more harmonious work environment and creativity. At the same time, you are building their confidence to trust and to look up to other professionals.

2. ***Be an open book and also share your struggles.*** It is a stigma that having mental issues equates to insanity. There are many leaders in history who struggled, and the difficulties they experienced helped them to be renowned pillars in their fields. According to the research conducted by a psychiatrist, Professor Nassir Ghaemi, people who are suffering from mental illness can be great leaders and can lead better. Mania unleashes creativity and resilience to trauma. Depression, on the other hand, intensifies empathy and practicality. To break such stigma, leaders must come forward and be an inspiration by sharing what they've been through to reach happiness and success. To act as a model reinforces people around you and to let them know that there are others who are suffering as well and might be in greater difficulties. Sharing your struggles and how you succeed will give them the message that *there is a rainbow always after the rain.*

3. ***Be an advocate of self-love.*** Leaders must always be presentable and must command respect. Showing that you are always prepared because of good time management allows you to juggle with your professional and personal life efficiently. You can relax, have fun, have eight hours of sleep, and maintain an impressive physical, mental, emotional, and spiritual state. With these qualities, you are a model that everyone can follow for a healthier living. Also, showing warmth and compassion to your coworkers deepens your connection to them. Having very positive attributes can affect your surroundings and the people within your circle that leads to a very good flow of business.

More Mental Models to Make Effective Decisions

It is time for me to unleash more mental models for you to create wise decisions that will resonate with a long-lasting impact not just to you, but everything around you. Effective and efficient decision-making processes are hard to find but once you recognize mental models and utilize them correctly, they will give you promising results. Unleash the great leader that has been dormant on your very core by reading the pointers ahead.

1. ***The Two-List System of Warren Buffet.*** Mr. Buffet had tried this with his pilot by asking him to create a list that contains his 25 most important things to accomplish and after doing so, he was instructed to encircle his top 5 out of that 25. Later, this list was known as the two-list system. You have to segregate the more important priorities by having your **List A** and **List B** that contains the things you must avoid in order to accomplish the first list. Somehow, these lists are also reminders of the process of elimination. Reminders are great so you will be constantly reminded of the most important things that you must achieve and set aside those that are preventing you from attaining them.
2. ***The 10/10/10 Rule.*** You might have regrets about your past decisions because you didn't think about their long-term impact. This rule will help you to reflect on the long-term implications of your decisions by asking yourself: *how will you feel it 10 minutes from now? How about after 10 months? How about after 10 years?* Exercising yourself to ask these questions before executing a decision helps you eliminate emotion from influencing your decision. That is because you will force yourself to think about the long-term effects of your decisions.

Emotions are catalysts that permit you to be biased with the decision that you are about to formulate.

3. ***The Outcome Blind Approach.*** You will always acquire inaccurate information, but you are always in control of your decisions and the processes that you are about to utilize in order to generate good decisions. If you are making a big decision, ask the input of the people who have involvement with the decision you have to make because they will be affected as well with the formulated decision. Always hold your ground whether your decision is a success or a failure. By getting through both scenarios, you avoid ***attribution bias*** – judging others with their actions without giving consideration to the situation they are in. Applying this mental model gives you a high probability of making successful decisions because you don't allow any form of bias to affect your decision-making mechanism.

4. ***The Right and Non-Consensus.*** The idea of this mental model is you have to be different and be bolder with your choices. This is quite risky, and yet very rewarding. In order to win, you have to be unconventional and be right at the same time. You have to muster all your strength and be positive all the time if you will apply this mental model.

5. ***The Rule of Three.*** The rule of three is an effective writing principle that can actually work with your decisions. Try to give three reasons, not two, not four, just three in persuading a client. Or you can also apply it when you are making your priority list. The lesser is much better for this principle.
6. ***The Moat.*** During the medieval era and the era directly succeeding it, a moat is a deep ditch filled with water that serves as the first line of defense of a castle, town, or fortress. No doubt that a moat diagram has been recreated and used in business as well. When you want to have a competitive edge and a powerful strategy, you can always utilize the moat and defend your business against competitors and win the game.
7. ***The Combination of Network Effects and Critical Mass.*** In order for you to expand your market and to reach the mass, you have to create a network. You need a medium to promote what you have to offer. The fastest, easiest, and affordable way is through the use of social media. Of course, to effectively participate in the market, you have to learn your **critical mass** – it refers to the ideal size of your business.

8. ***Utilization of Decentralized, and Distributed Infrastructure.*** One of the essential factors in reaching an effective network impact is to create a distributed and decentralized model to balance the power between the company and the individuals.
9. ***The Famous Game Theory.*** How people behave in strategic situations is the primary concern of *game theory*. Being used by famous scientists and high-ranking officials, this mental model allows you to think of strategies where you can use your advantage to a maximum level and your competitors are reduced.
10. ***The Economies of Scale.*** They are cost advantages cultivated by businesses and other organizations when production becomes effective. It can be achieved by companies by having an increase in production and lowering the prices of the products. This is possible because prices are distributed over a large volume of products. Prices or costs can be fixed or variable. In this principle, the size of the business is the main factor because the larger it is, the more savings will be generated. It can also be external and internal. External deals with the outside elements, while internal is concerned with managerial factors. This model

allows your business to grow faster without having a high fixed cost or overhead.

11. ***The Pyramid Principle.*** Under a thought, written ideas should always form a pyramid, and this is the advocacy *pyramid principle*. To effectively use it, you must begin with the answer, group and summarize your underlying arguments, and finally put your supporting ideas in order. You should try this model when you are communicating or pitching a proposal. Start with the answer first instead of unveiling your agenda at the end of the presentation. So, you will allow your clients or the people you are dealing with to have their conclusions and get aligned with you. Also, you can save more time and effort.

12. ***The 99/50/1.*** If you dissect the numbers, you will get 99%, 50%, and 1% which actually denotes your commitment to a project. You have to be highly and physically involved at the beginning of the production and getting involved less if you secured its smooth transition until the final phase. Utilizing this model will allow you to focus more on other tasks.

13. ***Become a Directly Responsible Individual (DRI).*** A concept that was highly adhered to by Apple, *DRI* is explicitly responsible for something,

especially decisions. Being or having one lessens time and energy consumption during meetings and other scenarios. It always about efficiency and results and DRIs leave no space for vagueness on the issue of who has the authority and final say on every question that a project or team has. They should also be fully focused on their goals and tasks, as well as being open to collaboration in order to real success. They have the tendency to make all the final decisions but they should also learn how and when to trust the capability of their coworkers.

14. ***The Team of Teams.*** This is an operating model that connects together different teams as well as their members forming a network of an organization. Decision making is conducted by team leaders of each group making them responsible for success or failure. This model is a dramatic example of the proverb: *united we stand, divided we fall.*

15. ***The Radical Candor.*** Let's make this fast and simple, be an aggressive leader with an ultra-empathy to others. One of the most successful ways of becoming a great leader is by building positive relationships with your coworkers. You have to possess and be known as someone who is kind, genuine, reliably honest, and caring. If you cannot love your coworkers, it must be an indication that

you cannot love your work for a longer time frame because of that manifestation. The atomic building block of good management is *honest feedback*. There is nothing more destructive to a relationship than an imbalance of influence and power. The honest destroyer of truth that neutralizes this imbalance is **candor**. One more pointer, there is this thing called *ruinous empathy* or when you tend to care too much because of attachment that you have for some. To get past through it, you must identify that enjoying near-term empathy bypasses long-term impacts. You could lead your people to a bigger failure and more undesirable feelings in the future. Forgetting your true intention while you help people can be fatal and destructive for the business.

16. ***The Listen, Decide, Communicate Sequence.*** A communication model from Dick Costolo, the former CEO of Twitter, the *listen, decide, communicate sequence* is important in decision-making. You have to listen first, if not to people, by the factors that you need to consider. Then you decide and communicate it with those involved.

Those mental models might not lead you to find necessary decisions easier, but it would definitely provide a clear platform for you to find success as a leader in progress. Since this chapter is dedicated to mental models, I have more latticework of models that you may use to optimize your results while spending less time and money. As you may observe, mental models are like handy applications you installed on your smartphone. You installed them because you know that they are helpful and fun. So, let me give you more applications that you can utilize.5

1. ***Regret Minimization Framework (Jeff Bezos).*** Jeff Bezos is a successful American entrepreneur and investor. He is famously known as the founder and president of Amazon.com, Inc. –– one of the Big Four technology companies along with Google, Facebook, and Apple. *Regret minimization framework* allows you to make difficult decisions by visualizing your future and looking backward about your current decision. This mental model might help you fulfill your goal of building a business of your own or doing things that you are craving to do for a long time. Also, it will make you a risk taker and better try things and be optimistic that you will succeed. You might regret it if you don't give it a shot.

2. ***Idea Maze (Balaji Srinivasan).*** Balaji Srinivasan is the co-founder of Counsyl, a genetic test company that tells couples whether they are safe or not of having children. It has won the Wall Street

Journal's Innovation Award for Medicine. This mental model is about thinking and planning on different paths and detours your decision will take.

3. ***Schlep Blindness (Paul Graham).*** Paul Graham is an English computer scientist and entrepreneur who is best known for his work on Lisp – a high-level programming language that is used by different tech professionals around the globe. *Schlep* was a Yiddish word which means *a tedious and unpleasant work.* This mental model prevents you from overlooking possible risks of your decisions. It tells you that you must learn the things and cure your ignorance about a certain venture.

4. ***Jobs to be Done (Clayton Christensen).*** Clayton Christensen is an American academic and business consultant who is currently serving as a professor at the Harvard Business School. This mental model allows you to understand why a consumer may buy your product. With this, you can accurately create and improve products that satisfy the need of your customers.

5. ***Minimum Viable Product (Frank Robinson).*** Frank Robinson was an American professional baseball player and manager in Major League Baseball. Throughout his career, he won the MVP on both American and National Leagues. *Minimum*

Viable Product, a mental model formulated by a legendary MVP, is originally a process for trying assumptions and guarantees that there is a need for a certain idea. The MVP process starts by identifying your riskiest assumption. Then, knowing the simplest experiment that you can undertake to test that assumption.

6. **Please Keep in Mind: *Confirmation Bias of Thucydides.*** We have discussed *confirmation bias* in Chapter 2. As a recap, it is a form of thinking that you agree with what confirms your assumptions and disagree with the opposing evidence. You have to avoid this type of thinking and be transparent because it doesn't get well with other models like the MVP and idea maze.

7. ***Product Market Fit (Andy Rachleff).*** Andy Rachleff is the founder and chairman of Wealthfront Inc. – an investment firm in California. *Product-market fit* is a model that puts you in good condition and your products satisfy your consumer.

8. ***100 People Love (Paul Graham).*** Good reviews and positive word-of-the-mouth-promotion are effective ways to propel your little business and be widely known. Paul Graham believes in this strategy of getting 100 people to love you and what you are promoting. From them, you build a network that

expands to others until your business acquires a stronghold in your industry. Advertisement from people who know you is cheaper than applying for an ad in radio, television, or publication. Also, social media platforms are out there for your disposal. So, you better have a list and write down if you got 100 people who love you personally.

9. ***AARRR (Dave McClure).*** Dave McClure is an entrepreneur and investor who founded the 500 Startups, a business accelerator company. *AARRR* stands for *Acquisition, Retention, Referral, Revenue* and it is a model for the customer lifecycle. It measures and optimizes each step of the funnel to grow rapidly and widen your market. It helps you also understand your consumers and a perfect tool for you to formulate a data-driven decision. And that is a powerful startup.

10. ***Network Effects (Robert Metcalfe).*** Robert Metcalfe is a tech-savvy, American entrepreneur and who co-invented the Ethernet and assisted the evolution of the internet. *Network effects* take place when a service or product increases its value as more consumers use it. This model also allows you to assemble a better business as you effectively strategize the market of your product or service.

11. ***Disruptive Innovation (Clayton Christensen).*** Ever wonder how the Billboard charts work? Billboard monitors the demands of albums and songs then ranks them according to their sales and streams. The *disruptive innovation* has the same concept. It is when you create a method, product, or service that is at the bottom of a market at first and relentlessly climbs up, outranking your competitors because you are redefining the industry with what you can offer in the market.
12. ***Conjoined Triangles of Success (Jack Barker).*** A fictional main character in HBO's hit series Silicon Valley, Jack "Action" Barker shows us how ridiculous and thrilling startups can be. The *conjoined triangles of success* allow you to shape decisions by looking at every market of your success and avoid overlapping them because it might lead to your downfall. Gaining a unique perspective on reality between sales and engineering will give you an absolute edge in making wise decisions.

Aside from learning and applying different mental models in your every decision, I suggest that you must develop a system for your regular progress. In this specific section, I will teach you how to develop the systems which will definitely upgrade your way of thinking. And in order to make it happen, I will introduce to you another set of mental models from **systems**

thinking which created the core to the approaches towards the success of many prominent figures. It is also a dynamic tool that can make improvements in all areas of your life possible. Possessing a big goal can stimulate you to act in order to achieve it, but only for a short period. You must remember that a system or process will always exceed your motivation.

A ***system*** as defined by Merriam-Webster Dictionary is a regularly interacting or interdependent group of items forming a unified whole. This unified whole is led to a definite objective. The system as a whole is greater than the sum of its components and can achieve more with better results. You take away a single component from the system that can lead to unpredictable changes. Everything in this world is a system. The best example is the universe and it consists of interacting components in which we are connected. We are an essential part of these many systems that exist in the universe and we are unique because we are constantly evolving. With our gift to think rationally, we can always emerge from the systems rather than being imprisoned to them. We can become the masters of the systems and formulate our own rules.

For you to be able to write your own rules in the infinite games of life, let me give you the vital mental models for systems thinking.

- **Theory of Constraints.** This mental model was developed from the realm of manufacturing systems. Every single system is reduced by different constraints but has one constraint which is tighter compared to the rest. Just like in a chain, there is always one weakest link and there will be a single weakest constraint in a system. This constraint is known as the **bottleneck** – the area where overwhelming congestion takes place that causes an interruption in a system. Its implication affects the performance of any system basically making it limited by the products that are coming out from the bottleneck. So, there must be an action that will address the bottleneck to see a gradual change, if not in an instant. This mental model opens our eyes to the reality that most of our ways of self-improvement are fruitless because of our failure to recognize their bottlenecks. We find ourselves in the middle of the ocean, floating and swimming but not getting ashore. You have to remember that you don't need more labor, but efforts that are applied effectively. You have to focus on removing your bottleneck and ignore the others for the meantime. Once it is removed, your system will smoothly run as it should be, and you will feel a big change in your life.
- **Having concrete leverage.** You've got to have leverage in order to influence your system positively

and in a way that your efforts will have maximum effect. Leverage is the answer to your limited time, focus, and energy. Having it, you can fully maximize your return of investment from your resources. Beginning leaders use willpower to create motivation while professionals use it for fortifying their systems of execution. The **Pareto Principle**, also known as the 80/20 rule, states that it is on the power-law distribution where the majority of the phenomena fall. It also adheres that 80% of the outcomes can be attained using 20% of the effort which is not actually impressive. Why is this so? Because you can have 50% of the outcomes by just using 1% effort. This fact wants to imply that you must understand the level of expertise or skill your objective is requiring you before you undergo diminishing marginal returns. You really have to choose your areas of mastery to equip yourself better. Your leverage tells you the opportunities in small changes in your life that might lead to expanded success. To better improve and maximize the power of your leverage, you have to use the following approach in your systems.

- You have to **change the rules** so you can define what to do within your system.

- You can design and customize your own systems **build in self-organization**. This way, they will naturally improve as time goes by.
- You must **improve your information flow** by making more objective and accurate measurements by frequently checking on them. Reflecting regularly on information gained from the measurements will improve your systems.

Getting Feedback. The distribution and returning of information to a system are called ***feedback***. Its primary function is to inform the system about its status relative to the goal. Feedback is like a loop because the connection between the measurement and the factor that is being measured is circular. Feedback is very vital to the system because of the information they hold if the measurements are getting closer to the desired outcome. Feedback is creating a loop that affects the overall system. We have two types of feedback loops. First is the ***balancing feedback loop*** which is the most common and it tries to stabilize the equilibrium or status quo. The second is the ***reinforcing feedback loop*** which delivers growth (+) or decline (−) to a system. You need feedback loops to keep your most wanted outcomes stable and minimize the setbacks when you lose your way towards your goal. You have to be vigilant in balancing feedback loops. Counterbalancing it will cause delays and problems in achieving what you desire.

The additional mental models above are very powerful when you combine together because they form a mechanism for advancement. You are now aware that measurement and awareness are vital keeps for you to learn how to overcome any obstacles that are halting you in reaching your goals. It is also important that you have to undertake minor behavioral experiments to clarify your assumptions. One tiny problem might change everything else, but identifying your bottlenecks allows you to be well prepared. Giving your full attention, time, and energy in fixing your bottlenecks, with the help of your leverage, will make your productivity fast and smooth over time. Be vigilant for all the time and observe for samples in your everyday existence and use them as a reference. Once you fully understand the nature of every system, you will begin to see it everywhere.

The more references that you have, you will also begin to form many ideas for enhancement that are not connected to your bottlenecks anymore. I would like you to try this, find one bottleneck that is limiting you now, focus on how you would fix it...without thinking about your other bottlenecks. Problems are a lot easier to solve one at a time so you won't feel stressed in the process.

Digging More About Mental Models

Imagine that you are in a garden one sunny morning, then it suddenly rains. You look at the falling droplets, you feel them on your skin. As you are observing, the lenses of your eyes concentrate photons from the light emitted by the sun into your retinas. There are photosensitive cells residing in your retinas that respond by distributing neural impulses to the brain. The brain works on these signals and creates an image of the rain in your head. That's the scientific explanation of how images of things you see form in your brain. The question is, what makes the picture of the rain an authentic one? This is how we use the **mental model**. The rain is an idea that really exists in reality and that is the model right in front of you. It is what you see and what you feel as of the moment. Understanding the model is demanding more information aside from your sensory experience. You can use information from your experiences and education.

Rain is defined as water in the form of droplets caused by the condensation of water vapor. It can be predicted and can occur seasonally. It is vital for drylands and plants, especially in farms where rice fields and other crops grow. You are confident by those facts that are related to the rain because you got the basic knowledge about it and the weather patterns remind you of it. Mental models are packed with knowledge that can also help you create other ideas.

More About Systems

Our brain is great at simulating mental models for our instant form of reality. Factors are getting difficult when you begin to think about the abstract. The best example that we can use for the abstract system in the market. The market system has products that which value is determined by their price. This price acts as a signal if a consumer can afford the product. Unlike our first sample, the rain, you cannot see the market physically. Obviously, the market is an abstract idea that lives in the minds of people who patronize it. There was an overwhelming economic crisis in late 2008, before the holiday shopping season. It was when retailers struggled financially due to the rapid decline of consumer purchases. People were troubled about the economy that they started saving money instead of spending it. In order to boost demand, retailers started dropping prices of their commodities. This option led to *price deflation.* Consumers observed the pattern of rapid price drop resulting in delayed spending and waiting for commodities to drop their value. This result of simulating the consumers' mental models of the market affected their decision-making that the more they delay buying, the cheaper the commodities would be.

It is difficult to describe the boundaries of a mental model. We are capable of narrowing our concentration and work on temporary facts within the scope of our mental models. Also, we are not good enough at mentally processing complex systems with lots of parts, variables, and interruptions. This is when we need to use the software. With software, we can change the state of our mental models into functional models. It also aids us in creating new knowledge and perception, as well as to build better mental models in the coming situations.

Pareto Principle

We have discussed this mental model earlier and as a recap, it is also known as **80/20 principle** which is a form of **power-law** -- a special mathematical connection between two variables in which one works as the power of the other. The *Pareto Principle* states that 20% of a set of factors pave the way for 80% of the outcomes. Anyway, it doesn't always have to be 80/20, it can also be 25/95 or 5/70. As you may observe, they don't always have to be summed up to 100%. This principle tells the idea that many causes and cases are not linear in nature, the small percentage of causes result in the majority of the effects. There are many simple examples of this principle like 20% of consumers can generate 80% of the revenue.

This mental model can be utilized if you can find out the main motivators for a specific effect that you are able to observe, then you optimize it for more promising outcomes. In a typical work setting, there are tasks or projects that are valuable to a company or a boss. By identifying them, you can focus on them and do your best. By doing so, you have a chance to be promoted or your presence be felt in the company. Charlie Munger is one of the most successful investors who utilized this principle and according to him, it does the heavy lifting and only a few mental models he had known can do such a thing.

Law of Small Numbers

This concept is part of probability which tells that you will witness the majority of variation in small samples. Obviously, it is the opposite of the *Law of Large Numbers* which discusses that the real probability will come out using a large number of samples. The main idea of the **law of small numbers** is that a small portion of samples will have outcomes that have many variations which can also be misleading.

The best example that we use is the performance of a specific school. Many people would give an assumption that schools with small population tend to perform better than those that are bigger. But in reality, they can also be the worst performers. It is easy to see that having a small number can propel a school's ranking by selecting the best through entrance examinations and removal of students who don't reach the average required in a specific program. This action can definitely propel a school's ranking against its bigger competitors. While there are several small schools which are parts of smaller communities and don't require anything in accepting students. If you see in the research in 2018 by a member of the National Association for College Admission Counseling, where they listed the 100 top-performing public schools in the United States, there are smaller schools in the top and bottom of the list.[10] The sample population in smaller schools are not large enough to measure the quality of education of the school in a specific time frame. By using the law of small numbers in ranking the schools, it would be easy for parents to put their children in the best schools if they want to have a quality education. In the corporate world, this mental model is the reason why Charlie Munger quoted that personal interviews as a classic medium of the hiring process are a terrible way. He suggested that it is best to look at the applicant's portfolio and qualifications. Munger believes that interviews have a sample size of one and a bad indicator of how the applicant will perform at the posted job or how he will communicate with other employees.

This mental model is highly associated and directly inclined to probability and can also have harmony with other mental models. It can lead to overconfidence and to huge losses when it is paired with *leverage.* There are random events that may happen all the time and when a business or a businessman decides to borrow resources from other corporations to support growth, they have the mentality that things will stay as long as they are paying their debt. The same concept is the main motivation for *redundancy* in engineering -- adding backups to the systems to survive possible setbacks.

The Circle of Competence

Having an awareness of your circle of competence gives you the power to avoid problems, recognize opportunities for growth, and to accept learning from others. The idea of the circle of competence has been utilized for so many years by Warren Buffet as a path to concentrate investors on working in areas they have mastered. Learning the boundaries of your capacity is essential. This mental model has a very simple concept. Every one of us has amassed helpful information in certain realms of the world through learning and experience. Some of these realms are very easy for us to understand, while other areas need more intelligence or information to be fully understood. Like in school, there are subjects that we love the most because we excel in them. We hate or we get bored with some of these bodies of knowledge because we have a hard time understanding their concept. Buffet believed that we do not need to gain a full understanding of the areas we have a hard time comprehending. We have to stick to the things that we really know. Our circle of competence can become broader as time goes by. Always remember that in order for us to learn more, we have to accept the errors. Surely, we will commit mistakes along the process and learn from them. Unless you are a perfect creature.

If you want to improve your chances of becoming a successful person in life and as a leader or entrepreneur, then identify the scope of your circle of competence and work hard inside. As time goes by, do your best to expand your circle but never, ever be afraid to accept your limitations.

More, more mental models…

I have given you several proven and tested mental models and I would like you to know that I am not done yet in giving you more for you to utilize and experiment as you make day-to-day decisions. Indulge the list again!

- **Checklist** – it is a tool that you can utilize to form a list or outline the things that you need to accomplish. It will help you to set your priorities and also will serve as a remember since your memory is limited. A checklist also increases your consistency and accuracy by providing you the proper sequence of repetitive processes.
- **Advantages of Scale** – it refers to the concept that as a system works more of the same kind of task, it will achieve efficiencies after a long time. There is a greater range of efficiencies that can be acquired as business flourishes such as employees getting better at their tasks which leads the way to meet deadlines ahead of time.

- **Redundancy** – it is originally a model from engineering which refers to the methods of allowing extra parts within a system. They act as substitutes or backups that can be utilized once a part is broken so the system continues to function and to avoid delay. Therefore, redundancy is very important within a system because it reduces the chance of system failure.
- **Division of Labor** – is a model that allows each person without an organization to specialize in different tasks or skills. Once a specific skill or process has been mastered, everyone can share the knowledge learned to provide growth and efficiency not just to the organization, but as well as to its members.
- **Incentives** – also known as **rewards** is a strategy that you can use to motivate your people. By providing people with the incentives that they deserve, you can change their behavior and reach for the goal that you have in mind.

Chapter 5: Negotiation and How to Make it a Win-Win

In the previous chapters, you have learned how powerful mental models can affect your decision-making and predict the long-term effects of your decisions with thorough contemplation and scientific analysis. There are so many mental models and I know that you have observed that they are not just for decision-making, but to sort your priorities in life and to make successful methods that will help you find success. Mental models are giving you tactics and pointers on how to make effective negotiations and powerful persuasion. If you are dreaming of a business of your own or winning deals that will put you on the pedestal, it is vital for you to learn things on how to master the art of negotiation and persuasion.

One of the most common errors that business negotiators or managers commit is rushing into a proposal without enough preparation. In order to create strong arguments and persuasive clauses, you need ample time to study the content of what you are doing. Because of ambition and taking shortcuts to be recognized, negotiators and managers are prone to create unreasonable demands and other dirty tactics to win deals. You always have to see room for improvement and always have an open mind for collaboration. A flashy bonus is a good motivator, but being a good leader, you must think not just your own sake but for the betterment of those people who are looking up to you. Emotions play a very important factor in making negotiations and proposals. Negotiators and managers are not able to do their best once they let emotional biases get into their way. Anger and sadness can lead to risky and unhealthy decisions. They are also prone to ethical shortcuts and behave unethically during negotiations because of financial incentives because of the mentality that they are already experts in their respective fields and won't be caught in doing anomalies.

Yes, most of the mistakes that you will encounter, or you have encountered already as a leader, negotiator, or manager, root from your dark side. I fully understand that because our nature says that we are *innately good and innately evil*. We tend to do things, in case you have, against our moral code because we are in a situation, or because of the success it can bring, or whatever reasons, we must avoid it at all costs. Once you did something that you think will never be uncovered, it is like a drug, very addictive and it will consume you until you lose control. I strongly believe in the *law of karma* and I must say that you must live in the golden rule, "*do not do unto others what you don't want others to do unto you.*"

Robert Cialdini and the Influence: The Psychology of Persuasion

Robert Cialdini is the celebrated author of the best-selling book entitled *Influence: The Psychology of Persuasion.* He is a professor and a social psychologist who has conducted complex and important research –– making him the most cited expert in the psychology of negotiation, influence, and persuasion. Cialdini introduced in his book the **six universal principles of influence** which are also called the *six weapons of influence.* Since its publication 35 years ago, the concepts from the book are still in use by businesses and organizations around the globe.

The creation of the book began with the author's theoretical perspective to deal with a complicated world, our brains evolved fluidly, and we respond to different situations. The six principles revolve primarily on human instincts. Other ordinary circumstances are good traits but can be utilized against us by those who want to destroy or control us. The author was hoping by understanding these principles of persuasion, we are better to identify events where they will act against their influence and to have the shield to fight undesirable social impact.

The first principle is ***reciprocity*** which states that individuals always want to return favors, pay debts, and to be kind to others who showed kindness as well. These samples are leading to the conclusion that we always tend to say *yes*. It is already a cultural standard that we have to return gifts and favors. This principle tells that people feel that they owe people who something good to them. People tend to feel uncomfortable when they are indebted to others. So, they will find ways to *reciprocate* the good deeds, just to satisfy or lessen the weight of obligation. This principle can also be utilized for unexpected exchanges as well. Its occurrence affected our ability to decide without restrictions and led us to respond involuntarily or automatically. To defend yourself from reciprocity, you must reject the offers. If you see offers as tricks or bait to control you, then you don't have to be obligated to reciprocate that offer. Unless you know that you can trust the person who offered and see meaningful exchanges. Always remember that you are the captain of your own ship and you can always decline to avoid reciprocity.

The second principle is **commitment and consistency** where the author argues that people have a longing to be consistent and they also value consistency from other things. It is a powerful social influence and highly valued by our society. Its principle suggests that we have an urge to be acknowledged as consistent and that we honor our commitments. Once we give our commitment to someone or to something, we are doing our best to keep our end of the bargain. Like we support projects that have an appeal to us. For Cialdini, commitments are very powerful to influence someone who is motivated or uncorrupted by power. To fight this principle, you have to stay cool and do not be pressured by accommodating requests that you really don't want to be involved in. You have to identify personal signals that can you help the right decisions.

The third principle talks about safety in considering numbers or the wisdom of the masses – the concept of **social proof**. Because of uncertainties or doubts that we have in making decisions, we seek validation for our actions from people. It is like you want to drink milk tea and you want the best-tasting store, you will conduct your own research to find the best shop where many people buy and generally have positive reviews from its customers. You have to be very careful in looking into others because you might be following a questionable person. It is vital for you to identify that the actions of others should not be the absolute basis of your decisions.

The fourth principle is the acceptance of **authority**. We have been taught since we were young that we need to comply with the demands of people who have power over us and respect them as well. Then, as we mature, we want to be like the people that we admired the most because of their influence. Sometimes, we are blinded by titles, possessions, and fiscal outlook that we forget to look for a true substance. There are authorities who abused their influence and power. In order for you to protect yourself, ask first if a person of considerable status has triggered your respect for authority genuinely and not because they imposed the power of their symbol.

Cialdini believes that we are more likely to be influenced by people we like –– and the fifth principle talks about **liking**. If we like the person who asks for a favor, admit it, we are more than happy and willing to be at that person's disposal. We feel that we are needed, and we can use and go back to the first principle, reciprocity. Cialdini enumerated factors why we are inclined to like a person. It might be because of appearance, influence, social circle, commonality, and flattery. Someone may compliment you when they want something from you. To counter this and for you not to be used by people who want to take advantage, you must learn how to separate emotional attachments and focus more on the weight of the favor. Assess the favor if you or others would benefit from it. Even if you like the person, you still have to be extra careful and be transparent.

The last and the sixth principle is the **scarcity** which is super powerful and works on the worth that individuals apply to things. Scarcity in economics is connected to supply and demand. The rarer the item is, the more valuable it can become, and people have the mentality to want it. The author exerts that people are defied emotionally when their freedoms are endangered, and scarcity has the tendency to limit free choice. It may cause people to want to have possession of the item. People find opportunities valuable when they are actually less valuable. It is a lesson that you must incorporate into your life; you must analyze the item, or an opportunity before you take it. Ask yourself what kind of value you would get and reflect on its long-term effect.

Referrals

- ***Social Proof*** We have already discussed this principle which is part of the book of the famous psychologist Robert Cialdini. Let us find out more about ***social proof.*** Social proof is a form of cognitive bias that defines how we are greatly persuaded by what the people around us are practicing. It is sometimes called as Herd Mentality, it is a kind of shortcut (heuristic) where we depend big time on the ideas and acts of the people around us, especially when we are creating a decision. This possibility is more likely to materialize when we are clouded with uncertainties. In any event, especially when you are stressed or confused, you tend to look for the crowd and seek confirmation from the majority. Social proof is one of the most utilized and effective tools if you want to persuade a person and influence their decisions. Salespeople are very good at it. So, if you are inclined corporately, you must learn the tricks of this cognitive bias. It can also be combined with other mental models like ***authority*** or you can also partner it with **scarcity** to create unusual patterns such as sell-offs and bank runs.

- **Getting to Yes** It is a book based on the efforts of the Harvard Negotiation Project, *Getting to Yes* is a good material on effective negotiation that leads both parties in a win-win situation. This book also thoughtfully combined different mental models, transforming them into a very beneficial discussion of how to reach winning solutions when problems emerge. Primarily more on business and professional discussions, there are pointers that you can use in personal matters too. It contains practical, concise, and applicable content and gives thoughtful solutions for a lot of issues.

It is not actually a good idea to eliminate conflict because it can actually lead to better opportunities. We can actually prevent it by altering our ways and work on our differences. Like, collaborate and transform that collaboration to win-win situations instead of proving who's the best. We have to focus more on interests rather than positions — for example, a landowner and a tenant. The tenant rents land and pays rent regularly. To maximize the rented land, the landowner allows the tenant to build a business that would boost the tenant's income. It is a win-win situation where the landowner is getting rental payments from the tenant while the latter is earning and is able to pay rentals in advance because of the business he builds. Different interests or having different utility functions can pave the way to **mutual gain** – this is the foundation of capitalism. So, you better hold and prevent your confirmation bias in getting your way to have a mutual understanding and harmony with your collaborator.

Traditional negotiation can be classified as ***soft*** or ***hard*** and both have their own downsides. Practically, the hard one dominates the soft, but being too hard can really be exhausting and suffocating. A principled negotiation is an approach where the one proposing separates people from the conflict, concentrates on interests and not for positions, formulates choices for common growth, and asserts on utilizing objective criteria. Always remember that when you deal, you must have empathy and deal with the interest of the other party. Failing to build rapport can also lead to the dismissal of the negotiation. You should proactively bring out some emotions. Be confident when you are pitching because conflict exists not in physical reality, but in your head. You need to deal and overcome your fears like feeling inferior or building pessimistic thoughts which include rejection. Do not blame others for your personal issues and you must solve it on your own or you could ask for help from the people who care for you. There are certain issues that might be unimportant for you but meaningful for others. Therefore, if you have business issues, allow your people to help by joining the process because no matter what the outcome is, they will be happy because they felt needed. The success of their production will give them happiness and they will see failure as a room for great improvements.

There are moments when people around you feel exhaustion and emotional stress. You always have to display empathy and be very welcome to their anger. Venting out is a good choice if you want to loosen up. If other people attack you, be silent and do not respond to show how professional you are. You have to be open to criticisms because harsh comments can give you the motivation to work harder and prove to those people who are letting you down that you are not the person that they are projecting just to mock you. Sometimes, you can conduct an interview and ask people about the areas that need further improvement. Through this, you are becoming an effective leader because you need to learn more about the welfare of those who are working with you. You need to negotiate under legal circumstances and do not undertake illegal things like using dirty tricks just to get what they want from you.

- ***The Humans vs. Econs Mental Model*** One of the most common bottlenecks that we have around is that we often see things in accordance with our perspective, or the way we desire them to be. That is a very inconvenient habit because our surroundings are changing in forms or events that we don't expect. So, you have to pattern your life to accommodate reality itself. Humans are "us", so what about ***econs***? Well, it simply refers to **economics** and **economists**. We already have a clue all along. Econs are doing their best to get incentives and be motivated by it and boost their interests. While normal humans always value fairness and rely heavily on social proof. They have the tendency to take away what is rightfully theirs to return a favor or to show consistency. But they can also be destructive when someone wronged them, or they are being threatened by an unfair and unjust system. We can put that it is the critical point of negotiation.

Humans, not econs, are the foundation of the *human-centered design approach* or *structural problem-solving*. This approach asserts that you cannot expect people around you to behave the way you want them to behave. Expect them to behave the way they want instead. Various professionals like lawyers, engineers, scientists, and people in the business world are trying to control things based on their designs simply because they are too analytical and imagine the things around them as the same. These professionals are like econs because of their education and they lean on the concept of sunk and opportunity costs. Such a concept can blind leaders and ignore human interests like fairness or memory that can lead to theoretical systems that don't work in reality. The most common complaint of leaders of big corporations about investors is they see companies as disorganized cash machines moving on spreadsheets rather than actual living things that breathe vital entities and facing standard human challenges. You might fail to consider the loss aversion, fairness, endowment effect, and self-justification – you have to see that people tend to overvalue their possessions and as time goes by, they feel entitled and boast what they have no matter what their sources are. There are so many business people and investors who are focusing so much on the records of their spreadsheets. Incentives, in reality, are complicated topics to be discussed and well-understood human psychology provides a more accurate solution.

One of the most overlooked mental models is **local vs. globalization** that tells the idea that decisions that are created for the short-term are not applicable in the long-term and vice versa. It is always present in businesses and badly dealt with. Most managers can adopt cost-saving materials because it is a rational decision, but they tend to see human needs and invoke fairness in any given circumstance. Loss aversion is being applied when businesses put fairness by applying discounts to their products and sacrificing whopping profits that they could gain.

Business managers who are already a veteran in their fields can have mercy and give in to human needs by applying discounts and prioritize fairness and other concerns therein for a long-term harmony between profit and consumers' approval. While most human traits should be considered as adaptive and like water, they do follow the shape of the frame created in the economy.

- ***Reason Respecting*** The word **because** is one of the most powerful words in the English language. As humans, we were given the capacity to think and to reason out which separate us from other life forms. Our intellect allows us to inquire about the things we don't know. Our inquisition gives way to the concept that we have to understand the reasons for everything in this universe. When we learn the answers to our why's, we are willing to comply, to remember, and to finish an order successfully. ***Because*** is a powerful motivator or tool for persuasion for both positive and negative goals.

One basic scenario that we can observe by utilizing the powerful effect of "because" is when you are falling in line. So, it is common that when there is a long line, some are patiently waiting while others are irritated because of what it seems to be a very long time for waiting. Then, there are individuals who have special cases that will use their status or situation like pregnancy, old age, and disabilities and cut into the line. Since they have a "because" or valid reason, anyone who is perfectly normal accepts the reason and understands the situation. Or, in the business world, you have to act professionally and be presentable all the time "*because*" they are part of the company rules that you must abide.

Because is a very potent word as you can persuade people to do things that you want, whether they are good or bad, and they can do the same for you. In a corporate setup, when you have a project and you have to finish it urgently, by simply explaining *why* this project is vital to your company and *why* you have to finish it urgently, you can influence that willingness to your coworkers pushing them to focus and finish the project. If you also want an increase, use *because* and write down detailed information on the important tasks or projects you completed, include your performance and functions, and how you made an impact on your company. You can also use the word to adapt to right-hand issues to solve them.

Every professional, even the average person, is always looking for reasons and *reason-respecting* is a cognitive bias and a persuasion tactic at the same time. By simply adding *because* to different media like verbal communication or email, it will increase the chances that your request will be granted, or people will comply with what you want. To add more, adding the question of *why* when you need a certain thing like a project to be done in time can help your resources to focus and do their best to adapt along the process.

So, the use of the words *because* and *why* will help you to meet your goals and influence people within your circle to actively and willingly participate in your demand as long as you have the will and goals to achieve. Reasons are very important because it is a validation and a form of justification of where efforts and resources will be used.

In using mental models, you have to recognize the issues and problems before you use them. There are always at your disposal, but you must be careful because you may use the wrong one or the wrong combination. Anyway, for what I have mentioned for so many times, it is okay to fail because utilizing mental models on the wrong occasion will let you know where it is best suited. Do not be afraid to experiment because it will lead you to better opportunities. You just have to be optimistic and find what is best suited to your system.

You can also develop your own mental models over time, especially when you are already leading. Part of leadership is the obstacles that you have to conquer and find what your strengths and weaknesses are, and where you have to be hard or soft. Be empathic in with the people around you and share a part of you that will empower them. Showing how human you are despite your achievements and position will definitely make a mark to the people that you shared a part of you. Be a great inspiration and always do legal things no matter how much you can make. Always believe in the *law of karma*. Find opportunities in every collaboration because it will bring harmony as you achieve your goals. You must allow others to participate to let them feel that they are wanted. Finishing a project through group effort, you are giving every single member self-worth. Every entity in the universe will conspire and will give you what you truly deserve. You can be hard on people who will trick you or those who tricked you already but be smart enough on plotting against them and make it sure that they will learn the lesson that they deserve. Through this, they might learn not to victimize others.

Let your system be in perfect harmony and work on first with your bottlenecks to guarantee a smooth-sailing business. Do not forget the maintenance of your system and install concepts that will keep it running towards your goals. Learning the business that you will work on and mastering the art of effective negotiation by providing powerful proposals leads to your success and the success of the people involved with it.

And when you reach all your goals, be grounded and do not forget to look back and thank the people who help you achieve your goals. Always believe in yourself and be confident. Be bolder with your choices and be different because you have to believe that you are a trendsetter.

Your decisions define you as a leader. Mental models are always there to help you out. Be analytic and review things that will lead you on the winning side. Optimism and letting others help you as long as you consider their merits increase the chances that you will generate the best decisions.

Conclusion

This book is created to help you analyze factors and construct wise decisions using mental models. To be a part of your start, or to be applied in your growing endeavor, is a great thing because it means that the purpose of this book has been greatly satisfied. Unlocking your mental abilities to explore what you think is impossible with the help of different concepts and methods written in this book equates to your long-term growth.

There might be concepts in this book that are new to you and I know that it is fun to experience new things, while it could be the opposite for others. You have to practice working on them so you can see their full potential and apply them to the most suitable situations. Exploring the different mental models will tell you where and when they are most suited.

The way in accumulating various mental models is like fortifying your eyesight by supplying your system with vitamin A. Our eyes can see something deeper in the surface. You need them together to have a better vision of things. Try to cover one of them, and you will have a very limited view. It is similar to mental models – they provide an abstract figure of how physical and theoretical things work in this universe. You should always be alert and vigilant in your surroundings so you can have pointers and improve the way you see things.

Read often, learn from other people, and gather experience from important events in your life. The mind is essentially in need of different mental models to have a complete understanding of how the world works. The more references that you have, the more you open your mind with possibilities. Remember that the archenemy of good decisions is an insufficient understanding of the real problem.

During our academic pursuit, we have learned different areas of knowledge like mathematics, science, history, and so on. In practical application, information is not often segregated into different categories. As quoted by Charlie Munger, all the wisdom in this world is not found in one tiny academic faculty. Philosophers and other thinkers are free thinkers which means that they do not actually think based on a specific discipline. They acquire practical and personal wisdom of things that also work for them personally. They are trying their best to look at things not just in a single context. So, you have to consider other perspectives about a specific subject and develop flexible knowledge that can be connected from one idea to another. That is the importance of learning mental models, by learning how to relate them with each other for you to generate good decisions. You have to be creative and innovative in concluding your own ideas. Spotting the connection between different mental models, you can recognize answers to several questions that other people are overlooking.

You have to keep on reminding yourself that it is not necessary to gain mastery in every subject in order to gain a great decision-making mechanism. Of all the existing mental models that have existed in history, created and developed from the ancient times up to the present generation, there are only a few that you have to master and understand fully and work in combinations to see how the universe works. Most of the important mental models are large ideas from all disciplines like math, science, psychology, philosophy and the like. Each of them has a selection of mental models that create the spine of the subject. Like in science, we have learned experimentation, the theory of relativity and game theory to name a few that we may also apply in decision-making. If you are able to gain fluency in the ***foundations*** and the ***basics*** of every existing discipline, you can definitely acquire an extraordinarily precise and helpful image of life. Once again, according to Charlie Munger, 80 or 90 essential models will handle about 90 percent of the journey in transforming you as an effective decision-maker. And from those mental models, only a few would last and endure the weight of the journey. It is best if you could make it a personal mission to dismantle the great models that lift heavy factors of life. After you've learned more than a thousand different mental models, slowly try to select a few that really work.

I hope that you would create your personal list of the most essential and memorable mental models that you have already applied in various situations in your personal and corporate life. Also, give it a try to explain and remember their actual application. Explain to them in an easy and meaningful way to perceive by everyone. Make it your goal to share your experiences with mental models and help everyone within your social circle the way you help yourself to think and make decisions much better.

If you want to learn more about effective and helpful leadership strategies, please grab your copy of Emotional Intelligence for Leadership: 4 Week Booster Plan to Increase Your Self-Awareness, Assertiveness and Your Ability to Manage People written by yours truly, Jonatan Slane.

Bibliography

Burnett, Jane. (2017). Majority of workers are unhappy employees, study finds. Ladders $100K Club. Retrieved from https://www.theladders.com/career-advice/majority-unhappy-at-work

Cherry, Kendra (2018). "The 6 Types of Basic Emotions and Their Effect on Human Behavior." Verywellmind. Retrieved from https://www.verywellmind.com/an-overview-of-the-types-of-emotions-4163976

Chignell, Berry. (2018). The importance of emotional intelligence in the workplace. CIPHR. Retrieved from https://www.ciphr.com/features/emotional-intelligence/

Clark, Josh (n.d.) "What are emotions, and why do we have them?" How Stuff Works. Retrieved from https://science.howstuffworks.com/life/what-are-emotions1.htm

Goleman, Daniel. (2015). Emotional Intelligence. [blog] Daniel Goleman. Retrieved from http://www.danielgoleman.info/daniel-goleman-how-emotionally-intelligent-are-you/

Grant, Jim and Susan David. (n.d.) Recognizing Emotions: A Core Positioning Skill. MSCEIT Self-Development Workbook.

Kraus, Michael W. (2017). Voice-Only Communication Enhances Empathic Accuracy. American Psychologist. 72 (7), pp. 644-654.

Positive Psychology Program: Your One-Stop Positive Psychology Resource. (2018). Emotion regulation worksheets & strategies: Improve your DBT skills. Retrieved from https://positivepsychologyprogram.com/emotion-regulation-worksheets-strategies-dbt-skills/

Practical Emotional Intelligence (n.d.) Emotional Intelligence blog. Retrieved from http://www.emotionalintelligencecourse.com/history-of-eq/

Salazar, Alejandra (2017). "Emotional Intelligence: What is it, interpretation models and controversies." CogniFit Health, Brain, and Neuroscience. Retrieved from https://blog.cognifit.com/emotional-intelligence/

References

Aventis (2018). Effective presentation skills: Engage your audience with NLP Strategies. *Aventis Learning Group.* Retrieved from https://aventislearning.com/effective-presentation-skills-engage-your-audience-with-nlp-strategies/ on 24th August 2019

Bandler, R. (2018). Time management and task-switching by Dr. Richard Bandler. *NLP Life.* Retrieved from https://www.nlplifetraining.com/content/time-management-and-task-switching-dr-richard-bandler on 22nd August 2019

Basu, R. (2009). NLP techniques, decision making with timeline. *The NLP Company.* Retrieved from http://www.thenlpcompany.com/therapy/nlp-techniques-decision-making-with-time-line/ on 22nd August 2019

Basu, R. (2016). Feel good techniques to increase productivity. *The NLP Company.* Retrieved from http://www.thenlpcompany.com/job-hunting/feel-good-techniques-increase-productivity/ on 22nd August 2019

Beale, M. (2019). What is NLP | Confirmation bias. *NLP Techniques.* Retrieved from https://www.nlp-techniques.org/what-is-nlp/confirmation-bias/ on 21st August 2019

Chang, C. (2014). NLP Singapore – Greatest entrepreneurs of all times & what we can learn from them (part 2 of 3). *N.L.P. Academy.* Retrieved from http://www.nlpinsingapore.com/tag/richard-branson on 19th August 2019

Excellence Academy. (2018). How to find your higher purpose using NLP. *Excellence Academy.* Retrieved from https://excellenceacademy.com.au/how-to-find-your-higher-purpose-using-nlp/ on 20th August 2019

Excellence Assured. (2017). Goal setting with your timeline in mind. *Excellency Assured.* Retrieved from https://excellenceassured.com/2402/goal-setting-with-your-timeline-in-mind on 20th August 2019

Excellence Assured (n.d). NLP language technique for negotiation. *Excellence Assured.* Retrieved from https://excellenceassured.com/1906/nlp-language-technique-for-negotiation on 25th August 2019

Farrell, W. (2016). The 4 D's of time management. *Coaching with NLP.* Retrieved from https://www.coachingwithnlp.co/4-ds-of-time-management/ on 22nd August 2019

Frossell, S. (2007). Communicating more effectively with NLP. *Sarah Frossell LLP.* Retrieved from http://www.sarahfrossell.com/article4.htm on 24th August 2019

Gallo, C. (2012). 11 presentation lessons you can still learn from Steve Jobs. *Forbes*. Retrieved from https://www.forbes.com/sites/carminegallo/2012/10/04/11-presentation-lessons-you-can-still-learn-from-steve-jobs/#5b75bfd8dde3 on 24th August 2019

Harrison, C. (2012). NLP business benefits – What are the benefits of NLP in a business or sales environment? *Planet NLP*. Retrieved from http://www.planetnlp.com/nlp_business_benefits.html on 19th August 2019

Harrison, C. (2013) NLP techniques. *Planet NLP*. Retrieved from http://www.planetnlp.com/nlp_techniques.html on 20th August 2019

Illiopoulos, A. (2018). 5 critical mental models to add to your cognitive repertoire. *Medium*. Retrieved from https://medium.com/personal-growth/mental-models-898f70438075 on 21st August 2019

Illumine (2012). NLP and effective communication. *Illumine Training*. Retrieved from https://www.illumine.co.uk/2012/02/nlp-and-effective-communication/ on 23rd August 2019

James, T. (2019). What is NLP? A model of communication and personality. *The Tad James Company.* Retrieved from https://www.nlpcoaching.com/what-is-nlp-a-model-of-communication-and-personality/ on 24th August 2019

Marquis, D. (2019). What is NLP? These 4 techniques could change how you think. *Happiness.* Retrieved from https://www.happiness.com/en/magazine/personal-growth/nlp-happiness-techniques/ on 21st August 2019

Matthew, B. J. (2019). What is NLP? *The Empowerment Partnership.* Retrieved from http://www.nlp.com/what-is-nlp/ on 19th August 2019

NLP Notes (2019). Internal Maps of The World. *NLP Notes.* Retrieved from http://nlpnotes.com/internal-maps-of-the-world/ on 19th August 2019

Sanders, R. (2016). 3 NLP techniques to reduce anxiety right now. *Robert Sanders Coaching.* Retrieved from http://www.robertsanders.me.uk/3-nlp-techniques-to-reduce-anxiety-right-now/ on 26th August 2019

Schneider, N. (2017). 5 ways to improve your productivity. *Global NLP Training.* Retrieved from https://www.globalnlptraining.com/blog/5-ways-improve-productivity/ on 22nd August 2019

Schneider, N. (2017). NLP motivation strategy. *Global NLP*. Retrieved from https://www.globalnlptraining.com/blog/nlp-motivation-strategy/ on 28th August 2019

Shervington, M. (2018). How to use NLP to skyrocket your negotiation skills. *The Coaching Room*. Retrieved from https://www.thecoachingroom.com.au/blog/how-to-use-nlp-to-skyrocket-your-negotiation-skills 25th August 2019

Sussman, A. (2016). Stress reduction using NLP: 3 part exercise. *Anxiety Control Center*. Retrieved from https://anxietycontrolcenter.com/stress-reduction-using-nlp-part-1/ on 26th August 2019

The Coaching Room. (n.d.). 15 ways to boost your motivation with NLP. *The Coaching Room*. Retrieved from https://www.thecoachingroom.com.au/hubfs/15_Tips/15_Tips_to_Boost_Motivation.pdf on 28th August 2019

The Maven Circle (2016). A basic guide to NLP and managing anxiety. *The Maven Circle*. Retrieved from https://www.themavencircle.com/managing-anxiety-with-nlp/ on 26th August 2019

Young, M. (2015). 3 powerful techniques to create rapport – fast! *The Coaching Room*. Retrieved from https://www.thecoachingroom.com.au/blog/3-powerful-nlp-techniques-to-create-rapport-fast on 23rd August 20

Weinschenk, S. (2019, February 7). How People Make Decisions. Retrieved August 12, 2019, from https://www.smashingmagazine.com/2019/02/human-decision-making/.

Soon, Chun & Brass, Marcel & Heinze, Hans-Jochen & Haynes, John-Dylan. (2008). Unconscious determinants of free decisions in the human brain. Nature neuroscience. 11. 543-5. 10.1038/nn.2112.

Adams, S. (2019, February 17). The Spanish Armada. Retrieved August 19, 2017, from http://www.bbc.co.uk/history/british/tudors/adams_armada_01.shtml.

History.com Editors. (2010, February 9). Spanish Armada defeated. Retrieved August 19, 2019, from https://www.history.com/this-day-in-history/spanish-armada-defeated.

Foroux, D. (2018, September 13). Mental Models and Making Decisions You Don't Regret. Retrieved August 7, 2019, from https://dariusforoux.com/mental-models/.

Rana, Z. (2017, September 7). Charlie Munger: How to Get Smarter by Using Mental Models. Retrieved August 19, 2019, from https://fs.blog/charlie-munger/.

Chen, J. (2019, June 25). Charlie Munger. Retrieved August 19, 2019, from https://www.investopedia.com/terms/c/charlie-munger.asp.

Heshmat, S. (2015, April 23). What Is Confirmation Bias? Retrieved August 22, 2019, from https://www.psychologytoday.com/us/blog/science-choice/201504/what-is-confirmation-bias.

Lewis, S. (1995). Alfred Korzybski. Retrieved September 4, 2019, from http://stevenlewis.info/gs/akbio.htm.

Wahba, P. (2015, March 13). Apple extends lead in the U.S. top 10 retailers by sales per square foot. Retrieved September 5, 2019, from https://fortune.com/2015/03/13/apples-holiday-top-10-retailers-iphone/.

History of mobile phones and the first mobile phone. (2019, February 21). Retrieved September 8, 2019, from https://www.uswitch.com/mobiles/guides/history-of-mobile-phones/.

Sincero, S. M. (2013, August 1). Selective Perception. Retrieved September 8, 2019, from https://explorable.com/selective-perception.

Stimulus [Def. 5]. (n.d.). In Dictionary.com, Retrieved September 8, 2019, from https://www.dictionary.com/browse/stimuli.

Chabris, C., & Simons, D. (n.d.). The Invisible Gorilla. Retrieved September 9, 2019, from http://www.theinvisiblegorilla.com/gorilla_experiment.html.

Burrowes, R. J. (2016, July 17). The Psychology of Ideology and Religion. Retrieved September 10, 2019, from http://www.ipsnews.net/2016/07/the-psychology-of-ideology-and-religion/.

Kolbert, E. (2008, February 17). What was I thinking. Retrieved September 9, 2019, from https://www.newyorker.com/magazine/2008/02/25/what-was-i-thinking.

Forbes Coaches Council. (2018, June 4). Learning from Mistakes: 10 Things Beginning Leaders Should Know. Retrieved September 10, 2019, from https://www.forbes.com/sites/forbescoachescouncil/2018/06/04/learning-from-mistakes-10-things-beginning-leaders-should-know/#fe0ee47235b0.

Farnam Street. (n.d.). First Principles: The Building Blocks of True Knowledge. Retrieved September 10, 2019, from https://fs.blog/2018/04/first-principles/.

Farnam Street. (n.d.). Thought Experiment: How Einstein Solved Difficult Problems. Retrieved September 11, 2019, from https://fs.blog/2017/06/thought-experiment-how-einstein-solved-difficult-problems/.

Farnam Street. (n.d.). Second-Order Thinking: What Smart People Use to Outperform. Retrieved September 10, 2019, from https://fs.blog/2016/04/second-order-thinking/.

Hayes II, J. (2018, September 29). 1 Powerful but Simple Technique Ray Dalio Uses to Make Better Decisions. Retrieved September 2019, from https://www.inc.com/julian-hayes-ii/ray-dalios-technique-to-instantly-becoming-a-better-decision-maker-boils-down-to-8-words.html.

Farnam Street. (n.d.). The Value of Probabilistic Thinking: Spies, Crime, and Lightning Strikes. Retrieved September 2019, from https://fs.blog/2018/05/probabilistic-thinking/.

Muñoz, S. (2018, October 24). Mental Models for Product Managers: The Inversion Principle. Retrieved September 11, 2019, from https://medium.com/@simonmunoz/mental-models-for-product-managers-the-inversion-principle-4f7692bddc2.

SUNK COSTS / COMMITMENT + CONSISTENCY BIAS MENTAL MODEL (INCL THESIS DRIFT). (n.d.). Retrieved September 12, 2019, from http://www.askeladdencapital.com/sunk-costs-commitment-consistency-bias-mental-model-incl-thesis-drift/.

PRODUCT VS. PACKAGING / ACTION BIAS MENTAL MODEL (INCL PRECISION VS. ACCURACY, BUSYNESS VS. PRODUCTIVITY). (n.d.). Retrieved September 12, 2019, from http://www.askeladdencapital.com/product-vs-packaging-action-bias-mental-model-incl-precision-vs-accuracy-busyness-vs-productivity/

Tuck. (2019, July 20). Chronotypes. Retrieved September 12, 2019, from https://www.tuck.com/chronotypes/.

McVagh, Andrew. (2018, August 7). Mental Model Summary: Base Rates. Retrieved September 12, 2019, from https://www.mymentalmodels.info/mms-base-rates/.

Pressure [Def. 1]. (n.d.). In Merriam-Webster, Retrieved September 13, 2019, from https://www.merriam-webster.com/dictionary/pressure.

Center for Creative Leadership. (2019). The #1 Reason You Are Stressed and How to Change It. Retrieved September 13, 2019, from https://www.ccl.org/articles/leading-effectively-articles/banish-stress-stop-ruminating/.

Bonnevalle, N. (2018, October 10). Leaders should care about mental health (including their own). Retrieved September 13, 2019, from https://medium.com/thnk-school-of-creative-leadership/leaders-should-care-about-mental-health-including-their-own-4c8ab9a4a57b.

Karnjanaprakorn, M. (2017, May 23). 16 Mental Models for Founders and Leaders. Retrieved September 13, 2019, from https://medium.com/personal-growth/16-mental-models-for-founders-and-leaders-25c3724a5208.

Hoffman, Jayme. (2016, May 21). 13 Mental Models Every Founder Should Know. Retrieved September 15, 2019, from https://medium.com/the-mission/13-mental-models-every-founder-should-know-c4d44afdcdd.

System [Def. 1]. (n.d.). In Merriam-Webster, Retrieved September 15, 2019, from https://www.merriam-webster.com/dictionary/pressure.

Sparks, C. (2017, August 15). 104: Systems Thinking — The Essential Mental Models Needed for Growth. Retrieved September 15, 2019, from https://medium.com/@SparksRemarks/systems-thinking-the-essential-mental-models-needed-for-growth-5d3e7f93b420.

Merritt, J. (n.d.). WHAT ARE MENTAL MODELS? Retrieved September 16, 2019, from https://thesystemsthinker.com/what-are-mental-models/.

Farnam Street. (n.d.). Understanding your Circle of Competence: How Warren Buffett Avoids Problems. Retrieved September 16, 2019, from https://fs.blog/2013/12/circle-of-competence/.

The Best Schools. (2018). The 100 Best Public High Schools in the U.S. Retrieved September 18, 2019, from https://thebestschools.org/rankings/best-public-high-schools-us/#top.

Shonk, K. (2019, May 9). 5 Common Negotiation Mistakes and How You Can Avoid Them. Retrieved September 26, 2019, from https://www.pon.harvard.edu/daily/negotiation-skills-daily/5-common-negotiation-mistakes-and-how-you-can-avoid-them/.

British Library. (n.d.). Robert Cialdini. Retrieved September 17, 2019, from https://www.bl.uk/people/robert-cialdini.

Poor Ash's Almanac. (n.d.). FISHER, URY, AND PATTON'S "GETTING TO YES": BOOK REVIEW, NOTES + ANALYSIS. Retrieved September 17, 2019, from http://www.askeladdencapital.com/fisher-ury-and-pattons-getting-to-yes-book-review/

Poor Ash's Almanac. (n.d.). HUMANS VS. ECONS MENTAL MODEL. Retrieved September 17, 2019, from http://www.askeladdencapital.com/humans-vs-econs-mental-model/.

McVagh, A. (2018, May 23). Mental Model Summary: Reason Respecting (Because Why). Retrieved September 27, 2019, from https://www.mymentalmodels.info/mms-reason-respecting/.

www.ingramcontent.com/pod-product-compliance
Lightning Source LLC
Chambersburg PA
CBHW071950110526
44592CB00012B/1045